BAROQUE NAPLES
1600–1800

Figure 1

BAROQUE NAPLES
A DOCUMENTARY HISTORY
1600–1800

Edited by
Jeanne Chenault Porter

ITALICA PRESS
NEW YORK
2000

ITALICA PRESS, INC.
595 MAIN STREET
NEW YORK, NY 10044

Library of Congress Cataloging-in-Publication Data

Baroque Naples : a documentary history, 1600–1800 / edited by Jeanne Chenault Porter.
    p. cm.
    Includes bibliographical references and index.
    ISBN 978-0-934977-52-4 (pbk. : alk. paper)
    1. Naples (Italy)—History—1503-1734. 2. Naples (Italy)—History—1734-1860.
    3. Arts, Italian—Italy—Naples. 4. Arts, Baroque—Italy—Naples. I. Porter,
Jeanne Chenault.

    DG848.1 .B37 2000

    945'.7307—dc21   99-088391

Printed in the USA and EU
5 4 3 2 1

Cover Art: Detail of the Palazzo Reale, Naples c.1757. From "Palazzo Reale con la Cuccagna a S. Spirito," by Antonio Jolli c.1700–1777. Oil on Canvas. Palace House, Beaulieu. The Lord Montagu of Beaulieu.

Unless otherwise noted, all other artwork used by permission of the source cited in List of Illustrations on p. XIII.

VISIT OUR WEB SITE AT:
WWW.ITALICAPRESS.COM

"Translating, when not pedantic, deserves more praise than blame.... Even I have translated to pass the time or to please someone...."

— Giovanni Battista Marino (1579–1625)

For Richard,
Andrew,
and Julia

Figure 2

CONTENTS

D. Pietro Fernando di Castro Conte di Lemos.
V. Re. Logot.̂ Cap. Gente nel
Regno di Napoli. 1616.

Pesche.

Figure 3

NUMERICAL
LIST OF READINGS

BAROQUE NAPLES, 1600–1800

NUMERICAL LIST OF READINGS

ILLUSTRATIONS

ILLUSTRATIONS

TRANSLATORS

Isabel Innocenti-Darrah	(I.I.-D.)
Vieva McClure	(V.M.)
Lisa Noetzel	(L.N.)
Jeanne Chenault Porter	(J.C.P.)
Marco Rossi-Doria	(M.R.-D.)
Jeff Veenstra	(J.V.)

FOREWORD

Naples, and the kingdom that took its name, has long been a neglected field of history in the United States. There have traditionally been several reasons for this. While the classical heritage of the Bay of Naples, of Pompeii, Herculaneum, Baia, Cumae, Pozzuoli, and Posillipo and their treasures in Naples' museums have long been a central focus of classical studies, both in Italy and in the United States, medieval studies have focused on northern Europe, especially France, Germany, and England; while Renaissance history, even of Italy, has tended to concentrate on the northern and republican centers of the period. This fit well with the liberal and democratic tendencies of the students of Italy in the United States through most of the nineteenth and twentieth centuries. Naples, both the city as capital, and the Regno, as the kingdom was called, were long associated with royalty: with the new Norman dynasty, the imperial dreams of the Hohenstaufen, the dynastic conflicts of Angevins and the house of Aragon, and then with the absolutist monarchies of early-modern Europe: the Spanish and Austrian Hapsburgs and the Spanish and Neapolitan Bourbons.

Coincident with this has been the emphasis of historians to examine the origins and development of medieval and Renaissance culture as expressions of urban and democratic tendencies, of a "civic humanism" that expressed the desires and values of a bourgeois and republican way of life. Thus, again, historians have concentrated on the northern centers of the Middle Ages and Renaissance: Florence, Siena, Venice; and in the High Renaissance, Rome. This tendency has been reinforced by the legacy of Romanticism in the nineteenth and the canons of artistic taste of the twentieth century, which viewed first the Gothic of the North and of northern Italy, and then the flowering of Renaissance style in Tuscany, Lombardy, and the Veneto as the norms of Italian art. Naples, long associated with the glory of the Baroque, shared the disdain of much of the twentieth century for its style and ethic.

More mundane reasons, of course, have contributed to this long neglect of Neapolitan history. Perhaps the most pervasive of these is the tourist image of Italy formed by Americans. With the end of the Grand Tour in the late nineteenth century, Rome, Florence, and Venice became the points of an ironclad triangle of travel, both for the obvious attractions and beauties of these cities and their environs, and for the cultural framework with which Americans have come to view Italy.

This attitude, moreover, belies another American outlook, one that is, unfortunately, still shared by a great many Italians and Europeans themselves: that the Mezzogiorno, the "South" of Italy, is a land of poverty and cultural deprivation: a region—and a capital city—beset by corruption, crime, and the stereotype of the *"far niente"* southern Italian. This is an image reinforced in the United States by the daily occurrence of Italian dichotomies: the cultured art, literature, even cuisine, of the North, as opposed to the supposedly poor, peasant culture of Naples and the South.

Such attitudes have long contributed to a certain shyness among Americans to devote much time and effort to the study of things Neapolitan: why contend with so many negative attitudes, such a relatively remote, and perhaps unrewarding, field of research when the bright cities of the North offer much better areas for study? Again, while the Neapolitan kingdom and city have witnessed many events and personalities that have been central to European—and Western—history, they have also suffered the repeated ravages to their historical records: from occasional loses of itinerant archives during the Middle Ages to such popular revolts as those of 1585 and 1647 against Spanish rule (in which tax, court, and other records were destroyed), to the most recent destruction of the State Archives on September 30, 1943 at the hands of the retreating Nazis that forever removed most of the records of the high Middle Ages and Renaissance in Naples. Indeed, Naples never seemed to have recovered from World War II and the impoverishment of the city and its culture that the war left behind.

Recently, however, much of this has begun to change. There has long been a tradition of serious Italian historical and art historical scholarship for Naples and the South. One need only consult the multi-volume *Storia di Napoli*, the *Storia di Campania* or the works of Bologna, Capasso, De Seta, and Gliejeses, among many others, to get some idea of the very well developed field of Italian research there. Indeed, the city and its cultural treasures have once again begun to attract both historians and art historians: the former to the age of the Aragonese monarchy in the Renaissance, the latter to the Baroque. Even medieval Naples has begun to attract its students. The reasons are numerous: the broadening of the horizon of historical studies in the United States toward more Mediterranean fields, the search for new areas of fruitful scholarly investigation — now that the chief northern centers of Italian culture have been analyzed with such wonderful results for over a century — and an understanding that Neapolitan politics, culture, and economic life had profound influences on Italy and Europe into the modern world. These trends happily coincide with renewed development in the Italian Mezzogiorno by the Italian government and private groups that, though slow in materializing, have now restored many of Naples' most important monuments, reinvigorated its urban life and political culture, and given new force to its social and economic potential.

For many of these reasons, in 1995 we conceived the notion of offering a complete documentary history of Naples that would present to English-speaking readers a comprehensive survey of the city's history, economy, politics, culture, arts, and spiritual and intellectual life. A series of carefully selected original texts, translated into English, with brief introductions to their authors' lives and work, is intended to offer a sampling of the rich materials still to be uncovered or further explored. In so doing, we hope to present to the professional researcher the status quo on Neapolitan studies in the United States and offer a base for further study and exploration; and to give the student and general reader a first introduction to the rich and complex history of this famous capital. To accomplish this task we asked many of the most prominent students of Naples and southern Italy in the United States to collaborate on this project. They agreed to participate and responded with equal amounts of enthusiasm and caution: enthusiasm for the enterprise but caution because so much of this territory is either uncharted or still poorly mapped out.

The following volume, *Baroque Naples, 1600–1800*, the fourth in the series, is the work of Jeanne Chenault Porter, professor of art history at The Pennsylvania State University, who has specialized in Italian, baroque, and Neapolitan themes. As befits the period, her book focuses on Naples as a cultural capital, one whose brilliant achievements in the arts and letters belied — and to an extent masked — the profound social, economic, and political problems of the kingdom of Naples and of the Ancien Régime throughout Europe. These would come to a crisis in the wake of the French Revolution and prepare the way for a century of "marginalization" from which the city is only now emerging. Thus, while no one can ignore the deep structural shortcomings of the city and its kingdom during the two centuries covered in the following volume, so too no one can deny the essential truth that the years 1600 to 1800 were indeed, "the Golden Age of Naples."

— Ronald G. Musto, Series Editor
New York City, January 2000

Figure 4

OMNIBVS VIIS ACCVRATA, ET
AB ANTONIO BVLIFON 1685.
Cum Priuilegio

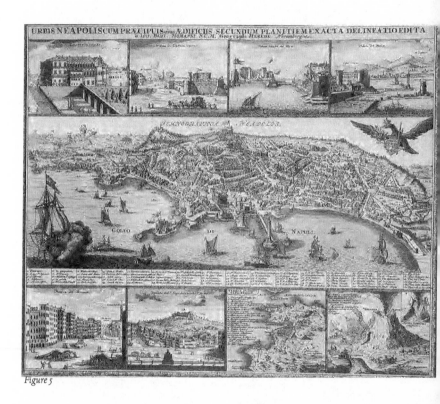

Figure 5

PREFACE

Not unlike the other portions of the five-volume *Documentary History of Naples*, volume 4, *Baroque Naples, 1600–1800*, offers a contextual approach to these two hundred years in the kingdom. Because its content is interdisciplinary, general as well as particular references are indicated in the notes for the benefit of the specialist and non-specialist alike. It is hoped that this anthology will serve as an introduction and guide to Neapolitan history, literature, and culture of this period. It is my intention to encourage the reader to explore further and become familiar with the additional works of many of these authors who, as indicated in the biographical introductions, produced far more than has been transcribed here. Several of the writers, such as Tommaso Campanella (1578–1639), Giovanni Battista Marino (1569–1625), and Giambattista Vico (1668–1774) were remarkably versatile and the range of their interests is reflected in the multiple entries by which they are represented.

The selections present a mixture that includes excerpts from obscure writings, such as an anonymous account of the royal marriage of Carlos II of Spain in 1679, as well as such classics as Tommaso Campanella's *City of the Sun* of 1602. A number of primary sources of literature, guide books, historical accounts, economic treatises, and philosophical writings are published here for the first time in English. Perhaps the most previously inaccessible for the reader of English are the earthy poems in Neapolitan dialect by Giulio Cesare Cortese (1575–1621/7) and those attributed to his alleged shadowy contemporary, Filippo Sgruttendio.

The kingdom's rich and complex culture is illuminated by these texts. During the seventeenth and eighteenth centuries Naples, the largest city in Italy and the fourth-largest in Europe, attracted visitors from all over western Europe, hence the numerous travel accounts and guide books. Although "baroque" is a stylistic term indicative of the richness and grandeur of the artistic creativity of the period, there are various and more appropriate adjectives for the other aspects of its intellectual, economic, and political context. While this period in Naples might be referred to as the Age of the Spanish Viceroys, it was equally that of the Counter Reformation and with it blossomed a cultural Golden Age that was rich especially in poetry, philosophy, music, law, and economic theory.

Baroque Naples, 1600–1800

Our terminal date of 1800, which approximates that of the French invasion and beginning of the Parthenopean Republic, seems more decisive than this volume's initial year of 1600. It often appears arbitrary to abide by the rigid dates of 1600–1800 when one is dealing with material of this sort. Whereas the Dominican philosopher and poet, Giordano Bruno (1548–1600) has not been included since his death is the very year in which this volume is to begin, an excerpt from *Albumazar*, the last play of Giovanni Battista della Porta (1535–1615), appears in the section on music and theater. In similar fashion, the commentaries of writers such as Michael Kelly (1764–1826) and Francesco Cerlone (1750–1800/5), both of whom lived into the early years of the nineteenth century, have been utilized. I have made such decisions realizing that they may be open to debate and keeping in mind the integrity of the other portions of this five-volume opus. Not all the primary sources are from authors who were born and died in Naples; neither were they all published in Naples or even in Italy. Although excerpts are translated from several languages including Italian, Neapolitan dialect, Latin, French, and Spanish, some, such as that of Sir John Evelyn, are in their original English. This choice expands our view of Neapolitan culture and history through every possible means including the observations of foreigners, often travelers on the Grand Tour for which Naples was usually the final destination. On occasion, as with Fr. San Felix's seventeenth-century biography of Saint Andrea Avellino, a passage was chosen less for its intrinsic value than for its implication, in this case to demonstrate the far-reaching influence of Naples on Mexico. Likewise, the excerpt from Lionardo Di Capua's treatise on medicine is adapted from an English translation of 1684 even though a modern English version is available.

There are many challenges in presenting such a literary kaleidoscope. It seems perverse not to take advantage of accessible and excellent modern English translations of sources such as the early seventeenth-century guide to Naples by Enrico Bacco which has been published by Italica Press in 1991 (see Bibliography). Likewise there have been superior anthologies written in English, such as that of Brendan Dooley and Robert Enggass (see Bibliography) from which some excerpts have been gleaned. Subsequent borrowing only brings further attention to these valuable publications. In order to emphasize the complexity of the process of translation, I have intentionally chosen two very diverse versions of Giovanni Battista Basile's early seventeenth-century tales, one interpreted by Richard Burton and the other by Benedetto Croce. Early English translations, such as Crashaw's of Marino's *Massacre of the Innocents*, or adaptations such as Thomas Tomkis' of Della Porta's comedy *Albumazar*, are in their original format rather than in modern English.

Not all of the original writing was in accordance with the rules of acceptable grammar and syntax. The guide books and diaries, often written hastily while in transit, are frequently in need of some editing. When British English, early or modern, is reproduced, that spelling is maintained to preserve the integrity of the writing with the result that both English and American spellings appear in this volume. When poetry is translated into English, it is usually impossible to maintain the original linear structure let alone appropriate attributes such as rhyme. There is also the question of how much should be translated into English. In order to remind the reader of the Neapolitan source, names of churches, monarchs, saints, locations, etc., unless themselves foreign, remain in Italian, Spanish, or Neapolitan.

Information concerning our authors is not always available. Several, such as the elusive seventeenth-century "W.B." who provides an account of Innocent XII, the Pignatelli pope, are undeniably obscure. On occasion there are alternative spellings of writers' names as in the case of Ranieri Calsabigi or Calzabigi. It is generally assumed that Filippo Sgruttendio is the nom de plume of the famous dialect poet Giulio Cesare Cortese. Some original accounts, such as another of Capaccio's guides, specifically one mentioned but not quoted from and designed for foreigners traveling to the Neapolitan suburb of Pozzuoli, were revised considerably in later editions such as that of Pompeo Sarnelli. The question arises as to how much of the text is by Capaccio and how much by Sarnelli. Many accounts, such as that of the English Evelyn, echo those of earlier writers, such as George Sandys and Pflaumern, to the extent that phrases have a very familiar ring. In fact, it was not uncommon for these guides to include sites the author had himself never visited.

Although music was a crowning achievement of Naples during this period, it is obviously difficult if not impossible to effectively recreate this mode of expression. By presenting it with theater and recalling Joseph-LaLande's account of the Teatro di San Carlo, it is hoped that this tip-of-the-iceberg reference will be preferable to simple omission. Such a challenge exists as well for the other arts such as painting and, to some extent, drama.

There are several scholars, professionals, and institutions I would like to thank for their assistance in this project. The Pennsylvania State University granted me a timely sabbatical leave for the spring term in 1996 allowing me some necessary time to work on this anthology. I wish to recognize several individuals in particular including Charles W. Mann, Jr., Professor of English and Comparative Literature, Fellow of the Institute of the Arts and Humanistic Studies, Chief of Rare Books and Special Collections at Penn State. Also from Pattee Library are Noelene P. Martin, former Head of Inter-Library Loan, and Sandra K. Stelts, Rare Books Specialist. Paul B. Harvey, Jr., Associate Professor of History and Classics and author of volume I of this series, was particularly helpful in his partial translation and analysis of the esoteric sacred books of Domenico Aulisio. I am especially indebted to Marco Rossi-Doria who heroically recomposed the never-before-translated dialect poetry of Cortese and Sgruttendio. Appreciation is sent as well to my other four translators whose names are listed at the end of the text and whose initials appear next to particular excerpts. Special gratitude is given to Dottoressa Anna Tuck-Scala for her assistance in getting access to several original sources available only in the Biblioteca Nazionale in Naples, and to her and her husband, Prof. Felice Scala, for their very special role as a liaison to their wonderful city of Naples.

Photographs were processed by the Still Photography department of The Pennsylvania State University.

Jeanne Chenault Porter
Associate Professor
Department of Art History
The Pennsylvania State University
University Park, PA
November 1999

INTRODUCTION
The Golden Age of Naples

GENERAL PERSPECTIVES

Although for the sake of clarity this volume has been separated into chapters, it is difficult if not impossible to discuss the city as it existed between 1600 and 1800 without acknowledging the interrelationships among its history, society, and culture. This is especially true in the eighteenth century when the "new philosophy" that had been introduced as early as 1650 permeated so many aspects of Neapolitan thinking. Although the sixteenth century had produced remarkable versatility, a legacy of Renaissance humanism, the seventeenth century affords more of an opportunity to consider disciplines, such as the fine arts or scientific development, as separate entities. Primarily because of its shifting foreign rule, the Seicento and Settecento in Naples emerge as remarkably opposed. The former seems in many ways still linked to the preceding Cinquecento, the age of the Spanish viceroys; the latter — primarily under the auspices of the Spanish Bourbons — achieves a new maturity associated with the Age of Enlightenment elsewhere in Europe. Despite its political expansions and contractions, each century has its particular triumph: the earlier in painting and literature, the later in philosophy and music.

This introduction will therefore offer a brief overview of some of the facets of Neapolitan history during this period revealed in the texts that follow. It makes no attempt at a comprehensive history but does offer some guideposts to the documents below. The Chronology of Neapolitan History and lists of Viceroys and Sovereigns of Naples in the Appendices will help round out the historical background. Any history of Naples must take into account two important facts: the city's uninterrupted survival from the period of antiquity to the present day, and its consecutive foreign rulers. Rome is not the only "eternal city": Naples has been referred to as "a Pompeii that was never buried." Through both written and physical evidence Naples' links to the ancient past are constant and varied. We have included two chapters dealing with the city, its history, and description in Part I below. Among the most relevant ancient memories of Naples are the *Letters* of Pliny the Younger who gives us an eyewitness account of the great eruption of Vesuvius in 79 C.E., an event recalled later by Giulio Cesare Braccini [see reading 2] and Pietro Castelli [3]. Also available are numerous references to monuments, lost and still extant. Whereas Plutarch describes the elegant coastal villa of Lucullus, other writers introduce us to Virgil's tomb [FIG. 24], Cicero's baths, Nero's palace, and the "paradise" known as Capri. Almost as an accompaniment to its history were its myths and legends. Naples' original name was derived from Parthenope [FIG. 9], the siren rejected by Odysseus. The city's present name is merely a derivation of the Greek *Nea polis* (new city).

The history of this city can be traced for almost three thousand years, perhaps from the ninth century B.C.E. when the area around the Sebeto River was settled by the Achaean Greeks and merchants from Asia Minor. By the seventh century B.C.E. settlers from Rhodes, off Asia Minor, had established a settlement on the site of the present Pizzofalcone and Santa Lucia, called Parthenope. Some time around 550 B.C.E., Greeks from Chalcis, who had settled neighboring Cumae, took the city; and c.474 B.C.E., they and Greeks from Syracuse in Sicily moved their settlement slightly off the shore to a new town they called *Neapolis*. Naples was taken by the inland tribe of Italic people called the Samnites c.400 B.C.E. and in 326 B.C.E. by the Romans. Naples was successively an early Christian and Byzantine center (325–568 C.E.), controlled by Lombard dukes (568–1130), Norman princes (1137–1194), Hohenstaufen emperors (1194–1266), Angevin (1266–1442), and Aragonese (1442–1495) kings, before becoming a viceroyalty of the Spanish Hapsburgs from 1504 to 1707. In 1707, it was taken over by the Austrians; and from 1734 by the Spanish who founded a cadet branch of the Bourbon dynasty there. The Bourbons remained in control until 1799 when the French invaded the kingdom and a revolution established the Second Parthenopean Republic. With the defeat of Napoleon at Waterloo in 1815, the Bourbons returned to the throne and ruled until 1860 when Garibaldi's expedition to Naples and Sicily led to Cavour's proclamation of the Kingdom of Italy in 1861. This was the great unification or *Risorgimento* of a country that had hitherto never been united. It is ironic that in the long run Naples failed to benefit from this "marriage" since it was its innovative "new philosophy" that had largely inspired such nationalism. For centuries the capital of the Kingdom of the Two Sicilies, Naples is now the major city of the Italian region known as Campania.

THE CITY AND ITS PEOPLE

During the seventeenth and eighteenth centuries the population of the city of Naples was probably about 300,000, although some estimates have been as high as 450,000 just prior to the major plague of 1656 when half of the city perished [FIG. 10]. The population did not reach this level again until the late eighteenth century: the total just before the Neapolitan Revolution of 1799 has been estimated at almost 500,000. Throughout this period Naples was the largest city in Italy, about three times the size of Rome, and in Europe smaller than only London (860,000, c.1800), Istanbul (700,000), and Paris (547,000). This population was cramped into an urban area of 1200 by 2500 meters, on a street grid laid out in the middle of the first millennium B.C.E. As a result of its foreign rulers and commercial contracts as a port city, Naples' populace consisted of various ethnic groups: Italians from all over the peninsula, particularly the south, Greeks, Arabs, Catalans, French, Ragusans, Austrians, Jews, as well as the predominant Spanish. As a reflection of the internationally complex Hapsburg Empire, there were close ties with its other member nations, with the result that many foreign visitors were from Flanders and Austria as well as Spain. Provincial taxes, administrative centralization, the topography of the surrounding mountainous regions, and the correspondingly impoverished rural economy all encouraged migration into the cosmopolitan city. Within a coastal basin of about 55 km. around the city there lived about 40 percent of the population of the entire kingdom, which probably totaled 2.9 million in 1650, 3.3 in 1700, 3.9 in 1750, and 4.8 million in 1800. The result was extreme overcrowding and poverty. In addition to social oppression there were also natural disasters and the constant fear of disease. Following upon the great fire in the western suburb of Pozzuoli, these two catastrophic centuries witnessed several plagues, the most devastating in 1656 [8]; frequent volcanic eruptions [2-3], particularly in 1631, 1672, and 1715; and the great famine of 1764. Much of Naples' history was continually characterized by drama and death.

As the texts in Chapters 1 and 2 reveal, class distinction was pronounced and rigidly maintained with a system whereby the Spanish monarchy governed through an appointed viceroy charged with both subordinating Naples and protecting her from foreign invasion. Because of Spain's repeated entanglements abroad, especially with the French and the Turks, as well as such debilitating conflicts as the Thirty Years War (1618–1648), Naples was exploited both strategically and financially. The city was not isolated militarily and often found herself utilized in local and foreign campaigns. Individual accounts as well as feats of the city's military heroes are preserved for us by Raffaelle Maria Filamondo [10]. In 1620 Neapolitan militia helped to bring about the victory of the White Mountain and the retaking of Prague, which restored the House of Austria's fortunes and generally strengthened the rest of the Hapsburg Empire. In 1650 the city was able to defeat the French at Portolongone. In spite of its oppressive viceroys, internal restructurings of the government of Naples did occur. In 1642 the three-part parliament, which used the same form as that of Sicily, was disbanded leaving the voting on taxes to six ancient civic institutions known as the *seggi* (local boards).

Within its walls — demolished only between 1740 and 1787 — there coexisted luxury and leisure, suffering and starvation. The baronial aristocracy offered dramatic contrast to the lowest stratum of society, the so-called *lazzaroni* (those like Lazarus of the parable) who survived through desperate means. The aristocracy, identified so accurately by Francesco Zazzera [1], Giuseppe Campanile [16], and Nicolo Toppi [17], was frequently able to manipulate the lower classes into antidemocratic movements that resulted in self-defeat. Unlike the rest of Europe, and despite the presence of an artisan class (25% of the population involved in the textile industry by 1650), as well as merchants, bankers, and a disproportionately large number of lawyers, Naples during this period failed to give rise to a strong upper-middle class, a sustaining and stabilizing bourgeoisie that might have served as a strong social and financial intermediary. Thus underneath Spain's simultaneously protective and despotic rule, the Neapolitans instigated lively political intrigue with their own internal forms of resistance. In 1546, during the initial years of the Counter Reformation, the citizens of Naples had rioted to protest the introduction of the Spanish Inquisition into the city [FIG. 6]. Their refusal thwarted its presence until over a century later when it did persecute identified "atheists."

In 1639/40 Giovanni Orefice, prince of Sanza, had conspired with the French ambassador in opposition to Spanish rule, as mentioned by Giuseppe Donzelli [5]. But without doubt the most recorded event in the seventeenth century was the brief and unsuccessful revolt in 1647 led by a young fisherman from Amalfi named Tommaso Aniello, called "Masaniello." This popular uprising resulted from the imposition of a fruit tax but was part of a larger protest among all of Naples' classes. Mayhem resulted when Don Giuseppe of the aristocratic Carafa family was mur-

dered on the order of Masaniello because he had attempted to lead a counter-revolution against the people's rebellion; and the revolt was soon crushed. Masaniello's revolutionaries were designated the First Parthenopean Republic. Vivid retellings, such as that of Donzelli [5], Lord Alexander Giraffi [6], and Pietro Giannone [7, FIG. 8], baroque paintings by Domenico Gargiulo and others [FIG. 12], and several later operatic productions record the rise and gory death of this hero of the people. Masaniello's uprising was accompanied by other less colorful rebellions. In 1648, for example, Giovanni Sanseverino, count of Saponara, joined Henry, duke of Guise, and the Neapolitan militias against Spanish rule. While they were unsuccessful militarily, some reforms did follow. But 1647/48 marked the last remnants of baronial rebellion against the monarchy.

In 1707, as a result of the War of the Spanish Succession, the Hapsburg Archduke Charles VI of Austria became ruler of Naples, a situation that was confirmed by the Treaty of Utrecht in 1713. While the city welcomed its new rulers, the Austrians gradually fell into popular disfavor, not because of the Hapsburgs' tax policies, much in the tradition of their Spanish predecessors, but rather because of their anti-papal attitudes. During the War of the Polish Succession between Bourbon France and Spain on the one side and Hapsburg Austria on the other, the Bourbons seized the kingdom in 1734 and established a third branch of the dynasty there. In 1746, during the reign of Charles III, the population of Naples rebelled once again against a final attempt to install the Inquisition. At this point the Bourbon king was forced to swear that such a purge would never again be imposed upon the city. With the establishment of the Second Parthenopean Republic in 1799 the French General Jeanne Antoine Étienne Championnet promised peace and prosperity as he led a Napoleanic army into Naples. What followed was oppression, taxes, and famine, a disastrous failure according to the historian Vincenzo Cuoco [12]. It was not until Napoleon's defeat at Waterloo in 1815 that the Bourbon rule of Naples was restored.

TRAVELERS AND THEIR GUIDES

There were still other illuminating facets of Naples during this period of the seventeenth and eighteenth centuries. One was its identity as the vacation resort of Italy, a theme treated in Chapter 2. Since antiquity it had continued to be a destination for all sorts of travelers. Under the Romans Naples had had a variety of famous visitors including Virgil, Nero, Seneca, Cicero, and somewhat later on Saint Paul, whose first landfall in Europe was at Pozzuoli. Centuries later Thomas Aquinas (c.1225–1274) attended the University of Naples. In the fourteenth century the city received the painter Giotto, as well as Saint Bridget of Sweden. Famous locations included its church of San Lorenzo where Boccaccio encountered his beloved Fiammetta, and the Castel Nuovo, where King Robert entertained Petrarch. During the eighteenth century, when so many tourists visited this southern paradise, it became known as the last stop on the Grand Tour. The traveler's view was in general superficial and optimistic, often the result of only a few days in the city. As is often the case with guidebooks, the hedonistic aspects of Naples were magnified; her underlying hardships overlooked. The pleasurable, exotic characteristics of the city loomed conspicuously and are recorded in the numerous travel accounts that are supplied for us mainly by visitors from other European countries.

Through these personal diaries and practical itineraries we become aware of the great physical beauty of Naples, its sunny climate, abundance of fruit and flowers, of its unusual and exceptional natural resources and wonders. We have evidence that many Roman visitors came here purely for the air, which was lauded into the late nineteenth century. In 1616 Enrico Bacco [13] referred to it as a haven for relaxation, a place of escape. In 1634 Giulio Cesare Capaccio's guide for foreigners [14] stated that "there is nobody who does not desire to see it and who does not desire to die here. Naples is the whole world." John Evelyn [15], who saw the city in 1645, called it "the *non ultra* of my travels." There are numerous descriptions of the *Molo Grande*, where one could walk along the shore in the evening and which, because of the depth of the water, ships could approach at close range. Evelyn recalled one of the annual city carnivals that included processions and masquerades of courtesans, "30,000 registered sinners who pay tax to the state for the Costome of their bodys…flinging eggs of sweete-water, into our Coach." Especially during the ostentatious eighteenth century, when the Bourbons were in power, there were elaborate celebrations and festivals, such as the annual Feast of Piedigrotta during which carpets hung from balconies, elegant costumes and jewelry were worn by the wealthy, and King Ferdinando IV (1759–1825, FIG. 47) traveled in the first of a long line of coaches — all in order to pay homage to the Virgin. There were others that were purely secular where giant gilded and decorated barges glided before the Royal Palace. Such ceremony is recreated in the accounts of Scipio Mazzella [4], as well as the anonymous chronicler who described the royal marriage of Charles II in 1679 [9]. Famous artists and writers who visited Naples from the sixteenth through the eighteenth century included Christopher Marlowe, John Milton (who was there during the late 1630s), Handel who wrote his opera *Parthenope* in 1730, and numerous painters, including the Spanish Jusepe de Ribera and the French Jean Honoré Fragonard and Mme. Vigée le Brun.

Major points of interest, many still extant, had been famous since antiquity. Many of the diaries and travel guides of the period gain their information either directly or indirectly from ancient texts. Some authors attempted to edit and correct these early accounts, whereas others relied upon them slavishly and even claimed, falsely, to have visited monuments they themselves never actually saw. Capaccio [14] was one of several who referred to natural phenomena, such as La Solfatara, deemed "the gates of hell," an area to the west of the city where sulfuric fumes rise from the ground. Neapolitan history and legends merge frequently, creating actual and imagined sites. Such was the legendary promontory of Misenum where Aeneas supposedly came to shore, and the cave of the Cumaean Sibyl just up the coast. More in the category of natural wonders were the Cave of the Dog [FIG. 23] known to Pliny and mentioned by Pompeo Sarnelli [19], the nearby mountaintop town of snow where liquor was manufactured, and the natural underground tunnel in Posillipo wide enough for several carriages to travel through.

In addition to such historical and mythical points of interest there were also those contrived by the Neapolitans themselves. These included Ferdinando Imperato's museum of exotic plants, animals, and "notable rarities" recorded in a woodcut of 1599 [FIG. 20] and decades later described by Evelyn [15]. The great Cocagna, mentioned by Pietro Colletta [11], consisted of temporary architecture upon which food, including live animals, had been nailed for the consumption of a ravenous mob [cover, FIG. 13]. In the eighteenth century — as still today — one could visit the elegant and bizarre Sansevero Chapel, built as a human laboratory by the mad alchemist Prince Raimondo. Preserved, clothed corpses of citizens were on display in the lower level of the Castel Nuovo as well as in the crypt of the church of the Carmine. Whereas the latter were destroyed during World War II. The former are still on view.

Many travelers commented upon the crowding, bustle, and noise of Naples, which Capaccio [14] described as similar to a swarm of bees. Not all observations of the city were favorable. Whereas the poet Percy Bysshe Shelley called Naples "a paradise of exiles," his compatriot Augustus Hare referred to it as "a paradise of devils" but added that they were lively and amusing devils with a spirit of irresistible fun. It was this sense of the dramatic and outrageous, as well as its breathtaking natural beauty, that made the city so popular with the Romantics of the nineteenth century. Naples, which had nourished poets, such as Shelley and Byron, inspired Goethe to utter his famous declaration: "Nobody who has seen Naples could ever be really unhappy.... To be enabled to dream like this is worth all difficulties.... See Naples and then die!"

There was always great interest in Vesuvius. Descriptions of its topography and accounts of its major eruptions are prevalent. Many writers, some in guidebooks, describe their personal encounter with the volcano. Using Pliny and other classical texts, many boast about having scaled the great mountain. Not all the claims were accurate, however, and only some of their daring feats are genuine. In the seventeenth century those who claim to have actually climbed Vesuvius include the Irish traveler Fynes Moryson, George Sandys, Evelyn, Capaccio, and Montfaucon. In the eighteenth century the event is recorded by Sir William Hamilton, the British ambassador and his wife, Emma who, accompanied by the Neapolitan sovereigns, witnessed the inferno through dark glasses. Paintings by Pietro Fabris record their night visits to the fiery volcano. Several nineteenth-century Romantics actually experienced, as well as recorded, Vesuvius. Among them were Shelley and Charles Dickens.

PAINTING, ARCHITECTURE, AND ARCHAEOLOGY

Naples as a cultural magnet is the subject of Part II of the readings. Despite the poverty and suffering of a significant portion of the population and the continued oppression of foreign rule, during the seventeenth and eighteenth centuries Naples was an important center of baroque painting, literature, philosophy, sociological and economic theory, jurisprudence, music, and theater. In this it presents something of a parallel to seventeenth-century Spain, which was being depleted by war and taxation yet simultaneously produced a golden age of art, literature, and theater. The southern capital had strong connections with cultural centers elsewhere in Europe engendered both by its Mediterranean trade and by its Hapsburg and then Bourbon court connections. Especially from the 1740s on, the creative tradition of Naples was magnified by the excavations of Pompeii and Herculaneum. It was this discovery, as well as its innovative rationalist philosophy, that caused the world to focus upon Naples during the Settecento. In retrospect, it might well be considered the city's last truly remarkable century.

It is difficult to characterize the culture of Naples during the period of 1600–1800 with a simple assessment. Creative changes tended to follow shifts in its foreign rule. Whereas the seventeenth century produced superlative painting as well as literature, it was primarily in the eighteenth that music, opera, theater, and architecture flourished. This transition from what has been glibly characterized as the "darkness," a jocular reference to the tenebrist technique of many Neapolitan paintings, into the "light," contemporary with the Age of Enlightenment, was due largely to the change in patronage from the exclusive Spanish viceroys to the more inclusive and free-spending Bourbons. Prior to the rediscovery of Pompeii and Herculaneum during the second quarter of the eighteenth century, Naples and its environs possessed a collection of ancient monuments, such as the amphitheater and temple of Serapide at outlying Pozzuoli. Despite the inheritance of the Farnese art collection through Charles III, much of the ancient sculpture had been sent previously to ruling Spain, causing its ancient legacy, prior to the unearthing of Pompeii, to consist primarily of architecture, sometimes no more than substructures of later buildings.

Chapter 3 surveys Neapolitan arts, architecture, and archaeological discovery in the seventeenth and early eighteenth centuries. During the Seicento Naples was, along with Rome and Bologna, one of the three major centers of baroque painting. Although at this period the city did not excel in the medium of sculpture, Rome's greatest practitioner, Gianlorenzo Bernini (1598–1680), was of Neapolitan origin. There was, in addition, a rich heritage of medieval art exemplified by the ten miles of early Christian catacombs and centuries later by gothic sculpture and architecture, such as the church known as the Donnaregina, the church of San Lorenzo Maggiore, the Franciscan church of Santa Chiara, and the cathedral of San Gennaro. During the early Trecento, for example, the Florentine master Giotto had executed frescoes for King Robert and Queen Sancia in the Great Hall of Castel Nuovo and at Santa Chiara, now lost. Many noble palaces, such as the Cuomo, and urban projects of the Renaissance period still grace the city.

Although there were several competent artists in the city during the sixteenth century, including Fabrizio Santafede and Belisario Corenzio, it was not until the seventeenth that Naples developed a major school of painting following the arrival of the unprecedented Michelangelo da Caravaggio who, fleeing a murder charge in Rome, was in the city in 1606 and again in 1608. There was no Neapolitan academy of painting until 1666, considerably later than those in Rome, Florence, and Bologna. It was Caravaggio's revolutionary naturalistic chiaroscuro mode, a contrast of light and shade, that was adopted initially by Neapolitan painters, such as Giovanni Battista Caracciolo, Massimo Stanzione, and Bernardo Cavallino. Jusepe de Ribera, one of the greatest Spanish artists, arrived in 1616 and stayed in Naples for the rest of his life. In his early years he too followed the precedent of Caravaggio, who had died six years earlier. He, Corenzio, and Caracciolo formed a triumvirate of power in the Neapolitan art world. Another outstanding Roman import was the extraordinary Artemisia Gentileschi (1593–1652/3) who, unlike her gentle father, specialized in violent depictions of triumphant women. In addition to these so-called *Caravaggeschi*, or followers of Caravaggio, there were the more classical painters from Bologna. Guido Reni (1581–1642) left the city when his assistant was assaulted; whereas a few years later Domenico Zampieri, called Domenichino (1581–1641), also from Bologna, and Giovanni Lanfranco (1580–1647) from Parma received many major commissions and thrived within the Neapolitan artistic milieu. Domenichino succeeded despite the constant fear of being poisoned that he shared with other outsiders (non-Neapolitans). Although archival records indicate that a great number of artists died in the terrible plague of 1656, the Neapolitan school of painting continued during the second half of the century and on into the early eighteenth with such painters as the dramatic Salvator Rosa (1615–1673, FIG. 26) and the facile and prolific Luca Giordano (1632–1705) who was known as *Fa Presto* ("Speedy").

In addition to the Neapolitan painters and those from elsewhere in Italy, there were a number of renowned foreign artists active in the city. Early in the Seicento, the Flemish painter Anthony Van Dyck (1599–1641) passed through on his way to Sicily; and later in the eighteenth century the English portraitist Allan Ramsay (1713–1784) set up a famous studio there. Like Pompeo Batoni of Lucca (1708–1787), he catered to the numerous English tourists who collected art while on the Grand Tour. For such travelers there was not only portraiture available but detailed naturalistic views *(vedute)* of the port and environs. Especially during the eighteenth century these served as picture postcards to record Naples in much the same way that Canaletto's depictions reproduced Venice. Despite the excavations at Pompeii and Herculaneum during the mid-eighteenth century, and Octavio Antonio Bayardi's engravings of them [FIGS. 30-31], the neoclassical style was not as relevant to Neapolitan painting, as it was to architecture and the minor arts. An exception was the numerous portrayals of the notorious Lady Emma Hamilton (c.1761–1815), mistress and later wife of the British ambassador. These present her draped in classical garb and assuming poses derived from those in the classical images at Pompeii. One example of the Neoclassical style applied to architecture would be the design of the famous church of San Francesco di Paola begun in 1818 and opposite the Royal Palace.

During the seventeenth century patrons of the arts included the Spanish royalty and their appointed viceroys, the Church, amply represented in what has been estimated at over three hundred edifices, the aristocracy, and a few foreign members of the minuscule bourgeoisie. The latter provided some of the most interesting independent commissions. As with many of the painters, patrons were not always originally from Naples. The Flemish shipping magnate Gaspar Roomer (late 16th c.–1674), possessed one of the most famous private collections, which included depictions of mythological subjects by some of the outstanding northern and southern European masters, including the Spanish Ribera. Roomer was so wealthy that the populace would often quip: "Do you take me for a Roomer?" During the latter part of the century another foreigner, the Marchese Ferdinand Van der Einden, commissioned the talented Mattia Preti (1613–1699) and others. The viceroys themselves, although often disreputable in their political and personal behavior, did support Neapolitan artists, thereby projecting their own tastes and interests. The duke of Alcalá (1629–1631) was obviously an admirer of classical antiquity, and his preference flavored the projects that he commissioned during his years in power. Not all of the art from Naples stayed in the city. Over forty shiploads of paintings were sent back to Spain where they usually found their way into royal collections, such as those in the Escorial and Alcazar in Madrid.

In the tradition of the great Renaissance biographer Giorgio Vasari, Bernardo De Dominici (1648–1750, **25**, FIG. **28**) gives us interesting, if often embellished, accounts of these Neapolitan painters, sculptors, and architects. His accounts refer frequently to famous commissions and particular monuments of the period. According to most accounts, such as those in diaries and guidebooks, domestic architecture in Naples was on the whole unexceptional. The buildings tended to emphasize the vertical, were located on minimal plots, and often used inexpensive details, such as paper window hangings. Conversely, the grand palaces, such as those belonging to the viceroys and later Bourbons, including the Royal Palace, Capodimonte, and Caserta, "the Versailles of the south," [FIGS. **32–33**] were sumptuous and contained the finest art collections. The prevalence of painters in Seicento Italy was not equaled by the number of architects. There were few as distinguished as Cosimo Fanzago (1591–1678), whose projects were ubiquitous in Naples an⟨ cluded the redecoration of the beautiful Certosa di San Martino. Unlike the painters, almost all the architects, including Fanzago, Luigi Vanvitelli (1700–1773), and his son Carlo Vanvitelli (1739–1821), who designed the great palace of Caserta, were native Neapolitans.

Some of Naples' monuments were as outstanding for their interior paintings and decoration as for their architectural design. These were not merely art collections but special works executed specifically for predetermined settings. The church of San Domenico Maggiore and the Pio Monte della Misericordia contained huge oils of religious themes by Caravaggio and other masters. The walls and vaults of the baroque Tesoro [FIGS. 29, 55-56] adjacent to the gothic cathedral of San Gennaro, where the patron saint's blood miraculously liquefies three times each year, were covered with frescoes by Domenichino and Lanfranco. One of the most spectacular monuments was the Carthusian complex of San Martino next to the Castel Sant'Elmo on its mountaintop overlooking the city. This richly decorated church included oils and frescoes by Ribera, Lanfranco, and such natives as Giovanni Battista Caracciolo (1570–1637) and Massimo Stanzione (1585–1656). During this period there were many visitors to this famous monument, including the French rococo painters Jean Honoré Fragonard (1732–1806) and Hubert Robert (1703–1808), the painter of ruins.

In the second quarter of the eighteenth century the golden age of painting came to an end during Bourbon rule. At this time the Church, less powerful and favored than during the reign of the Spanish viceroys, declined as a major patron. Naples was nevertheless still a center of interest because of the subsequent excavations of Pompeii, Herculaneum, and Stabiae. As a city of painters, however, it never again gained prominence; and there was a shift in focus as Venice reemerged triumphantly with the luminary Giovanni Battista Tiepolo (1696–1770). The Risorgimento proved to be unconducive to artistic production, and it was not until the twentieth century that a few Italian movements, such a Futurism, surfaced here.

LITERATURE

Many of the characteristics displayed by Naples' artistic world during this period are discernible also in its literature, which is sampled in Chapter 4. As with painting, some of the Neapolitan writers and poets, especially those of the Seicento, were among the most famous in Italy. The legacy of antiquity persisted. There was access to ancient works of literature in the great libraries, such as that of Giuseppe Valletta (1636–1714), which was said by Bernard de Montfaucon to have contained copies of Catullus, Livy, Apuleius, Horace, and Pliny. Many academies, such as the mid-eighteenth century Ercolanese, venerated the antique tradition. There was frequent mention of the ancients in literature, including the renowned poet Giovanni Battista Marino's [**29**, FIGS. **25-26, 34-35**] references to Virgil.

If the sixteenth century revealed a general indifference to literature on the part of the viceroys, from the seventeenth century on these royal appointees began commissioning works from such poets as Marino, the most famous of his time, who died in 1625. The poet Giovanni Battista Manso [**32**, FIG. **38**], author of a voluminous encyclopedia of academic Platonism and himself a poet, became a special patron of Marino. Although the court poet Luigi Tansillo from Barcelona was in Italy at that time, it was not until the period of the enlightened viceroy, the count of Lemos (1610–1616, FIG. 3) that numerous Spanish writers came to Naples. During the subsequent viceregency of the duke of Ossuna (1616–1620), his counselor, the satirist Francisco Quevedo, lived in Naples. Interchange with Spain increased, and such poets as Giulio Cesare Cortese [**28**], the father of dialect literature, spent time in Spain as well. Neapolitan literature of the seventeenth and eighteenth centuries pointed in two directions: one elevated and the other common. Centuries after the Florentine establishment of *la lingua toscana*, there were three major languages in Naples: Italian, Latin, and Neapolitan. Although the latter began to flourish in Neapolitan literature during the early seventeenth century, real pride in the Neapolitan language did not develop until the nineteenth and twentieth centuries. Giovanni Battista Basile's *Tale of Tales*, a collection of charming and fanciful short stories [**30**, FIG. **36**], is a good example. Its author was inspired by his friend Cortese, who displayed patriotic and genuine preference for Neapolitan dialect coupled with an obvious love for his city. Cortese described the common people of Naples, their everyday life, adventures, duels, and all types of human interactions. His verbal renditions do not idealize but appear to be accurate observations flavored with earthiness and a pinch of satire. Still more passionate were the Italian poems and prose of the versatile Salvator Rosa [**34**], who wrote satires but was known primarily as a painter of romantic landscapes.

As with its fine arts, literature in Naples had the legacy not only of classical antiquity but of the late Middle Ages. Thomas Aquinas in the thirteenth century, Boccaccio in the fourteenth, and the Renaissance Giovanni Pontano (1426–1503) and Jacopo Sannazaro (1458–1530) formed a continued and admirable native tradition. As late as 1724 Ciccareli published the annotated *editio princeps* of Boccaccio's commentary on Dante. Sannazaro was venerated in somewhat the same mythical way Virgil had been with visitations to his tomb and elegies composed in his honor. Sannazaro's pastoral romance of 1504, *Arcadia*, had influenced many, including Sir Philip Sidney and even Shakespeare. The great Torquato Tasso (1544–1595), the last of the great Italian classical poets and author of *Gerusalemme Liberata* completed in 1575, had been born in nearby Sorrento. It was, in fact, Tasso who was an inspiration to Marino. The city abounded with many foreign writers as well; but most of these were either totally removed from Neapolitan culture: tourists who observed as outsiders or writers intent upon producing pragmatic and lucrative guides. There were the occasional foreign literary giants, such as Milton for whom Manso gave a tour of the city in 1638.

Marino's numerous Italian followers, the so-called *Marinisti* [33], were not necessarily Neapolitan, but these poets continued Marino's flamboyant style for a hundred years until it was out of favor due, in part, to the "new philosophy" that rejected its baroque ideals. Marino and his disciples offer examples of farfetched artifice, hyperbole, and extravagant analogies expressed through seemingly musical verse. Such flamboyance was perhaps inherited from the Spanish whose formality had exerted a marked influence upon Neapolitan manners and customs as well as its art and literature. The facility, sensuousness, exaggeration, and elaboration of Marino's poetry has been compared to the slightly earlier, often startling, art of Caravaggio who had so influenced the world of Neapolitan painting. Marino, who claimed that surprise was the true end of art, amassed outrageous comparisons, thus creating the "conceit." In his epic poem *Adone* of 1623 he offers this sort of hyperbole with his one hundred comparisons to jealousy. As Caravaggio's art was often unpredictable, Marino's elaborate epic shocked the censors, even though he associated moral allegories with each canto. Richard Crashaw's well-known translation of the *Sospetto d'Herode* [29] is relatively dry and does not reflect the vibrancy of the original. Marino's legacy was eventually replaced by a purity of style and an accommodation of the vernacular.

After the phenomenal popularity of Marino began to subside, the Settecento reacted with rationalist analyses of literature as exemplified by Gian Vincenzo Gravina's 1708 treatise *On the Nature of Poetry*, followed by another on tragedy in 1715. Literature often merged either with contemporary opera libretti, such as those of the renowned Pietro Metastasio [36, FIG. 40], or with historical accounts, such as that of Vincenzo Cuoco [12]. There was a pervasive and continued love of poetry that persisted on into the nineteenth century when it frequently came from foreign inspiration, most notably the English Romantics. As Joseph Addison, an eighteenth-century visitor, wrote:

> *The Town in soft Solemnities delights,*
> *And gentle Poets to her Arms invites....*

This was the century before the influx of Percy Bysshe Shelley who in 1819 wrote his "Julian and Maddalo" in this southern resort.

MUSIC AND THEATER

Chapter 5 presents another aspect of Neapolitan culture, especially during the eighteenth century: music and its relative, opera. Eighteenth-century Naples has been called the European capital of music. The Chevalier LaLande's travel accounts of 1769 [42] stated "music is the Neapolitan's triumph...the entire nation sings." As with poetry, there was the common and the elevated. While the tarantella was danced in the streets, the classical Neapolitan composers and musicians formed a musical avant-garde. The list is impressive and includes Alessandro Scarlatti (1659–1725) [FIG. 44], Domenico Scarlatti (1683–1757), Leonardo Leo (1694–1744), Baldassare Galuppi (1706–1785), Giovanni Battista Pergolesi (1710–1736), Niccolò Piccini (1728–1800), Antonio Sacchini (1734–1786), Giovanni Paisiello (1741–1816), Domenico Cimarosa (1749–1801) [FIG. 45], and others. The city abounded with numerous conservatories and attracted musicians from elsewhere, including such famous composers as Handel and Mozart.

The first opera performed in Naples was during the middle of the seventeenth century when visiting companies provided theatrical recapitulations of Masaniello's recent revolt. Native Neapolitan opera, which had been initiated under Scarlatti, was reputed to represent a native style that was lighter in theme but more melodious and harmonically richer than that elsewhere. Famous castrati performed their unique soprano until their tradition was forbidden in 1798. In the field of music Naples was frequently an initiator. Pergolesi's *La Serva padrona* of 1733 was considered to be the first *opera buffa*, a form in which the hero was a common person. Later examples of this new mode were Paisiello's *Socrate immaginario* of 1775 and Cimarosa's *Matrimonio segreto* of 1792. The greatest librettists, such as Pietro Metastasio, and outstanding singers, such as the female soprano known as La Gabrielli *(la cochetta)* were idolized. By 1750 a complete Paris edition of Metastasio's works was available, indicating his reputation in that northern cultural capital of Europe.

Several operas, including Handel's *Parthenope* of 1730, were specific tributes to Naples. Domenico Sarro's (1679–1744) opera of the same title, although not well received by the seasoned native audience, coincided with the opening of the great palace theater of San Carlo [FIG. 43]. The dramatic history of the city was itself frequently inspirational, and there was still special commemoration of the unsuccessful revolution led by Masaniello in 1647. Prior to Handel's opera was Reinhard Keiser's *Massagnello* of 1706. The legend of the fisherman continued into the nineteenth century with Daniel François Auber's *La muette de Portici*, which opened in Paris in 1828.

Naples provided many theaters for musical and theatrical productions. In the eighteenth century it boasted five major ones, including the socially prestigious Teatro di San Carlo founded in 1737 as part of the Palazzo Reale complex, the Fiorentini, the

Teatro Nuovo, the San Carlino (especially for *opera buffa*), and the Teatro del Fondo. As with Neapolitan literature, its theater could be elitist or vulgar, and theatrical companies professional or amateur. Plays could present Spanish drama, mysticism, conventional comedy, or improvised slapstick. Whereas several of the Spanish viceroys, such as the duke of Ossuna, hesitated to attend; later rulers, such as the duke of Monterey, enforced attendance by the garrison and the city's numerous courtesans. Although some of the masked comedies were bawdy, an occasional monk might be seen in the audience. During the Settecento the Bourbon royalty frequented the palace theater where lengthy plays and operas were performed and where the empty royal box can still be seen today.

In contrast to the world of classical performance there was the popular theater. By the end of the seventeenth century the improvisational Italian comic theater (*Commedia dell'arte*) was in decline. With its charlatans, quack dentists and doctors, as well as standard characters, such as the amorous Harlequin, it had prevailed since the sixteenth century or earlier as the common entertainment. In France Louis XIV had forbidden performances by the *Commedia*, but it continued nevertheless into the early eighteenth century.

Naples has always been associated with the theater of Pulcinella (Eng. Punchinello), which was derived from the *Commedia dell'arte* and flourished from around 1620. The character and his chaotic world was largely the invention of Silvio Fiorillo (fl. c. 1630). The name *"Pulcinella"* was derived from the word *pulcino* (chick). The character was traditionally a portly male with a squeaky voice who wore a black mask with a hooked nose, a baggy white suit, and a peaked cap [FIG. 42]. Pulcinella is constantly the victim of a cruel master and, despite amorous intrigues, his love is unrequited. It is his cunning that enables the lovable buffoon to escape the worst consequences. On occasion he is depicted with his large family surrounding him. Francesco Cerlone provides a humorous and typical episode from a Pulcinella script [41]. Just as Basile's tales served as a foundation for some of our modern fairy stories [30], Pulcinella was the original Punch, counterpart to Judy, and immortalized through English puppetry. Such paid entertainment was yet another attraction for the foreign visitor, and many wrote of their memorable evenings spent in Neapolitan theaters.

ECONOMY AND SOCIETY

The sociological structure of Naples during the period of 1600–1800 reveals the complexity of this cosmopolitan city. As Chapter 6 documents, during this period Naples faced many challenges. Surrounding mountains closed in the city. Its plains were vulnerable, its soil depleted, and its sea lanes neglected. The kingdom of Naples was not one of the Italian city-states but an exception because of its royal tradition and association with Spain. Until the Settecento it was still basically a feudal society, a medieval system imported by the Normans, strengthened by the Hohenstaufen and Angevin monarchies, and by the eighteenth century atypical in Italy. In fact, the feudal system in Naples was so stagnant and mismanaged that even those in control of it did not benefit. It was not until 1806 and the arrival of the Napoleonic system that this outdated social structure was finally abolished.

The kingdom's natural and human resources were never adequately developed and, despite its rich natural produce and in Naples the possession of the most active port on the Mediterranean, it had little or no industry outside of textiles. Beyond the city there was little productive agriculture, partly due to poor technical knowledge and a dearth of manpower, which created a need for imported Albanian and Greek laborers. Naples' wealth was non-circulating. Its major products were primarily exports for the luxury trade, such as silk stockings, soap, marble tables, and tortoiseshell snuff boxes. In addition, there was a minor exportation of wheat, barley, hemp, flax, oil, and wine. The city was a major net importer, often from the provinces, especially of grain from Apulia, but also for most other commodities from the rest of Europe. Despite exuberant reviews in the guidebooks, which referred to the *abbondanza* of Naples, by the mid-eighteenth century such descriptions had been replaced by sober and realistic Bourbon surveys. The famine of 1764 was seen by many observers as the greatest failure of the European Ancien Régime to date.

Economic classes reflected the social and political strata already mentioned. In addition to the viceroy and Spanish aristocracy, there was the discontented baronial class, the slowly growing middle-class known as the *gentile civile*, which consisted of administrators and bureaucrats — almost entirely from the feudal class — the professionals, and the miserable and powerless proletariat who repeatedly looked in vain to the monarchy for better conditions. The rural peasants were forced to support a larger and larger urban aristocracy. Between 1590 and 1675, for example, titled baronries alone rose from 118 to 434 within the kingdom. These spent the vast majority of their landed income and bureaucratic stipends on conspicuous consumption within the city and the court. At the same time, the nobility were faced with ever-mounting debt and dreaded and thwarted the middle class who increasingly demanded participation in local and royal administration. Eventually these upstarts, with their primarily administrative and professional functions, became indispensable to both the state and the nobility. Nevertheless, there remained no real Neapolitan bourgeoisie in the sense of an intermediary commercial or business class. In the seventeenth century during the reign of the viceroys only about one in six Neapolitans was formally employed; and there were reportedly an additional 10,000 slaves in the city. Moryson dramatically illustrates this phenomenon by mentioning that in the market place there was a stone on which men played away their liberty at dice.

The king's officers lent them money to do so and then sent them to the galleys when they were unable to pay their debts. This was a means, he claims, by which Spain could obtain slaves of both sexes.

Naples suffered from high prices and taxes, as well as low wages; and its inflation was particularly high during the eighteenth century. Its debts, many to its rival port Genoa, were accompanied by heavy duties, export restrictions, currency depreciation, and by such rigid and corrupt state regulation as the *Annona*, which controlled the grain supply and which by 1750 was responsible for feeding almost 330,000 impoverished Neapolitans. Antonio Serra's brief treatise of 1613 [43] proposed the development of native manufacturing as well as "how to make kingdoms abound in gold and silver." During the period of 1638–1647 Naples' economy suffered greatly as a result of Spain's involvement in the Thirty Years War, which ended in 1648. By the eighteenth century, inflation had almost destroyed the economy. At the same time, due to strict regulation, the large population was extremely concentrated within the city walls. The relatively tall buildings and narrow streets created an unhealthy atmosphere made worse by resulting crime and crippled transportation. It was not until 1740 that the regime ordered the walls dismantled, a project that took until 1787 to complete. Meanwhile, as expansion became possible, suburbs were developed, which relieved considerable pressure. Until that time the city was the center of virtually all economic activity, an unmitigated socioeconomic concentration that further impoverished the rural economy.

This is not to say that the kingdom and city lacked the tools of economic analysis and individual writers to apply these in new and significant ways for the history of European economics. Serra's treatise on the comparative economics of Venice and Naples, already mentioned, was only one in a great school of economic thought exemplified by such students of currency and exchange as Gian Donato Turbolo [44] in the early Seicento, and Ferdinando Galiani [45, FIG. 48] and Carlo Antonio Broggia [46] in the Settecento. At the end of our period Giuseppe Palmieri [48] offered a skilled analysis of the kingdom's problems and recommendations for reforms, which never came.

LEGAL STUDIES AND LEGISLATION

Perhaps not coincidentally, during the period of 1600–1800 Naples was a city of lawyers, and legal theory and history fill the readings in Chapter 7. The seventeenth-century traveler Sandys had described Naples as "full of life and bustle; the tribunals pestered with clamorous advocates and litigious clients; the streets thronged…." At that time it was estimated that the kingdom had 20,000 or even as many as 30,000 solicitors, most of whom made their careers in Naples, which had a virtual monopoly on the realm's courts. When Pope Innocent XI wanted the marquis of Carpio to give him 30,000 swine for slaughter, this aristocrat amusingly offered lawyers, instead. Especially during the eighteenth century all of the litigation that took place between the progressives and conservatives, including the Church and local administrators, well served this disproportionate group. Legal education was an initiation for so many into the professions. The passage by Francesco D'Andrea [49, FIG. 49] indicates how the legal profession could improve one's social status.

Although the wealth of the baronial class was dwindling, they contributed to the growth of this legal system because of their own special needs and their control of the administrative system as the *ministero togato*. While the clergy sometimes benefited, as in the case of the archbishop of Santa Severina who pursued lawsuits against the local court in Rome and Naples, the professional class amassed great fortunes through the courts. With this wealth came titles, tax farms, and agricultural speculation; and by the 1680s a demand as well for formal equality of titles and dress. The laws were complex and fluctuated constantly with each succeeding wave, the legal process was slow, and the judges often corrupt. Many could easily be bribed to serve as a false witness. In the face of this reality the "new philosophy" inspired D'Andrea to develop a new concept of law — not just a rigid code but a functional reform system. In this light, from 1780 to 1788 Gaetano Filangieri's *La Scienze della legislazione* [50, FIG. 50] was also published.

PHILOSOPHES AND REFORMERS

Chapter 8 surveys Naples' growing interest in rationalist philosophy. In the Seicento Neapolitan philosophy was represented by such thinkers as Giacomo della Porta, Bernardo Telesio, Tommaso Campanella [FIG. 37], and Giordano Bruno the poet-philosopher, who was burned at the stake for heresy in Rome in 1600. During his viceregency from 1599 to 1601, the progressive Fernando Ruiz de Castro, count of Lemos, promoted humanistic learning and helped sponsor the Accademia degli Oziosi ("idlers"). He attempted as well to solve some of the city's problems, including its administrative corruption, by issuing *prammatiche* to regulate every organ of local and central government. The count was ahead of his time in his effort to harness these "pragmatic treatises" by knowledgeable men of letters for preventing abuses and obtaining new benefits for the city. This reform literature became a Neapolitan hallmark and did bring about some societal change. From the middle of the seventeenth century, Naples became one of the most innovative schools of political and economic thought in Italy and in this surpassed even Florence and Venice. Yet such an Enlightenment approach remained problematic. In the sixteenth century Bruno had already postulated that one truth existed for the masses and another for the cognoscenti. What followed was a continued rift between the avant-garde intellectuals and the masses that was not addressed until well into the eighteenth century. There remained subsequently an enormous gap between social ideals and practice as the *illuministi* thinkers outnumbered the doers. Many hoped for a "gradualism" whereby evolutionary change would inevitably and independently come about. Yet it became increasingly clear that economic reform would not occur without social and political change.

The process by which this was realized had to do with a great intellectual revival that began as early as the 1650s, the decade of the great plague, with the return from northern Italy of the young scientist and mathematics professor Tommaso Cornelio [68]. With him he brought back books by Galileo, who had many followers in Naples, as well as writings of Francis Bacon, Robert Boyle, and René Descartes. The scholarly library of Giuseppe Valletta was made accessible to students, and during the late 1720s the impressive library of the monastery of the Gerolomini was constructed. By 1707 the Spanish monarchy was no longer a factor of intellectual oppression; and by 1720 the Austrians were encouraging these "moderns." There began significant interchange with foreign schools, including contests with England's Royal Society. Naples' close-knit intelligentsia engaged in constant and lively debate. The writer Metastasio [36], for example, collaborated with the natural philosopher Giambattista Vico [54, FIG. 52], who in turn worked with the reformist Antonio Genovesi [55].

Many academies, such as the Investiganti and the Uniti, were initiated; and others, such as the Infuriati, were revived. While Viceroy Don Pedro de Toledo (1532–1553) had closed down several of these groups because he considered them to be anti-Spanish, by 1611 Giovanni Battista Manso had founded the Accademia degl' Oziosi in an attempt to unite Spanish and Italian, especially Neapolitan, writers. These institutions thrived well into the eighteenth century with the continuous admission of outstanding scholars, such as Vico, who was elected to the Academy of the Assorditi in 1730. Within this progressive context, the "new philosophy" was born. The roots of this philosophy were in Cartesian philosophy, the dissemination of which newly alarmed the previously expelled Inquisition, which by the 1690s had the power to stigmatize Vico's friends, such as Giovanni de Cristofaro and Basilio Giannelli. Descartes' metaphysics was alternately accepted and rejected by gifted Neapolitans. It has been said that the city's intellectuals were too skeptical to accept wholeheartedly any one abstract theory. As a result they tended to prefer Descartes' more tangible math and physics. French ideas both concrete and abstract continued to be widespread, however, and Genovesi's [60] belief that agriculture supported by a large population constituted the primary source of wealth was derived ultimately from the Physiocrats; like Galiani, Genovesi supported Newton's theories, and it was this that finally cost him his chair in theology in 1748. By the second quarter of the Settecento French rationalism was eclipsed increasingly by English theory. At this time Naples received several prominent foreign intellectuals, including Johann Schiller, Stendhal, and Goethe. The latter was especially impressed with the ideas of Gaetano Filangieri [50], who wrote against the backdrop of the American Revolution and whose sympathies clearly lay with its rationalist and democratic ideals.

The importance of this new thinking was first recognized by scientists and physicians from whom it spread to other fields of learning and branches of society. Thus the study of nature led to the examination of society and inspired a desire for reform. The need to change the thinking of conservative institutions was paramount. By 1720 the new philosophy had found its way into Naples' ultra-conservative, medieval university as well as into its courts and literary societies. Genovesi's lectures were instrumental in leading intellectuals back to the university; and in 1754 Naples created the first European university chair in political economy for Genovesi. Later in the eighteenth century the university gained importance as that of the academies waned. Although the new philosophy continued to be opposed both by conservative thinkers and the Church, by the middle of the eighteenth century it was triumphant, and practical government action was desired.

Although there had been a long tradition in Naples of religious charitable institutions, such as the Hospital of Santa Anna and the Albergo dei Poveri, sponsored in part by Charles IV (1734–1759) (III of Spain, 1759–1788), real social reform came out of the new scientific and rational thinking. The Bourbons also contributed to an atmosphere of nationalistic and humanitarian reform and in the process helped destroy the economic power of the nobility. During the second half of the century the famous Florentine politician and jurist Bernardo Tanucci ruled from 1759 to 1767 as an enlightened, if absolutist, regent who took up the reform program of the intellectuals against both the feudal nobility and the clergy until the forces of reaction within the realm forced him to resign from his ministerial post in 1776. Thus concrete social objectives often remained unrealized, due partly to the lack of a unified intellectual movement and of an effective progressive bourgeoisie to implement the ideas of the reformist intellectuals. Ironically the reformers themselves were primarily from the middle class, which tended to be socially conservative and in favor of the status quo.

Nevertheless, eighteenth-century Naples abounded in significant publications in philosophy, economics, and sociology. Probably the two greatest were Pietro Giannone's *Istoria civile del regno di Napoli* of 1723 [7] and Giambattista Vico's *Scienze nuova* [54] of 1725. The latter, which claimed that history or creative action is the only valid human knowledge, suggested reorganizing the state on a natural, rational basis defined in terms similar to those of Jean Jacques Rousseau and of Charles

Montesquieu who visited Naples in 1729. René Descartes' principles were also finally translated in 1722 and became a fundamental base for the new thinking. Genovesi's practical approach urged the abolition of feudalism through specific economic and juridical reforms, including the redistribution of land.

Early in his reign the vulgar but popular monarch Ferdinando IV (1759–1806, 1815–1825) tried to continue the reformist policy of his father Charles IV. During his reign the experimental, self-governing village of equals, known as San Leucio [47], was initiated, a good example of the immediate application of reform brought about through both compulsory instruction and vaccination. Located at the edge of Charles' royal palace at Caserta, San Leucio was to be an ideal society of the future.

RELIGIOUS LIFE

In Part IV (Chapter 9), "The Spiritual World," we offer texts dealing with Naples' spiritual life and thought. Christian religious establishments had a very long history in the city and included monasteries that dated from as early as 400 C.E. Its early Christian catacombs were extensive and remarkable. John Evelyn's diaries [15] stated that in churches and monasteries Naples exceeded all cities except Rome. Because of their number, estimated as high as 500 but probably fewer than 300, Neapolitan churches were often considered collectively by visitors, although the numerous guidebooks made references to their famous tombs, relics, and saints, which were visited and written about more than the great works of art in them. There were early Neapolitan saints, such as the city's patron San Gennaro and the martyr Sant'Aspreno [FIG. 53], and later ones, such as Sant'Andrea Avellino (died 1608, canonized

1712) [64, FIG. 58] and San Francesco Caracciolo (died 1608, canonized 1807). Despite the skepticism of such observers as Fynes Moryson [57] and Michael Kelly [61], devotion to San Gennaro was so intense that it was reported that one English consul was dismembered for "heresy" by the crowd when the saint's blood failed to liquefy.

By 1600 the occult had been suppressed, and all heresy had (at least officially) disappeared. During the Seicento great churches and confraternities were established, including the Pio Monte della Misericordia in 1601. By about 1620 the Neapolitan church of the Counter Reformation had obtained allegiance, unification, and obedience. But on a popular level Naples lived on as a city of great traditions and customs that were often unappreciated by foreigners. Like most popular religious life of the Ancien Régime throughout Europe, much of Neapolitan spirituality might seem superstitious and outmoded by modern standards. A penchant for legend and tradition is exemplified by the church of the Dominicans, which housed the famous crucifix that was said to have spoken to St. Thomas Aquinas [15]. A small painting of the Crucifixion attributed to Michelangelo was erroneously said to have been created by using as a model a peasant whom the artist had just crucified. One cynical French traveler stated that "religion here is mere superstition; it is also very convenient."

The city of Naples supplied no less than eighteen popes including the honest, educated, virtuous, and popular *"angelo"* Innocent XII (1691–1700) [62] of the Pignatelli family, the last southern Italian pope. But even a popular pope worked in a time-worn mode. In 1697, despite the opposition of some cardinals, Innocent exercised authoritative censorship when he shut down the new Tor di Nona Theater because it performed an "immoral" French comedy. In contrast to an age when Spanish viceroys controlled all actions of the clergy, and a Counter-Reformation clergy controlled many aspects of Neapolitan culture, the eighteenth century witnessed a government and church increasingly challenged by the Enlightenment. The "new philosophy" permeated every part of the society and began to dispel "fashionable and external baroque religiosity," sometimes with unexpected results. It was not only the intellectuals who reflected enlightened rationalism but also the Freemasons who were quite active in Naples by the late eighteenth century and were supported by Queen Maria Carolina (1752–1814) of Austria. Soon Freemasonry became the most vital force outside the university, with five active lodges supporting the revolutionary ones in Paris. In 1751 a papal bull forbade its continuance, and in 1789 these lodges were finally suppressed by the Neapolitan court.

There were other unorthodox reactions to the Catholic fervor and censorship that had permeated the period of the Spanish domination, including inward Quietism, severe Molinism, ascetic Jansenism, and even a formal atheism. The latter, which can be traced to a revival of Lucretius' attitude toward nature, had been prosecuted during the period of 1686–1693. In the eighteenth century Bourbon royal policy gradually came to side with the *illuministi* and against reactionary forces within the Church. By the 1760s, guided by Tanucci and an alliance dominated by otherwise devout Catholics, the crown aimed to promote less rigid, more progressive ideas and, above all, to stop Jesuit control of religious education. Although the conservatives were steadfast in their position, the unwavering stance of the Jesuits proved largely unsuccessful, and by 1769 they were expelled by the Bourbons not only from Naples itself but all their dominions. But it was not until the 1770s that non-religious primary and secondary schools were established. The communes of the kingdom won the right to teach in Italian and to control instruction of Latin and religious education. The books used to replace the Jesuits' texts were, in fact, printed at the Regia Stamperia (Royal Press) itself. In 1777 the Jesuits' extensive properties were also placed under royal control.

Pietro Giannone [7] became a leader of anticlerical sentiment, arguing that since the Church owned a great deal of land, thus perpetuating feudalism, it should be treated as a temporal power. In 1790 Giuseppe Maria Galanti had stated that the numerous clergy, larger than Rome's and consisting of about five percent of the population, possessed one third of the national wealth, including a great deal of land, while extending their privileges not only to relatives and friends but even to tenants. The practical efforts initiated by his appointment as religious Visitor of the Kingdom in March 1781 were frustrated by a baronial-clerical alliance and won only limited success. He was removed from office by the Bourbons in 1794. The writings of Giuseppe Capelcelatro concerning celibacy [65] reflects contemporary cynicism toward the clergy. Not all clergy were unpopular, however. Some, like Cardinal Ascanio Filomarino, the great autocratic archbishop of Naples from 1641 to 1666, had serious social concerns and gained popularity by arguing against the *gabelle* (excise taxes). There were major and minor victories and defeats for both the conservatives and progressives throughout the period.

NATURAL SCIENCE

When the "new philosophy" was introduced around 1650 it implications were first to scientists and physicians from whom it then spread to other branches of society and fields of learning. Whether or not Neapolitan philosophy had produced social improvement, as Part IV (Chapter 10) reveals, it had certainly exerted an influence upon physical science and experimentation. In the field of scientific discovery, Naples had its own disciples of Newton and Galileo. Tommaso Campanella [67] had been a defender of the latter [FIG. 59]. Natural philosophy had paved the way for experimental science, and there was considerable interchange among scholars in various disciplines as well as individual versatility. Naples, now recognized as an intellectual center, was visited during the seventeenth century by Francesco Redi (c.1626–1697/8) who had spent most of his life in Florence and was an expert on insects and vipers. Giulio Cesare Vanini [66, FIG. 51] both discussed the most arcane principles of philosophical/scientific inquiry and undertook the detailed, empirical study of botany. In 1649 Tommaso Cornelio [68] of Cosenza arrived in Naples, bringing with him many books by both Italian and foreign naturalists. Like Lionardo Di Capua [69], who held a chair in medicine at the University of Naples, Cornelio received one in mathematics; although the passage included here is from his writing on physical science, specifically the digestive system. It was probably Pierre Gassendi (1592–1655) who provided the strongest philosophical basis of the local experimental science. Later on some of the Church's greatest opposition came from this group of scientists, which by 1720 had penetrated the conservative University of Naples. Atheism was so strong among medical practitioners that the Inquisition began to arrest some of Naples' young aristocratic physicians. This action eventually created sympathy for the moderns and strengthened their position.

The late seventeenth and early eighteenth centuries were important for the natural sciences because the academies that flourished at that time encouraged the study of physics, math, and natural history. In Rome the Accademia dei Lincei elected foreign members who were to supply information concerning the latest scientific discoveries to the rest of Europe. The Lincei had a sister academy in Naples headed by the versatile Giovanni Battista della Porta [FIG. 41]. Arcadia was yet another, a society of naturalists whose members included the well-known Neapolitan painter of the early eighteenth century, Francesco Solimena (1657–1747). Naples' Società delle Scienze Naturali (Society of Natural Sciences) had been founded over a hundred years before the English Royal Society was created in 1660. The Reale Accademia delle Scienze (Royal Academy of Sciences) was established in 1732 through the efforts of Ferdinando Galiani. Because of a lack of finances — and Charles III's view that it was supported by the Austrians — it lasted only five years.

Any discussion of culture in Naples requires some mention of the strange and exotic. In the field of science these would include the already mentioned unorthodox museum of the nobleman Ferdinando Imperato, which housed natural rarities described by Evelyn, the Speciary for rare drugs and medicines at the convent of S. Caterina a Formello, and the still extant Sansevero Chapel built by the eccentric alchemist Prince Raimondo in the eighteenth century. It was he who had tried to extract phosphorus from wine, dissected two corpses in order to expose their nervous systems, and attempted to simulate the liquefaction of San Gennaro's blood by combining mercury and cinnabar. Excommunicated by the pope, he died after a botched experiment.

L

INTRODUCTION

The new philosophy of the enlightened eighteenth century combined with several political and social factors to contribute to the great Neapolitan Revolution of 1799 known as the Second Parthenopean Republic, which followed quickly on the heals of the French invasion of the kingdom. The invasion was spurred by an ill-advised anti-French alliance with Great Britain forged by Queen Maria Carolina's prime minister, Sir John Francis Acton, and by the queen's own alliance with Austria; but, according to Cuoco [12], the ensuing revolution did not understand and therefore satisfy the needs of the populace. Ferdinando IV returned to the city, only to be displaced in 1806 by the return of the French and the installation of Joseph Bonaparte as king. He was succeeded as king of Naples by Joachim Murat, who ruled until the defeat of Napoleon in 1815 and the restoration of the Bourbons. Despite the sweeping changes and modernizations brought about by nearly fifteen years of French revolutionary and imperial rule, the Bourbon restoration ended the Neapolitan Enlightenment and succeeded in slowing or stopping many progressive trends. After this point Naples never again regained its creative and intellectual fervor. The unification of Italy in the 1860s proved to be more of a conquest of the South than an assimilation. By mid-century churches and monasteries were already closed. Theaters were abandoned, and artistic production came to an end, as did the Grand Tour. The travelers and their guidebooks ceased. Naples entered into a new and difficult modernity for which she was ill-suited and from which she never recovered. Her Golden Age was no more, and would never be again. Sannazaro's prophecy echoes: *Poi che Napoli tua non è più Napoli.*

Figure 9

PART I:
CIVIC
PRIDE

Figure 10

CHAPTER 1
History of the Kingdom
and City of Naples

1. FRANCESCO ZAZZERA (16TH–EARLY 17TH C.)

Zazzera's account of the Neapolitan nobility, published early in the seventeenth century in 1615–18, is a reminder that ever since 1504 Naples was governed by a viceroy appointed by the Spanish crown. At that time the viceroy was Pedro Fernandez de Castro e Andrada, count of Lemos, who ruled from 1610 to 1616 [FIG. 3]. The viceroy resided at the Palazzo Reale, which had been designed just a few years earlier in 1600–1602 by Domenico Fontana and was centrally located in the city's old part nearest the port. Zazzera, who is concerned primarily with the Neapolitan nobility during the reign of Spain's Philip III (1598–1621), introduces us to the major aristocratic families, such as that of de Castro and Caracciolo. This passage is an excerpt from his rather lengthy account of the origins and history of the former. For a continuation of records concerning this privileged stratum of society, see the excerpt from Toppi's 1687 directory of prominent citizens [17].

FRANCESCO ZAZZERA, THE NEAPOLITAN NOBILITY, "CONCERNING THE DE CASTRO FAMILY"

> What we think of as the nobility of Spain was the broad, historical category developed by Don Alonso ["the Wise"] who supported the idea that de Castro's family was descended from Nugno Rasura and Laino Calvo, a position supported by the first father-in-law as well as the reporter, Loperizio. The Count Don Pietro of Portugal started this lineage with the name of Count Don Gottiere Fernandez de Castro, so-named because of his ruling Castroxeris in Castile. I believe all this is true, provided that "Figueros" is descended from the Count Don Fernando, son of the King Don Bermudo of Leone, the first with this name (and later with another) who succeeded to Maurecato around 786 A.D. He was known as "Signore" in Galizia of Manforte and Lemos, and remained the head of these states, later to

3

lose rule of them as well as other territories, in particular, Orseglion and Torogno. He eventually married the Countess Donna Nugna, with whom he had a son and, using the name of the mother, became known as Count Don Nugno Fernandez. He was a great and powerful prince in his time because he was married to Donna Geloira or Aluira, daughter of the Count Don Sancio Vglioa, sister of the Count Don Gonsalvo Sances Vglioa.... [Francesco Zazzera, *Della nobiltà dell'Italia*. Naples: Giovanni Battista Gargano e Lucretio Nucci, 1615–18. (Trans. I.I.-D.)]

2. GIULIO CESARE, "ABBATE," BRACCINI (EARLY 17TH C.)

This early seventeenth-century journalist gives us a detailed and analytical account of the eruption of Vesuvius which began on the 16th of December, 1631 and lasted through the following March. The volcano, which had frequently brought disaster to the city and continued to be a constant threat, has been documented from ancient times. In 79 C.E. the Elder Pliny had died while trying to rescue victims of what was probably the most devastating eruption. An account of the famous burial of Pompeii, Herculaneum, and Stabiae during the reign of Titus was provided by Pliny the Younger[1] who recorded his memories for Tacitus. Major eruptions of Vesuvius, located approximately six miles east of the city of Naples, were recorded as well in 1538, 1672 and 1715, as was a gigantic volcano-related earthquake in 1688. In 1631 Braccini took a copy of Pliny the Younger's account with him to the site of the eruption. This disaster of 1631 was not without religious significance for the citizens of Naples in that it was supposed to have not only verified the liquefaction of the blood of San Gennaro [61], the patron saint of the city, but caused the position of the saint's hand to turn subsequently toward Vesuvius. [See 3; FIGS. 11, 54.] Here Braccini sets the stage by giving a detailed description of the topography of the volcanic mountain and its surroundings. Castelli [3] is another writer who focuses upon various aspects of this 1631 eruption of Vesuvius.

GIULIO CESARE BRACCINI, "THE ERUPTION OF VESUVIUS IN 1631"

> The ancient and notorious Vesuvius looms over a loosely-defined, sunny plain out of which arise earthquakes and eruptions. On this site is the lovely Sebeto which flows into the famous basin of the Tyrrhenian Sea. Pliny named the highest levels of this peaceful region "the battle's fence" because of its incredible fertility, and it has a base from which this magnificent mountain shoots up between Ceres and Bacchus and from the Italian Merula Paradise. If one drops a plumb line from its highest peak down to the sea, it so happens that

not all of its sides are that steep, its slope being only a little over four miles long. At least one side of the slopes, with a round base of 24,[2] is lower as if disassociated from the other hills. Except for the part on the east where the slope was either formed in this steep manner or became that way due to debris vomited on top of it, its levels and strata are full of vineyards bearing fruit trees and herbs. Wild trees and useful kindling are everywhere here. The top of the volcano, somewhat divided or rather almost completely surrounded by another hollow mountain shaped like a half-moon, and known as the *atrio*, is actually separate; although some think that it used to be all one piece as described by Strabo and affirmed by Dione.[3] However, judging from the rocks and ashes that have been ejected, it is probable that separation started on the most western side.

Figure 11

Among the famous sites was the Torre del Greco, a tourist attraction and resort, where many Europeans went to escape the bitter winter, and a considerable number of invalids hoped to regain their health. And somewhat similar are the [nearby towns of] Annunziata, Resina and Portici[4] although the air in the former was very humid since it was so near the Sarno River as well as the duct of Molina and, in addition, not far from the Cava. As for the other two locations, they were sunny and warm due to the western wind with the thinner and colder north wind, dominated by the Mistral winds, restricted to either side. In short, Vesuvius was surrounded by delightful estates and farms that were irrigated not by gurgling streams but by rain water, which was abundant and made the land extremely fertile, a condition that I myself have observed and that is likewise recorded by both Strabo and Pliny. [Giulio Cesare Braccini, *Dell'Incendio fattosi nel Vesuvio*. Naples: Gioviano di Lucca, 1632, pp. 1-2. (Trans. I. I.-D.)]

3. PIETRO CASTELLI (1570–1657)

The Roman Castelli is an obscure writer and scholar who, like Braccini [2] provides a record of the 1631 eruption of Vesuvius. His account, published the following year in 1632, is a specific and accurate description of some of the particular aspects of the disaster and is presented with "a distinctive historical and philosophical method." In addition, like Braccini, Castelli offers a history of Vesuvius' eruptions including those from antiquity. He discusses as well probable causes, specific incidents and locations, and possible remedies. Castelli's verbose account mentions that of Braccini. Such documentaries underscore the magnitude of this eruption of 1631. [See **2.**]

Pietro Castelli, "Contemporary and Historical Vesuvius"

> With regard to this recent incident of 1631, I estimate that in all a total of twelve fires has occurred. And while many reported a greater number of fires, others claimed fewer reducing the number to that already indicated; we will let them debate the matter as to how many times this mountain has endured such explosions; but then it cooled down extinguishing every flame and all blasts of heat: the fact that it did indeed take place has been determined and underscored by the writings of Braccini [2] who was himself in the great chasm of the mountain [and who maintains that] a number of cows died despite their struggles to save themselves. Some were impaled on very large trees dangling from the mouth of the abyss whereas others were lowered by long suspended ropes attached to one of the trees. Many of the beasts could not be pulled out as in many cases these ropes were immersed in water; others that were visible met with great torrents of water, and it was reported that five or six years later a little smoke could be seen coming out of the chasm. Finally, after some so-called earthquakes, on the morning of December 16 an arch of fire was said to have been seen for a brief time, then flames, and a little ways from there a great peak of fire at the top of the mountain: then appeared the great puff of gas, then in a short period great thunder, enormous darkness, clouds of cinders, more fumes, a rain of stones, ashes, rivers of fire, more holes, and a gush of water; for four days there was enormous turmoil, then just the violence of the chasm, with earthquakes and simultaneous showers of ashes over all of the Gennaro.[5] This is when it occurred to me to record this account and insist that it is the most accurate, despite the fact that some record a greater number, up to twenty and even more, or a lesser: four were recorded in the time of the eruption during the reign of Titus, and nine for Theodoric who ruled in 484....[6] [Pietro Castelli, *Incendio del Monte Vesuvio*. Rome: Giacomo Mascardi, 1632, pp. 12-13. (Trans. J.C.P.)]

4. SCIPIO MAZZELLA (FL. 16TH –17TH C.)

Although Mazzella, a "famous antiquary," according to his volume's complete English title, might be associated primarily with the sixteenth rather than the seventeenth century, his volume on the Kingdom of Naples should be included here as part of a collective history because it was not completed until many years later by James Howell, who compiled the second part. Published in 1654, *Parthenopeia* (from the ancient Greek name for Naples, *"Parthenope"*)[7] includes not only a history of the kingdom and its "dominions thereunto annexed," but an account of the lives of all their ruling monarchs. The volume is illustrated with depictions of the kings and the heraldic arms of all the provinces. The prolific Howell derived his text from an early translation of Mazzella's account by Samson Lennard but added his own supplements concerning Naples' physical beauty and abundance. A probable source for this augmented history of Naples is Alexander Giraffi's *Exact History of the Revolution in Naples,* which Howell had translated in 1650 [see 6]. It should be remembered that Howell wrote this portrayal of a Catholic kingdom during the Puritan interregnum.

As with the description of the elusive B.W. [see 62], Mazzella's basic account is representative of the Neapolitan fascination with the ceremonial process, whether it be religious or secular.

SCIPIO MAZZELLA, "ON THE CORONATION OF THE KINGS OF NAPLES"

> I have thought it a thing very fit and convenient, having declared what the Kings were of this noble and renowned kingdom, to receive also the manner and the ceremony which is used in the time of their coronation. But before I proceed any further, it is to be understood, that there are but only four Kings that are crowned and anointed by the order of the Pope...the King of Jerusalem, the King of France, the King of Naples, commonly called Sicilia, and the King of England. All the rest are crowned by their Archbishops or Bishops by a certain custome. The Emperour is anointed and crowned in the same manner as are the said four Kings, and therefore all the other Kings are called by the name of Highness, and not Majesty, except those that are anointed by the order of the Pope, as is said. In the coronation then of the King of Naples the Pope sendeth a Cardinall his Legate, or a Patriarch, but he must have holy Orders, because the said Legate not having the said holy Orders, another ought to come which hath the said dignity. There also assembles (according to the accustomed manner) all the Archbishops of the kingdome

which crown this Prince with the greatest pomp and state that may
be done to any Christian King.

The principall thing before the King taketh this dignity, the seven
Officers of the kingdom, which are seven principall secular Lords, that
meet together at this coronation, are cloathed in Purple,[8] lined with
Ermins, with very rich attires upon their heads, and repair together
with the Recorder of the Citie into the Cathedrall Church of Naples,
where is the ancient Tomb of Charles of Angio,[9] which was the first
that was crowned with an Imperiall crown, and invested King of both
the Sicilies and Jerusalem; and there the Apostolike Legate, with the
other Archbishops pontifically clothed with Miters and Rochets, and
the other Prelats in Purple Vestments, attend the Kings coming at the
Church Dore. Afterward when the King cometh that is to be crowned,
he entreth into the said Church, accompanied with all the Princes,
Dukes, Marqueses, Earls, Barons and Lords of the kingdom, and the
Legat suddenly kissing [his] forehead, receiveth him, and saith unto
him with an high and intelligible voyce these words,

I AM COME BY THE APPOINTMENT AS THE SUPREAM BISHOP POPE (NAME) TO
CROWN THEE KING OF NAPLES AND JERUSALEM.

After the Archbishop with the other, that have charge to say Service
in the said Church, receive the King at the Altar, and there causing
him to kneel down, and after is made by the Archbishop of Naples,
of Capua, and of Salerno, devout prayers for his Majesty, one of the
Bishops demandeth of him in Latin, if he will promise to maintain
always the Faith and Christian Religion? Defend the Widows, the
Fatherless, and the Poor? Establish the kingdom and minister justice
to everyone? And last of all if he will always yeild due honor to the
supream Bishop? To all which things the King answering He will, two
Archbishops take him by the arm, and lead him to the Altar, where
he solemly sweareth to observe all that which the Archbishop hath
demanded of him.… [Scipio Mazzella, *Parthenopeia, or the History of
the Most Renowned Kingdom of Naples and the Dominions, There unto
Annexed and the Lives of All Their Kings… (The Second Part continued
to these Present Times, 1654 by James Howell)*. London: Humphrey
Moseley, 1654, 1:28-29.]

5. GIUSEPPE DONZELLI (1596–1670)

Donzelli, the Neapolitan baron of Dogliola, doctor, republican, and author of numerous scientific and medical treatises, dedicated his detailed 1647 account entitled *Naples Freed, the Heroic Solution Made by Its People, to Henry of Lorraine, Duke of Guise,*[10] whose coat of arms appears on the frontispiece. There exist several manuscript versions of this diary, which was divided into two parts and edited by Ottavio Beltrano. Because of changing political conditions, Donzelli's book was unauthorized and even the part already printed was suppressed. Almost all examples of it had been burned. The work begins with a short description of Naples and its environs followed by accounts, such as the following, recounting the 1647 Revolution led by Masaniello. [See **6, 7, FIGS. 1, 12.**] The narration stops on Nov. 14, 1647, the date when the duke of Guise entered the city. On the last page of the text the escutcheon of the Neapolitan Republic is featured.

GIUSEPPE DONZELLI, "A DESIRE FOR FREEDOM"

> That same day, Tomaso Anello (Masaniello) received a message from the viceroy[11] who invited him and his family to spend some time on the delightful and pleasant riviera of Posilipo.[12] He accepted the invitation and thanked the viceroy for the favor. In the meantime, the wife of the viceroy sent her usual carriage with six horses to transport Tomaso Anello's wife and her female relatives. The women entered the carriage wearing their cheap brocade clothing and were welcomed in grand style. The viceroy's wife gave Tomaso Anello's wife the title of Duchess since the viceroy himself had already bestowed the title of Duke of St. George to Tomaso himself. Anello, having been brought to the palace by the cardinal archbishop, was treated with only apparent politeness because not only was he hated but a cruel death had been already planned for him. So he found himself reunited with the viceroy and all the court as the Arpaja who had been elected. And there were others, too, including one person in authority who was accompanied by a royal visitor from Spain. To the latter Tomaso Anello said with determination as he held him by the shirt, "Honored visitor, I have been told that you have stolen six thousand ducats, and if I haven't already punished you, you deserve to be for the sake of His Eminence the cardinal here present, but for the future keep your wits about you because you will need them.") Soon after, everyone left and the honored cardinal excused himself. Tomaso Anello went on the viceroy's boat and the women on that of his wife. And on the

boats they were playing the same music heard at the palace; eight boats, armed in order to keep an eye on Anello, followed. After arriving at Posillipo, the viceroy welcomed all and offered a delicious lunch, entertaining them in the same way his wife treated the women guests; a necklace worth one thousand five hundred scudi was then given to Anello's wife. People muttered a lot about this meeting with the viceroy and most believed it was not the right time to go to Posillipo. Everyone returned home at a very late hour.

After this banquet, it became obvious that Tomaso Anello was acting rather strange, one might say in a frenetic manner: or maybe it was because his attitude had changed when he saw himself elevated socially by the viceroy. He began to talk constantly night and day with people and often forgot to eat, consequently becoming weak and losing his voice. The more clever and analytical minds were offering different explanations, which were lapped up by those who were vengeful and had been preferred politically to the Spaniards perpetually in command.

Monday the 15th, Tomaso Anello was behaving in such an excessive manner that everyone thought he had gone mad; the people began to contemplate the end of his rule; and some claimed to have seen him riding his horse around the market while alternately toss-

Figure 12

ing away and then demanding back a huge knife. Some of those wounded (by his weapon) sought revenge and started throwing stones back at him. Although he was never stationary, one stone did manage to hit him on the back of the head and he was lucky not to have been injured by the force of the blow. Then a man named Giovanni Panarella, commonly known as Vanni, one of the local leaders, was very upset by the serious wounds that Anello had inflicted upon two of his people from the Conciaria, and so he went that night to Tomaso's house intending to kill him but was subdued by Anello's guards. [Giuseppe Donzelli, *Parthenope liberata*, Antonio Altamura, F. Fiorentino, eds. Naples: F. Fiorentino, 1970, pp. 96-97. (Trans. I.I.-D.)]

6. LORD ALEXANDER (ALESSANDRO) GIRAFFI (17TH C.)

In 1650 James Howell had translated Giraffi's *Exact History of...the Revolution in Naples*, a publication of the Regia Stamperia (Royal Press), and it had become a probable inspiration for his expanded version of Mazzella's *Parthenopeia* [4]. Among the more than twenty accounts of the Revolution in 1647, which had been initiated by the fisherman Tommaso Aniello ("Masaniello") over an excessive fruit tax, this one by the obscure scholar Giraffi is perhaps the most dramatic and eloquent. Seemingly an eyewitness testimony of the event, it emerges also as a miniature masterpiece of humanist historical writing based upon the ancient Roman model of Sallust's *Conspiracy of Catiline*. Giraffi follows the late 16th- and early 17th-century tradition of including documentary evidence to buttress arguments. In all there are several participating authors, including Edward Hutton. In addition to its journalistic record, major topics include Christian development, avoidance of luxury, and good government.

LORD ALEXANDER (ALESSANDRO) GIRAFFI, "MASANIELLO'S REVOLUTION OF 1647"

Tenth Day: Tuesday, 16 July, 1647

That day was the feast of the glorious Virgin of the Carmine, a day of great devotion among the Neapolitans, especially among the common people, since the church [18] is situated in Piazza del Mercato, the favorite place of the most numerous gatherings. Having a little before managed to escape from his chains and his keepers, Masaniello went into the church to wait for the archbishop, who was supposed to come to celebrate High Mass as he did every year. As soon as His Eminence came near the door, Masaniello approached him and said: "Most eminent lord, I see that the people have abandoned and betrayed me. I desire, for my consolation, and of all this people, that a solemn procession be made for this Most Holy Lady, with the viceroy, the Collateral and all the tribunals of the city, so that if I have to die, at least I shall die happy. Therefore I beseech Your Eminence to send this letter to the viceroy." The archbishop embraced him, commending his devotion, and immediately sent a gentleman to the palace with the letter for the viceroy; he then went to the high altar of the Virgin of the Carmine, and bent over, intending to celebrate Mass. The church was tightly packed with as many people as it could hold. At that point Masaniello climbed to the pulpit with a crucifix in his hands and heartily recommended himself to the people. He told them they should not abandon him and reminded them of everything he had done for them, pointing out the courage he had demonstrated by embracing the enterprise, the dangers he had encountered, the hatred he had incurred for burning the property of so many scoundrels and the happy conclusion of all their negotiations. A little while later he started to rave, publicly blaming himself with furious words for the wickedness of his past life and exhorting everyone to make a similar confession at the feet of the confessor if they wanted to appease God's anger. Because he uttered many ridiculous expressions, many savouring of heresy, he was abandoned by his guard. When the archbishop, who was celebrating, could no longer endure listening to him, he managed to get him off the pulpit with the help of some priests. At this point Masaniello, seeing his sorry plight, threw himself at His Eminence's feet and begged him to send his theologian to the palace to tell the viceroy that he was willing to renounce his command. The archbishop gave him his word that he would do that and, considering him worthy of compassion, had him escorted to the friars' cells so that he could change his clothes, for he was in a sweat, and rest for a while. The archbishop then retired to his palace.

In the meantime, Masaniello, after changing his clothes, went out into a great hall and was leaning out of a window overlooking the sea to get some fresh air. Some bold and daring gentlemen rushed in accompanied by many people. They had first entered the church of the Carmine crying aloud, "Long live the king of Spain, and let no one, on pain of death, obey the commands of Masaniello." Then they entered the cloister of the convent under the pretext of wanting to talk and negotiate with him and found him there practically alone. When he heard somebody call his name, the unfortunate wretch turned toward the conspirators and said,

"Are you perhaps looking for me? Here I am, my people." The two brothers Carlo and Salvatore Catania, and Michelangelo Ardizzone and Andrea Rama shot at him, one shot each. He fell down after the first shot, and crying, "Ingrates! Traitors!" he breathed his last. A butcher then came and cut off his head with a big knife, and putting it on a lance, went with the assassins into the church of the Carmine, where there must have been at least eight thousand people. Then they went to Piazza del Mercato, continuously crying, "Long live the king of Spain, and let it be treason to mention Masaniello from now on! Masaniello is dead!" They fired salvos just to create panic and the very same base plebeians were frightened and disheartened who shortly before had scared the sky and terrified the earth. Without a leader, they scattered here and there, lacking the courage to say even a word to the assassins of their former leader Masaniello, whom they had feared, obeyed and respected so much. Therefore his assassins were allowed to go around the city without any obstacle, with his head on a pole, while the boys dragged his body through the public squares and streets. Both groups were cheered, receiving not only kisses, embraces and blessings as they went along, but also great amounts of doppie, zecchini, and scudi[13] from the people whose houses Masaniello had burnt or had offended in other ways, and especially from the gentry. The latter, who had shut themselves up in their houses out of fear and had been afraid to show themselves outside, on hearing the good news came out immediately, got on their horses and merrily rode towards the royal palace, all armed and triumphant, to rejoice with His Excellency over what had happened. The viceroy, who was beside himself with joy, received everyone with great demonstrations of affection. The archbishop, after leaving the Carmine, had gone back to his palace. He had hardly arrived home when, on hearing the news of the death of Masaniello, he immediately went to the royal palace to do his duty and congratulate the viceroy. The latter issued strict orders that all the *capitani* (of the *ottine*) should be on the alert along with the armed people and that, on pain of life, they should not dare to obey anybody but him. He also gave orders to apprehend Masaniello's accomplices, which was done: his wife, his sisters and his relatives were arrested and taken to the castle. Since his brother Matteo had gone to Benevento with others in order to capture, the reports said, the duke of Maddaloni, numerous bands, some on horseback and some on foot, were dispatched to apprehend him and take him back to Naples. He was taken and committed to the castle, although afterwards, to please the people, he and the others were set free.... Soldiers were also sent to the market, to restrain the people and guard the goods belonging to different owners that were there deposited.

After giving these good orders, the viceroy was exhorted by the archbishop, the whole nobility and the royal ministers, to show himself publicly around the city. Whereupon he got on a horse, accompanied by His Eminence and attended by the train of all the nobility and ministers of the royal tribunals. Well guarded by horse and foot, they went to the cathedral to give thanks to God and to the most glorious and important protector of Naples, San Gennaro,[14] whose holy head and blood was exposed on the high altar. Extraordinary thanks were given for the peace that had been regained by the death of so base a fellow, who, by the mysterious ways of God, had become formidable enough to terrify a city like Naples. He had been a clear instrument (it cannot be said otherwise) of the just indignation of God who, offended by the sins of the Neapolitans, had chosen the vilest man from the lowest plebeians to punish them and humiliate them, like he had punished the Egyptians with little flies....

That Tuesday evening, Masaniello's brother, who had gone out of Naples, was brought back to the city and imprisoned in the castle with his mother. As she passed, on her way to prison, everyone cried out, "Make way, make way for the duchess of sardines!" With the brother of Masaniello were brought the heads of four of his companions who had refused to surrender and had offered resistance by firing their muskets at the royal soldiers. Nine were taken alive; the rest of his followers were either wounded or put to flight.... [From Brendan Dooley, ed. and trans., *Italy in the Baroque, Selected Readings*. New York and London: Garland Publishers, 1995, pp. 272-75.]

7. PIETRO GIANNONE (1676–1748)

Born at Ischitella, Capitanata, Giannone was the greatest Neapolitan historian prior to Pietro Colletta. After graduating in law in 1698, he became interested in the new learning. He was known for his opposition to papal intervention in Naples and sided with civil power over Roman Catholic hierarchy and his criticism of ecclesiastical policies in the kingdom finally led to his excommunication and imprisonment. Giannone, who sketched the development of Neapolitan political institutions in his *Istoria civile del Regno di Napoli* of 1723, offers a polemical survey of Neapolitan history. After reaching Vienna where he received a pension from Charles VI and prepared his greatest work, *Il Triregno, ossia del regno del cielo (The Triple, that is, Heavenly Kingdom)*, Giannone traveled to Venice when Charles de Bourbon obtained the Neapolitan crown. From there he accepted refuge in Geneva in 1735 when Venice had deemed his views on maritime law unfavorable to the Republic. In the Piedmont Giannone was kidnapped by agents of the Sardinian government and taken to the castle of Miolans in 1736. There he wrote his autobiography. The last twelve years of his life he spent in prison in Turin. Giannone's history is divided into five chapters. The following passage underscores the frequency with which Masaniello's Revolution of 1647 continued to be recalled. [See **5, 6**.]

Pietro Giannone, "Masaniello Remembered"

> Masaniello, in tatters and half naked, had a scaffold as a background and a sword for a scepter. There were 150,000 men at his back, armed haphazardly but alarmingly enough, and they controlled the entire city. As the instigator of sedition and leader of the insurrection, he moved all motions, imposed silence, decided what was to be discussed and, as though everybody's destiny were in his power, killed with a nod or set fire to any house at which he glared. Heads were struck off, palaces burnt down. Through the Cardinal Archbishop's mediation, the Viceroy was induced to grant the edict of exemption which the mob had first demanded, and to accept a solemn agreement by which all taxes imposed since the time of Charles v were removed and no new ones levied. The commons and nobility were put on the same footing where voting was concerned. An amnesty was promised, and the rabble were to be allowed to continue to bear arms for the next three months until the King's consent had arrived. All this was ratified by a solemn oath in the church of the Carmelites [see **18**], thus giving a short breathing-space. Masaniello, flattered excessively by the Viceroy, as was his wife by the Vicereine, grew excessively conceited, then disturbed in his mind, and finally, from lack of sleep and too much wine, delirious. Unacceptable even to his supporters and cruel to everybody, he was killed on the morning of 16 July in the friary of the Carmelites by people hired for the purpose; some of his most trusted followers shared his fate. The populace appeared not in the least concerned about his death; on the contrary, they seemed overjoyed

at seeing his head on a pole. In consequence, general peace and calm were anticipated.

However, certain noblemen, with disastrous irresponsibility, snubbed some of the mob. On the following day, by extraordinary ill-judgment, the price of bread was raised. Rebellion immediately broke out again with such intensity that, after digging up Masaniello's body and re-uniting it with the head, his corpse lay in state in the Carmelites' church [see 18]. The enormous throng bent on seeing it would never have dispersed if he had not been re-buried with the same solemn and regal ceremony as a Captain-General. [From Desmond Seward, *Naples: A Traveller's Companion*. New York: Atheneum, 1986, pp. 89-90.]

8. FRA MASSIMO DE RITIJS (17TH C.)

During the seventeenth century volcanic eruptions and civil unrest were not the only threats to the welfare of the city. This document, written by a Dominican and published recently by James Clifton in his 1987 doctoral thesis, gives an account of the most famous and disastrous plague of 1656. It is estimated that at least fifty percent of the 450,000 population of this largest city in Italy was destroyed, including some of the city's most successful artists, such as Massimo Stanzione and Bernardo Cavallino, records of whom cease after this year. Other plagues are recorded to have taken place in 1526 and 1884 when a cholera epidemic reached epidemic proportions. In 1743 a plague from Messina was followed in 1764 by a major famine. At the end of this text is a list of some of the more prominent citizens who perished in the tragedy of 1656. In many ways this mid-century event was a turning point for Naples and had long-lasting consequences for the kingdom. It tends to divide the city's history and culture into two distinct halves during this period. [See FIG. 10.]

FRA MASSIMO DE RITIJS, "THE PLAGUE OF 1656"

Signor Cardinal Ascanio Filomarino,[15] archbishop of Naples since the beginning of the contagion, was a watchman, a prudent pastor, and a father who displayed the most ardent and necessary zeal, and gave himself more than ever to the spiritual government of his church and welfare of his parishioners. He published various timely health edicts: that one pray and beg for divine mercy; that confessors should be abundant throughout the entire city; that helpers be appointed to administer the sacrament and last rites to the dying. Furthermore, he gave permission to appoint approved confessors, secular and non, as well as appropriate priests to administer the sacrament of penance and absolve all previous chastisements. He insisted that the churches be always open; that they celebrate publicly outside accompanying other holy traditions; and that all customary rites be observed during the plague. Once the epidemic was over, many abuses, old and new, caused by the corruption, disorder, and governmental confusion, prevailed. With the same constant devotion, Cardinal Filomarino reorganized the government and once more established balance and rule; only with God's assistance did he operate at all times. He was left without vicars, officials, helpers, and government ministers because so many had perished. This eminent Cardinal obtained from the Holiness of Our Lord, Alessandro VII,[16] most generous care for the terminally ill. Always available to his parishioners who would come for charity and mercy, he continuously helped the needy with public and private alms and offered wheat and other charitable goods to the convents in order to maintain a sense of stability. [From James B. Clifton, "Images of the Plague and Other Contemporary Events in Seventeenth-Century Naples." Ph.D. Diss. Princeton, NJ: Princeton University, 1987, pp. 197-98. (Trans. L.N.)]

9. ANONYMOUS (17TH C.)

Seventeenth-century Naples was a city of celebration and festivity. There are numerous travelers' accounts of the carnivals, *Cuccagne* [see FIG. 13], royal balls, and spectacles. This romantic account of Neapolitan splendor, dated January 14, 1680 and published by Lodovico Canallo, recreates for us the pageantry, symbolic of extravagantly displayed loyalty to the Spanish Crown. The wedding celebration recounted was for Carlos II of Spain. Known as "the bewitched," because of physical and mental disabilities that prevented this or any other marriage from being auspicious, this childless monarch had married Maria Luisa of Orleans in 1679. She died ten years later, whereupon Carlos married for a second time and ruled until 1700. Upon his death, Hapsburg dominance of Spain came to an end; and with the settlement achieved with the Peace of Utrecht, which ended the War of the Spanish Succession (1702–13), Spain was ceded to the French Bourbons; while Naples became a possession of the Hapsburg dynasty of Austria.

ANONYMOUS, "ROYAL MARRIAGE OF 1679"

Finally, the long-awaited day arrived. With a display of true decorum, Naples had to show to all nations of the world the ardor with which it would serve its own Lord as well as the faithful and loyal citizens. As the nobility and population at large had always valued glory, they were pleased when ordered by his Excellency Signor Marchese de los Velez [viceroy of Naples, 1675–83][17] to solemnize with great pomp and decorum the marriage of His Majesty [Carlos II], whom God protects. However, before the marriage took place, the festivities started Saturday night — the thirteenth of the same month. The whole city attended and, as on the subsequent evenings, the night sky was so illuminated as to appear sun-filled. All the fortresses were surrounded by lights aligned in such a way that one could not tell them from a ball of flames that seemed to encroach upon the foliage present in the various depictions of Our Lady of Conception that had been painted on the banners of each castle. The flames seemed to compete with the pale moon [as it appeared in traditional depictions] at the feet of Our Lady. The royal palace and houses of noblemen and royal ministers were illuminated by the same quantity of torches and, in each one of these palaces, hearts were on fire because of the Neapolitans' love for His Majesty, reflected in the illumination of all the torches. [*Relatione della Cavalcata Reale: Seguita in questa fedelissima Città di Napoli il di 14 Gennaro 1680*. Naples: Lodovico Canallo, 1680, p. II. (Trans. L.N.)]

10. RAFFAELLE MARIA FILAMONDO (1650–1716)

The *Genio bellicoso*, published in 1694, is a collection of historical records of famous Neapolitan military heroes. The valor of the militia is emphasized; and celebrated generals, such as Andrea d'Avalos and Andrea Cicinello, are featured with an engraved portrait of each officer in full regalia. The following is an account of the 17th-century Captain Andrea Cantelmo.

RAFFAELLE MARIA FILAMONDO, "MILITARY HEROES"

Andrea Cantelmo

While introducing to you this famous captain, do not think that I will exaggerate the facts with the type of extravagant amplification often found in historical accounts. Exaggerated claims would only distort and not enhance him. That was experienced by Nero who, having received from Greece a bronze statue of Alexander the Great by Lycippus, had it gilded: when finished, it looked effeminate. So he used a file and took off the golden surface unfortunately scraping

and scarring it in several places and ultimately ruining it. At least it finally turned out to be the Alexander Lycippus had intended! The heroic
exploits of Andrea Cantelmo do not need embellishments because they
are representative of a truly iron man whose soul was not inferior to
that of the Macedonian. In fact, he was referred to as such in a eulogy
by Cornelio Schat of Anversa [Antwerp] which is included here, and
also in a eulogy by Ericio Pateano, (a man trusted by the Cedro and a
captain of unique value to Italy).

Born on August 2, 1598, Cantelmo excelled as a highly intelligent
child. His father, Fabrizio, a duke of the people, hoping to give his
son the best, sent him to the Roman seminary in order that he might
pursue ecclesiastical honors. The young Cantelmo, more inclined towards the warfare of Pallas [Athena] than the wisdom of the goddess
Minerva, returned to Naples. There he became accomplished in every
branch of chivalry, which he learned with style and ease. He continued to lust after glory, however, and, when still in his youth, left for
Milan. There he became captain of an infantry group that conducted
several heroic rescues in the regions of Valtellina, Chiavenna, Tirano
and Coiro.[18] In doing this, he showed maturity at a young age and
great courage in combat as if he had been born to rule and honor the
military. [Raffaelle Maria Filamondo, *Il genio bellicoso di Napoli*. Naples:
Domenico-Antonio Parrino, 1714, p. 30. (Trans. I.I.-D.)]

II. PIETRO COLLETTA (1775–1831)

After Giannone [7], Colletta is probably the most famous Neapolitan
historian. From the age of twenty-one he had been a soldier, originally in the
service of the Bourbons and later, a general in the army of Joseph Bonaparte and
Marshal Murat. As a result of his having been Minister for War in the Carbonari government of 1820, he spent two years in prison. Coletta took part in the revolution of 1799.
His famous *History of the Kingdom of Naples, 1734–1825* was not in print until 1834, three
years after his death. Here, on the lighter side, he describes the curious "Cocagna"
(cuccagna) celebration of 1734.[19] [See Cover and FIG. 13.]

PIETRO COLETTA, "CEREMONY AND CELEBRATION, THE COCAGNA OF 1734"

Now that the capital has been freed of all traces of the previous regime, the Infante entered it with royal pomp on 10 May. The people
greeted him with wild enthusiasm, since they had high hopes of
their new sovereign, and their rejoicing became almost ecstatic when

his equerries scattered large amounts of gold and silver coin in all the main streets. In the morning he made his solemn entrance through the Capuan Gate, but wishing to first of all give thanks to God for his victories he dismounted at the church of San Francesco on the outskirts, staying in the monastery till 4 o'clock in the afternoon. He then continued his entrance into the city, riding a fine charger, magnificently dressed and wearing splendid jewels. He took care to go first to the cathedral [FIGS. 29, 56-57] to receive Cardinal Pignatelli's blessing and to take part with due devotion in the ceremony of thanksgiving, and also to hang a rich collar of rubies and diamonds round the neck of San Gennaro's bust. When these pious duties were over, he proceeded to the palace. As he was passing the prisons of the Vicaria[20] and San Giacomo, their keys were presented to him in homage to his sovereignty, whereupon he gave orders for the cell doors to be opened and to release all the prisoners, an act of foolish generosity. The city was entirely given over to celebrations — its militia lined the streets and provided the guards at the palace, while the fireworks and illuminations went on all night....

On 15 June 1734 he published an edict of Philip V of Spain, in which the latter bestowed the ancient but newly established claim to The

Figure 13

Two Sicilies, once again united in an independent king, on his son Charles, born of his blessed marriage to Elizabeth Farnese. The new King had himself proclaimed "Charles, by the Grace of God, King of The Two Sicilies and Jerusalem, Infante of Spain, Duke of Parma, Piacenza and Castro, and Hereditary Grand Prince of Tuscany." He changed the royal coat of arms, adding to the national arms of The Two Sicilies the golden lilies of the House of Spain, the azure lilies of Parma, and the red balls of the Medici. The city renewed its public rejoicing and the priests continued to offer services of thanksgiving. The King introduced a new entertainment to the festivities. This was the Cocagna, a huge construction supposed to depict the Garden of the Hesperides, from which were hung costly gifts for which anyone was allowed to compete, though they were deliberately hung high up and very hard to reach — the object was to arouse the mob's greed and encourage it to show its agility. From the palace roof Charles watched the competition with boyish amusement, thoroughly enjoying the spectacle of such an amusing game. Suddenly part of the Cocagna's scaffolding, insecurely constructed and over-loaded with people, collapsed, pulling everything down with it and crushing those underneath. Many were killed and hundreds more injured. Very soon the piazza in front of the palace was deserted. The King at once issued an edict which forbade any repetition of this type of entertainment. [From Seward, *Naples: A Traveller's Companion*, pp. 139-41.]

12. VINCENZO CUOCO (1770–1823)

Awriter, historian, and politician, Cuoco was born near Molise. He came to Naples in 1787 to study law where he was interested as well in literary and philosophical studies, especially those dealing with economic theory. A pupil of the economist, Mario Pagano [56] and Antonio Genovesi [55, 60], Cuoco knew as well the famous eighteenth-century writer G.M. Galanti[21] and associated with all the famous intellectual and cultural circles. In 1799 he wrote his celebrated *History of the Revolution of Naples* demonstrating his expertise concerning the events of the late eighteenth century. Although exiled by the Bourbons, he nevertheless died in Naples. Cuoco's writings were not published until the very first years of the nineteenth century. In this excerpt, Cuoco analyzes the failure of the revolution and the mistakes made by the revolutionaries. Simultaneously he criticizes those abstract ideas that failed to take into account national differences between various countries while recognizing the incapacity of Neapolitan intellectuals to understand and sympathize with the real needs of the people.

VINCENZO CUOCO, "THE REVOLUTION OF 1799"

I should like to write about the history of a revolution which should have brought about the happiness of [the] nation but which, instead, has brought on its ruin. We will see, within the space of a year, a nation turned upside down, at a time when it was about to conquer the whole of Italy; an army of eighty thousand men beaten, scattered and destroyed by a handful of soldiers; a weak king, counseled by cowardly ministers, who abandoned his state when there was no danger; the birth and establishment of freedom just when nobody was expecting it; the struggle for a just cause, and the human errors which destroyed the results of their action, thereby creating the conditions for the return of an even fiercer despotism. Great political revolutions occupy in the history of Mankind the same place as do extraordinary phenomena in the history of Nature. For centuries, life goes on as normal, generation after generation, just as the days of the year: they differ only in name, and it is impossible to tell one from the other. But an extraordinary event gives new life to them: we suddenly notice new things and, in the general disorder which appears to be destroying a nation, we can discover the character, customs, and laws of an order of which earlier it had only been possible to see the surface effects. Posterity, which will be our judge, will write our history. But since it is our right to prepare the facts, then may we be permitted to clear the ground for their judgment. Without wishing to write the history of the Neapolitan Revolution, I should like to write about some events which I judge to be significant, and to express my opinion as to which were commendable and which were not. Dispassionate posterity is not always free of prejudice, with respect to the eventual winners, and our actions might be judged wrongly, in as much as they went wrong. I declare that I am not [a] member of any political party, other than that of Reason and Humanity. I am going to tell the story of my country, things I have seen and been part of; I am writing for my fellow countrymen whom I cannot, must not, and will not deceive. [From Massa Nunzia, ed., *Napoli Guida, Guide-Naples, Reiseführer Neapel*. Naples: Graphotronic Edizioni, 1994, pp. 139-40.]

CHAPTER 2
Guides, Diaries, Directories, and Travelers' Accounts

13. ENRICO BACCO (LATE 16TH–EARLY 17TH C.)

Bacco's *Description of the Kingdom of Naples*, divided into twelve provinces, dates from around 1616. The first part is concerned primarily with the city and environs. It contains information concerning its plan and topography as well as its various institutions including churches, monasteries, palaces, and fortresses. An extremely popular book in its own day, there were at least six editions of Bacco's guide by 1671. The author's description of the kingdom of Naples included references not only to the physical characteristics of the city itself but to its inhabitants categorized as nobles, saints, viceroys, dukes, counts, and others. In this passage we are provided with observations of the city as well as statistics relevant to its institutions.

ENRICO BACCO, "NAPLES' INSTITUTIONS AND POINTS OF INTEREST"

Figure 14

Near the port is the great Castel Nuovo of Charles I, both expanded and adorned by the above-mentioned Alfonso, and by el Gran Capitan brought to the form in which it is seen today, situated on the shores of the sea, built above the water that flows below it and on every side in order that it could not be damaged by sappers, which are the most important reason for every ruin. Inside appears a dwelling that exactly resembles a city. Here previously was the monastery or convent of S. Maria della Nova of the Observantine Friars of St. Francis and called the Torre Maestta. It was then moved by the said Charles to where it is seen today, giving in exchange this place where the said castle first stood. It was also fortified to such a degree by the Emperor Charles V that today it is considered one of the strongest fortresses in Italy.

Foreigners are astounded by so many war machines, so much artillery and such a great amount of balls of iron, helmets of gold and silver, shields, lances, swords and all the rest of the apparatus of war, tapestries of silk, and brocade of gold, magnificent sculpture, statues and paintings, and the rest of all their treasures of a pleasantness and beauty little less than regal. King Charles also built a tower in the sea to watch and defend the moats of the castle, inside of which ran the harbor. In ancient times it was called S. Vincenzo, because within it stood a small church dedicated to that holy martyr, as ancient tradition holds.

Figure 15

Quite nearby is the Royal Arsenal, where the galleys and other ships are made, where more than a hundred artisans of all the arts that pertain to the aforementioned manufacture continually work. A little further is the Castel dell'Ovo and that of S. Erasmo, which we will discuss in their appropriate places.

Predating these is the Castel Capuana, so named for the gate that leads to Capua, which was nearby, built by the previously mentioned King Charles I, before having begun the above-mentioned Castel Nuovo, although some are accustomed to say it was the work of the Normans. Later this castle was converted by the Viceroy Don Pedro of Toledo into a wide and most marvelous court to accommodate the merchants, as it is seen today divided into four parts, namely civil and criminal Vicaria, the council, and the Summaria, besides the other courts of the mint and of the bailiff.

The city is also very celebrated for so many beautiful and sumptuous churches of priests, monks, friars, nuns, and homes for women, children, and the aged, with their beautiful and spacious monasteries and convents, which will be discussed in their appropriate places.

Naples renders itself no less remarkable and beautiful than marvelous also for the great remains of the ancient buildings, of so many statues, columns, inscriptions, which are seen as much in the palaces of the lords as scattered throughout the city. Among others are the ruins of the Temple of Castor and Pollux. This temple was built to Castor and Pollux before the coming of our Lord Jesus Christ by Tiberius Julius Tarsus, a freedman of Augustus and procurator of the fleet, which the emperor kept on these shores. Today there can be seen the front of the portico of this temple, with six fronting columns of marble, and above them a great Corinthian architectural cornice, amazing for its size and skill, with the most beautiful capitals and baskets, from which hang flowers and folded acanthus leaves. In the embellishment of the marble architrave supported by these columns is carved an inscription to the aforementioned Tiberius and many gods. When this city was made Christian and Catholic, thanks to the majesty of God, the temple was appropriately dedicated to the truly heavenly lights, the apostles Saints Peter and Paul, as the inscription of the new church [S. Paolo Maggiore] makes note.

Already, in a calculation made in 1614, the number of souls was found to exceed 167,972. But today it is found to have grown so much more, and the number of hearths to sixty thousand, so that to give five to a hearth more or less, and no more, there are 500,000 people. Add to them the monasteries and ecclesiastics and the foreigners, and those who visit the city at every hour, besides those who come and go and do not make an ordinary residence, who increase in great numbers, so that every day in the city and in the borghi they eat more than six thousand *tomoli* [27.5–55.5 liters] of grain. This does not include those who make bread at home, which is a large part, or the different clerics, religious, or nuns who are numerous.

INSTITUTIONS IN THE CITY OF NAPLES

Fortresses (with garrisons)

Castel Nuovo	250
Castel dell'Ovo	128
Castel S. Elmo	250
Torre di S. Vincenzo	60
Spanish Infantry	1,500
Galleys	4,500

Prisons (with inmates)

Vicaria	1,000
Admiralty	80
The Archbishopric	30
The Nuncio	30

Silk Guild	70
Wool Guild	40
Justiciar	40
Moccia, or Portolan	25
Spanish	100
Bailiff	50
Mint	50

[From Enrico Bacco, *Naples: an Early Guide,* ed. and trans. by Eileen Gardiner, introd. essays by Caroline Bruzelius and Ronald G. Musto. New York: Italica Press, 1991, pp. 8-10.]

14. GIULIO CESARE CAPACCIO (1552–1631/2)

Capaccio wrote several illustrated city guides for "foreigners." In one he described the "true antiquity" of the ancient town of Pozzuoli, located to the west of Naples; in another he referred to the cites of Baja, Cuma, and Miseno. The following passage introduces the reader to Pozzuoli. Capaccio's other writings include *Piscatorial Eclogues of Mergellina* (in tribute to Sannazaro), the *Decoration of the Festivity for the Glorious St. John the Baptist, The Foreigner, Dialogues,* and *The Prince.*

GIULIO CESARE CAPACCIO, "THE TRUE ANTIQUITY OF POZZUOLI"

The greed for gold is such that, as generally happens with all avarice, it

Figure 16

has led man to madness and induced him to search for treasure without thinking of his own mortality let alone his soul. The greedy enter caves knowing well that they are filled with fire, sulfur and mephitis because, retaining diabolical superstitions, they believe that they can easily find treasure in Pozzuoli. Beggars come from various European locations and claim to have magic books. Either they are cunning and, relying upon people's tendency to lose all judgment in their desire to become rich, manage to fool the people; or they themselves are so limited, cowardly and superstitious that night and day they wander about, poking in holes covered with thorns, walking on dangerous cliffs, sweating, gasping, or perhaps discovering a tree root or a sign in some corner once owned by a rich Roman, a soldier from Lotrecco, or simply left behind by Hannibal's men. Thousands also firmly believe in a legendary king[22] and that gold is created in the Solfatara (sulfurous volcano). In the Barbaro mountain alone, there are said to be kings bearing that precious metal with emblems as big as a sun on their fore-heads. It is held that in many caves there are piles of shields, old coins, and chests filled with "philosopher's stone" *(Lapis Philosophorum)* which might easily be discovered were they not guarded by Larue[23] and spirits. You can well see what madness and what beastly types of men Virgil was alluding to. [Giulio Cesare Capaccio, *La vera antichità di Pozzuolo descritta da Giulio Cesare Capaccio secretario dell'inclita città di Napoli.* Rome: Filippo de Rossi, 1652, pp. 123-24. (Trans. L.N.)]

15. JOHN EVELYN (1620–1706)

Probably the most famous of the English chroniclers of Italy, including the city of Naples, Evelyn was a man of letters who displayed great versatility in his intellectual pursuits. Famous primarily for his diary *(Kalendarium)*, which documented his travels in England and abroad until 1649, Evelyn was both an Anglican and a supporter of the crown. He first became interested in the arts through Thomas Howard, earl of Arundel. In 1643 Evelyn traveled to Italy and then back to Paris where he married in 1647. Having studied anatomy and physiology at Padua, in Paris he pursued a knowledge of plants and chemistry. Evelyn returned to England in 1652 to await better times as Charles II's fortunes were at a low ebb. In his later years he wrote a variety of works including, in 1649, *Of Liberty and Servitude,* a brief moral treatise, and *De rerum natura* in 1656, a translation of Lucretius' original text. Evelyn held several charitable offices in England and during the 1660s became a member of the society of scientists that was to become the Royal Society in 1662. His *Sylva, or a Discourse on Forest-Trees* appeared in 1662 to be followed in the same year by a book on engraving and etching in which he introduced the practice of mezzotint. In 1664 he published *A Parallel of the Ancient Architecture with the Modern.* Finally, in 1697 he wrote *Numismata,* a discourse on medals, ancient and modern. The passage below, almost buried within his voluminous diary of European travels, was eventually published in full from manuscripts in 1955. In it Evelyn relies heavily upon George Sandys, *A Relation of a Journey Begun an. Dom. 1610…* (London, 1627), and Johann Heinrich von Pflaumern (Ioan. Henrici a Pflaumern IC.), *Mercurius italicus, hospiti fidus per Italiae praecipuas regiones & urbes dux…* (1628). Evelyn's is a brief and sensitive overview of his arrival in, and passage through, Naples in 1645.

JOHN EVELYN, "AN ENGLISHMAN'S VIEW OF THE CITY IN 1645"

> About noone We enterd the Citty of Naples, allighting at the 3 Kings, a Place of treatement to excesse, as we found by our very plentifull fare all the tyme we were in Naples, where provisions are miraculously cheape, & we seldome sat downe to fewer than

18 or 20 dishes of the most exquisite meate & fruites, enjoying the Creature:

The morrow after our arival in the afternoone We hired a Coach

Figure 17

to carry us about the Towne, & first we went to Visite the Castle of St. Elmo, built on an excessive high rock, whence we had an intire prospect of the whole Citty, which lyes in shape of a Theatre upon the Sea brinke, with all the circumjacent Ilands, as far as Capra, famous for the debauch'd recesses of Tiberius.

This fort is the bridle of the Whole Citty, and was well stor'd, & Garrisond with natural Spanyards: the strangenesse, of the precipice, & rarenesse of the Prospect in view of so many magnificent & stately Palaces, Churches & Monasteries, (with) the Arsenale, Mole, & distant Mount Vesuvius, all in full command of the Eye, is certainly one of the richest Landskips in the World: Hence we descended to another strong Castle, cald il Castello Nuovo, which protects the Shore, but they would by no intreaty permitt us to go in; the outward defence seemes to consist but in 4 tours very high, & an exceeding deepe graft, with thick Walls: Opposite to this is the Toure of St. Vincent,

Figure 18

which is also very Strong: Then we went to the Vice-Roy's Palace, which is realy one of the noblest that I had seene in all Italy, partly old, & part of a newer Work, but we did not stay long here. Towards the Evening we tooke the ayre upon the Mole, which is a streete upon the

rampart or banke raysed in the sea for security of their Gallys in Port, built as that of Genoa: here I observ'd an incomparable rich Fountaine built in the middst of the Piazza, & adornd with divers rare statues of Copper representing the Sirens & deities of (Parthenope), spouting large streames of Water into an ample Concha, all of cast mettall &

Figure 19

infinite Cost: this stands at the entrance of the Mole, where wee mett many of the Nobility, both on horse-back, & in their Coaches to take the fresco from the sea, as the manner is, it being in the

most advantagious quarter for good ayre, delight & prospect: Here
we saw divers goodly horses who handsomly become their riders,
the Neapolitan Gentlemen. This Mole is about 500 paces in length,
& pav'd with a square hewn stone.

From the Mole we ascend to a Church, a very greate antiquity
formerly sacred to Castor & Pollux, as the Greeke letters carv'd in the
Architrave testify, & the busts of their two statues, converted now into
a stately Oratory by the Theatines: Hence we went to the Cathedrall
which is a most magnificent pile: and unlesse St. Peters in Rome certainly Naples exceeds all Cittys in the World for stately Churches &
Monasteries: We were told that this day the Blood of St. Genuarius,
& his head should be expos'd, and so we found it; but obtain'd not to
see the miracle of the boiling of this blod, as was told us: The Next
we went to see was St. Peters, richly adornd; the Chapel especialy,
where the Apostle sayd Masse, as is testified on the Walle: After dinner we went to St. Dominic, where they shew'd us the Crucifix that
is reported to have sayd these Words to St. Thomas (Aquinas): *Bene
de me scripsisti, Thoma.*[24] Hence to the Padri Olivetani[25] famous for the
monument of the learned Alexand. *ab Alexandro*....[26]

From hence climbing a steepe hill we came to the Monastery of
the Carthusians and Church, where (after we had turn'd about &
considerd the goodly Prospect towards the Sea, and Citty; the one
full of Gallys, and ships, and Other of stately Palaces, Churches,
Monasteries, Castles, Gardens, delicious fields & meadows, Mount
Vesuvius smoaking, the Promontory of Minerva, & Misenum, Capra,
Prochyta, Ischia, Pausilipe, Puteoli and the rest, doubtless one of
the most divertisant & considerable Vistas in the World) we went
into the Church; which is most elegantly built; the very pavements
of the common Cloyster being all layd with variously polish'd &
rich marbles, richly figurd: here they shew'd a Massive Crosse of
silver, much celebrated for the Workmanship & carving, and sayd
to have ben 14 yeares in perfecting: The Quire also of this Church
is of rare arte.

But above all to be admir'd is the yet unfinished Jesuites Church; a
Piece, certainely if accomplish'd, not to me match'd in Europe: Hence
we pass'd the Palazza Caraffi full of antient & very noble statues; also
the Palace of the Ursini.

The next day little, but visite some friends that were English merchants resident for their negotiation; Onely this morning at the Viceroys Cavalerizzo, I saw the noblest horses that I had ever beheld, one of his sonns riding the Menage with that addresse & dexterity, as I had never seene any thing approch it.

Feb. 4th We were invited to the Collection of exotic rarities in the Museum of Ferdinando Imperati [FIG. 20] a Neapolitan Nobleman, and one of the most observable Palaces in the Citty: The repository full of incomparable rarities; amongst the Natural Herbals most remarkable was the Byssus Marina, & Pinna Marina: Male & femal Camelion; an Onacratulus[27] & an extraordinary greate Crocodile: a Salamander; some of the Orcades Anates, held here for a strange rarity: The Male & female Manucodiata,[28] the Male having an hollow on the back in which 'tis reported (the female) both layes, & hatches her Egg.

The Mandragoras also of both Sexes: Papyyrs made of severall reedes, & some of silke, tables of the rinds of Trees writen with Japonique characters; and another of the branches of Palme: many Indian fruites: a Chrystal that had a pretty quantity of uncongeal'd Water within its cavity, a petrified fishers net: divers sorts of Tarantulas, being a kind of monstrous spiders, with lark-like clawes and somewhat bigger....

Figure 20

The 6 We sent by Coach to take the ayre, and see the diversions, or rather maddnesse of the Carnoval; the Courtisans (who swarme in this Citty to the number — as we are told — of 30,000 registered sinners, who pay a tax to the state for the Costome of their bodys) flinging eggs of sweete-water, into our Coach as we passed by the houses and windoes; and indeede this towne is so pester'd with these Cattel, that there needes no small mortification to preserve from their inchantments, whilst they display all their naturall & artificially beauty, play, sing, feigne, compliment, & by a thousand studied devices seeke to inveagle foolish young persons: and some of our Company did purchase their repentance at a deare rate, after their returne. [From E.S. de Beer, ed., *The Diary of John Evelyn, Kalendarium 1620–49.* Oxford: Clarendon Press, 1955, 2:325-32.]

16. GIUSEPPE CAMPANILE (17TH C.)

Campanile described himself as an *"accademico umorista, e ozioso"* (a good-humored and indolent academician), referring to the moderate intent of the members of this academy. Although his introductory essay appears nevertheless to encompass encyclopedic knowledge, it is essentially a heraldic dictionary, complete with coats of arms, tracing the foundation of the families of Naples. In addition, the author wrote notices concerning the nobility and genealogy of the prominent citizens. These, which he refers to in the extended title as "letters" (or documents) were published in 1672. On the frontispiece of the *Notizie* is a copper-etched portrait of Campanile by F.P. (perhaps by Federico Pesche[29]). This work is reputed to contain, at the end of the volume, references to the Academies but this final portion is sometimes missing.

GIUSEPPE CAMPANILE, "PROMINENT CITIZENS"

Your lordship can be certain that after the first four families — to be specific, the Sersale, Vulcana, Capece and Mastrogiodice — who are found in the very old city of Sorrento, two major ones were the Acciapaccia and the Donorsi. The former died out during our own time whereas the latter is still in existence....

He who thinks he is divulging the truth, is mistaken. I confess in writing that I have a heart-felt obligation to the Sorrentines despite the fact that certain ones among them are not very admirable because of their unfair, acquired family connection. I often mention the luxuries which they have amassed, but must also announce to all the city I love so much that it has changed from being a capital of glory, which it was for some time, to a capital of indolence. Its noble sons have not faithfully carried on the qualities of their elders who loyally followed in the military (tradition) as well as in the humanities. From these princes they inherited estates, titles, magistrates, and other tributes which caused them to become highly esteemed. Furthermore, I insist that such benefits and payments have no place in a tradition of lineage. But there is never praise if the end result is shameful. Let us now satisfy your curiosity by expressing my attitude toward the Donorsi family. As I will prove they too were honored in the seggio di Nido.[30] If I consider the history of this house, I realize that it is very ancient indeed. I conclude that their line is one which represents both strength and fame. Since this century is one in which the Agareni barbarians, wielding bows and arrows, brought disturbance to this beautiful part of the Christian world, that cursed mob slipped in through the Donorsi city gate located where San Pietro della Maiella now stands. Typical of a town in the Kingdom of Naples, our fair city survived for a long time before her ruling power was divided. [Giuseppe Campanile, *Notizie di nobiltà, Lettere di Giuseppe Campanile.* Naples: Luc'Antonio di Fusco, 1672, pp. 351-52. (Trans. L.N.)]

17. NICOLO TOPPI (1603–1681)

Dottor Toppi, described in the frontispiece as a patriarch of Chieti (near Ancona in the Marches), published his *Biblioteca Napoletana* in 1678. It is an index, arranged according to profession, of all prominent residents of the city and kingdom of Naples. Among these are cardinals, ambassadors of the king, archbishops, doctors, lawyers and "those men illustrious in letters," that is, the educated and erudite. The entries in this directory are accompanied by short essays describing the particular subject, his biography, and outstanding accomplishments. Toppi's writing serves as an appropriate complement to that of Campanile [16] and it is interesting that both works were published in the third quarter of the century, a time when Naples was obviously basking in social pride and, according to Croce, demanding a list of the nobility.

NICOLO TOPPI, "RESIDENTS AND PROFESSIONS"

Rafaele Aversa from Sanseverino (near Salerno) was a philosopher and famous theologian of the Padri Cherici Regolari Minori Order. In his time, he was second to none as is shown by his works in both philosophy and theology which were known first in Rome and then elsewhere and will be mentioned below. In these writings he was able to bring together depth, clarity and brevity. All the scholars' schools and academies followed this worthy and admirable man to such an extent that many religious orders elected him as master and doctor. In particular, he was admired by the court of Rome where he spent most of his life. There, he lead the governing body of his religion five times as he had done for the Holy Congregations of the Holy Office, the Rituals, the Index, the Scrutiny of the Holy Orders, and the works of Giansenio. In all these responsibilities, he always demonstrated his rare and vivacious wit and knowledge. For some reason which I do not know it seems that he was never made a cardinal, and thus decorated with the holy purple,[31] although those in the know considered him worthy of it despite his disdain for ecclesiastical pomp. [Nicolo Toppi, *Biblioteca Napoletana, et apparato a gli Huomini illustri in lettere di Napoli, e del Regno....* Naples: Antonio Bulifon, 1678. (Trans. L.N.)]

18. CARLO CELANO (1617–1693)

Celano, born in Naples and a canon of the church of Santa Restituta, published his *Delle Notizie del bello, dell'antico e del curioso della città di Napoli* in 1692, the year prior to his death. He remains one of the most famous literary figures from the second half of the seventeenth century. This volume presents a journey of ten days, a scheme proposed earlier by the famous *Forestieri* of Capaccio [14]. Later editions of the *Notizie* appeared in up to ten volumes. Celano dedicated this work to Pope Innocent XII (1691–1700) [see 62] and his family, the Pignatelli. The modern historian Benedetto Croce referred to it as "a conductor for strangers, of a tour of Naples, in which he showed the beautiful and the curious, furnished the related historical notices...and interrupted the descriptions with effusions of sentiment and anecdotes." The frontispiece displays an engraving after a portrait of Celano by Luca Giordano. Celano received his degree in law in 1642 and practiced for several years. He was arrested for his controversial account of the revolution of 1647; freed by the intercession of the Reggente del Consiglio Collaterale, D. Giacomo Capece Galeota; and subsequently studied theology before finally embracing the religious life. In addition to his *Notizie*, Celano had written comedy, directing his works mainly to the theater. The following is his commentary on the famous church of Santa Maria del Carmine, which existed as early as the twelfth century but, with damages and restorations, was not completed until the eighteenth.

CARLO CELANO, "LANDMARKS, THE CHURCH OF THE CARMINE"

The beautiful and venerated church of the Carmine was founded in the following manner. There arrived at Naples some brethren called the Order of the Blessed Virgin of Mount Carmel who, as soon as their rule had been confirmed by Pope Honorius III in the year 1217, built a very small church and convent just outside the city from alms given by the Neapolitans. In it they placed a picture of the Blessed Virgin, known as Santa Maria della Bruna, which they had brought with them. Some say it was painted by St. Luke the Evangelist.

When the Empress [Elizabeth], mother of the luckless King Con-

Figure 22

radin,[32] came to Naples to ransom her son from Charles I she found that by order of the said Charles he was already dead, so she spent the treasure she had brought in giving honorable burial to his royal bones and in endowing chantries for his soul, since she was not allowed to bear away his body; a great part went to the Carmelite brethren, and out of her magnificent donation they built a new church and enlarged their friary. Then, in the year 1269, to demonstrate his piety, Charles gave the brothers a large field called the "Moricino." [Soon the city walls were extended and enclosed the field, which became the Piazza del Mercato]....

We must now say something of the strange and beautiful things to be seen in this church. Among the most important is the holy and miraculous picture (of the Virgin), which is kept in the sanctuary behind the high altar. Beneath the sanctuary's pavement lie buried the unfortunate King Conradin and also the duke of Austria who was beheaded with the said king....

Cardinal Ascanio Filomarino, by God's grace archbishop of Naples, had a deep devotion to the holy picture; every Wednesday he would visit it most devoutly and hear Mass. On the feastday he said Mass himself, celebrating it with altar vessels of very rich plate including a splendid chalice. This prelate thought it most improper that the acolytes who served the sanctuary, unveiling the picture or lighting the candles, could be seen over the top of the altar in consequence of the floor being almost as high as the altar itself.

He therefore made the friars lower the floor so that people would not have to watch all the coming and going. While lowering it, by good fortune a leaden coffin some six palms long and two palms deep was discovered; on it were inscribed three letters, an R and two Cs, which were interpreted as signifying REGIS CONRADINI CORPUS [The body of King Conradin]. When opened, all the bones inside were found to be fleshless though the head still kept its teeth; clearly the skull of a young man, it has been placed on the breast. I gather that at the time the sword which was there too was all but intact; its blade shone bright and polished as the day it left the swordmaker. One could also see a few fragments of clothing, though as soon as they were touched they crumbled into dust. These relics were replaced, covered up again, and reinterred deeper down, where they remain to this day.

Close by, almost under the holy picture, another coffin was discovered. This was left undisturbed, but people believed that it contained the bones of the duke of Austria. Some think that the coffins had been moved there when the church was altered during its enlargement by King Ferrante of Aragon.

Over the arch of the entrance to the gallery immediately opposite is placed a miraculous carved wooden crucifix held in deep and unfeigned veneration by all Neapolitans, a veneration demonstrated twice a year and whenever the city is suffering some affliction. It is well known that in AD 1439, when King Alfonso I of Aragon had closely invested the city, Don Pedro of Aragon, Infante of Castile, was shelling it with a great bombard brought from the town of Rieti, and had reduced the neighbourhood around the church to ruins – the place was bombarded to such an extent that part of the church itself was beginning to collapse. A cannonball of truly enormous size smashed through the gallery and was hurtling towards the crucifix, whereupon the sacred likeness on the cross turned its head away and the cannon ball did no more damage than to knock off its crown of thorns. So that the miracle should not be forgotten the head remained turned aside, as may be seen even now. A few days later, a shot fired from near the church smote off the head of that valiant Infante Don Pedro. [From Seward, *Naples: A Traveller's Companion*, pp. 90-92.]

19. POMPEO SARNELLI (1649–1724)

Sarnelli was born in Polignano and died at Bisceglie. His major literary contribution was in the form of very popular pocket guides to Naples, Pozzuoli, and environs. These portable volumes appeared in various similar editions for over a century. Sarnelli had traveled to the city in about 1665 to study jurisprudence. He knew the French writer and publisher Antonio Bulifon,[33] who had immigrated there and eventually served as literary editor for the later editions of the works of Basile [30], Capaccio [14], whose *Guida de' forestieri per Pozzuoli...* is traditionally associated with Sarnelli's revisions, and others. Around 1669 he was ordained a priest; and the future Benedict XIII (1724–1730) selected him to be archbishop of Manfredonia. Sarnelli continued as bishop of Bisceglie until his death in 1724. His writings, which include his ecclesiastical notes, are both sacred and profane and employ the same Latin grammar used in Neapolitan schools for some five hundred years. Sarnelli describes the outrageous practices at the famous Cave of the Dog [FIG. 23], located to the west of Naples. These experiments, a constant tourist attraction, were continued as late as 1906.

POMPEO SARNELLI, "A POCKET GUIDE TO THE CITY AND ENVIRONS"

The Cave of the Dog

Near the lake, about one hundred steps from the so-called saunas, there is a small cave at the foot of the mountain. It is about fourteen hands long, six wide, and seven high. It came to be known as the Cave of the Dog because it was this animal which most often was used in experimentation here and because, upon entering the cave, any animal will die immediately from the foul vapors of the *mofette*. The reasons for this phenomenon is due to the extremely hot spirits which come out of the innermost rock. At first in the form of condensation due to the high temperatures,

Figure 23

Lago di Agnano, e Grotta del Cane.

they change to water. One can see drops trickling from the cave's vault. They appear resplendent to those who look in from the outside. Usually the experiment is carried out using dogs. Their heads are forced to the ground and, within a minute, they appear dazed and near death. If they are then taken into the lake, which is no more than fifteen steps away, they recover their lost senses. However, if the animal stays longer (without oxygen), it dies and the water of the whole lake can not revive it. Pliny mentions this cave in his third book, chapter 99, where he says: *alii spiracula vocant, alii charoneas scrobes mortiferum spiritum exhalantes.*[34] Charles VIII, king of France, having conquered the kingdom of Naples, came to see this curiosity and attempted to carry out the experiment with a donkey which died very soon. Don Pietro di Toledo, viceroy of the kingdom, also wanted to try the experiment using two slaves. They too died quickly. On November 26, 1694, His Highness Cristiano Luigi, brother of Sir Margravio, elector of Brandenburg, tried it out on two dogs in order to satisfy his curiosity. One died and the other recovered when doused with the nearby water. Ducks, frogs, and other animals have also been tried. Almost all died.

In the same place and at the same time, another experiment is a favorite. If you take a lighted torch down into this cave, the torch will show no sign of being extinguished and its smoke will not rise but instead travel down quickly toward the fresh air. When one shoots off arquebuses[35] in this cave, grazing the surface of the earth, they do not catch fire if within the clouds of gases. [Pompeo Sarnelli, *Guida de' Forestieri per Pozzuoli, Baja, Cuma, e Miseno.* Naples: N. Rossi, 1789, pp. 7-9. (Trans. L.N.)]

20. DOMENICO ANTONIO PARRINO (17TH C.–C.1730)

B orn around the middle of the seventeenth century in Naples, the versatile Parrino was initially an actor celebrated primarily as the *"innamorato"* (lover) under the name of Florindo. In 1675 he joined the company of the duke of Modena and later of Mantua. Having returned to Naples in 1680, Parrino rejoined the theater and dedicated himself to the study of history. After this he became a writer of political subjects, including the *Teatro eroico,* which was an account of the Neapolitan viceroys. He wrote as well a "new guide for observing and enjoying" exotic Naples. This excerpt from it describes the church of the Annuziata located in the central part of Naples and containing numerous significant works of art. In existence in 1318, rebuilt in the sixteenth century, destroyed by fire in 1757, and finally restored in 1760 by Luigi Vanvitelli, it is an example of religious constancy as well as architectural regeneration within the city.

Domenico Antonio Parrino, "Observe and Enjoy Naples"

Following Forcella Road, returning to the place called Sopra Muro where there were walls of the ancient city, and going straight there is the church, home, hospital and bank of the most holy Annuciation.

The latter is one of the most outstanding charitable institutions. At one time it was the richest house in the Kingdom but, due to bankruptcy in 1701, it is now minimal and the bank closed down. We will offer a rather specific account, with much in the form of a summary, so as not to be too long-winded.

The sacred place originated in the time of weak princes during the period of Charles II and from Nicolo and Giacomo Sconditi. In 1304 in a place called Mal Passo which had been given to them by Giacomo Galeota, these two who were freed from captivity through the intercession of the Virgin built the small church of the most holy Annunciation which included a confraternity known as the Ripentiti Battenti. When Queen Sancia [1309–1345] wanted to build the Maddalena on the same location, they changed places with this [building, which is the] present location of her tomb. Giovanna II then enlarged the hospital. Queen Margarita with other devotees enriched it by means of feudal and city funds. The church is one of the most beautiful in Naples and was rebuilt around 1540 according to Ferdinando Manlio's design. The ceiling is the work of [Giovanni Bernardo] Lama, painted by Imparato, [Francesco] Curia and [Fabrizio] Santafede. The choir's frescoes and the dome are by Belisario [Corenzio]. The oil paintings in the choir — *The Disputà, The Marriage at Cana* — are by Massimo [Stanzione]; *The Presentation in the Temple* — by Carlo Merlini Lorenese; *Noah Leaving the Ark* is by the Cavalier Calabrese [Mattia Preti] who in his old age still has skill; *David, Jacob,* and *Jacob Wrestling with the Angel* are the works of [Luca] Giordano.

The paintings above the side vaults of the main altar, where the angel warns St. Joseph not to fear and another angel leads the flight into Egypt, are by [Giovanni] Lanfranco. The doors, adapted from the organs located in Santafede's vaults, along with many other paintings are also by Lanfranco. The paintings on the windows are by

many followers of Giordano and Vaccaro. Lama painted the Annuciation to the Virgin which graces the main door. The two sides are the
work of Santafede. The organs newly decorated in gold are (from) the
drawings of Lazzari. The church, all stuccoed and in gold, seems like
paradise. These stucco works of sculpture are by Lorenzo Vaccaro.
[Domenico Antonio Parrino, *Nuova guida de' forestieri per osservare, e
godere le curiosità piu vaghe, e piu rare della fedeliss(ima) gran Napoli, città
antica....* Naples: n.p., 1725, pp. 243-45. (Trans. L.N.)]

21. GIUSEPPE SIGISMONDO (1734–1826)

Sigismondo's description of the city of Naples and its surroundings is a combination of a history and guide book concerned primarily with recording inscriptions
on monuments and complimenting patrons. Although individual artists are referred
to, sometimes incorrectly, they are in general given little space with the occasional
exception of those such as the late seventeenth-century painter, "our own" Luca
Giordano. Giuseppe Alojaine is the engraver for the 1788/9 edition, which is presented
in three volumes, the third of which includes interesting accounts of the great collections in storage at the royal museum of Portici and excavations at Pompeii and
Herculaneum. The description of Luigi Vanvitelli's Royal Palace at Caserta includes
lists of the paintings in the royal apartments and the chapel. Sigismondo describes
the gardens and fountains as well as the aqueducts that transport water to the huge
complex [FIGS. 32-33].

The first passage included here, in the tradition of Celano [18], is concerned with
the famous church of the Carmine and it is interesting to see what the excerpts of
the two authors have in common and how they differ. The second is a rather dry
inventory of the sumptuous Carthusian church of San Martino, located just above
the Castel Sant'Elmo and decorated by some of the greatest seventeenth-century
painters from Naples, the rest of Italy, and elsewhere. Sigismondo is critical in the
sense that he calls attention to those artists and monuments at the Certosa that he
considers to be of primary importance.

GIUSEPPE SIGISMONDO, "RECORD AND DESCRIBE NAPLES"

The Church of Santa Maria del Carmine

Behind the main altar, and under the lower icon where the Holy
Image is located, the unhappy Corradino was buried. In fact, during the time of Ascanio Filomarino, archbishop of Naples and
also a cardinal, the level behind the altar was lowered in the mid
1700s. There, a coffin was found; on its top an R and two Cs were
engraved. These letters were interpreted as REGIS CORRADINI CORPUS

(the body of King Corradino). Another coffin was also found there. It is believed to contain the body of the duke of Austria who was decapitated with Corradino. These deposits were located here when the church, during the time of Ferdinand of Aragon, changed its shape. Before, the door was where the main altar is but now this is reversed. The altar and the tribune, all made of subtle marble bearing a design of the cosmos, was made by Pietro and Giuseppe Mozzetti at the expense of the duke of Giovenazzo — Don. Domenico Giudice. The work, begun in 1672 and completed in 1682, is now the legal property of this family who have always been affiliated with this order. At his own expense Don Nicola Giudice, prince of Cellamare, also rebuilt and expanded the Monistero della Croce which belongs to the Carmelite nuns. In the architrave of this tribune, a miraculous image of the Holy Crucifixion carved in wood is venerated. This image is unveiled on the day of Saint Sylvester P.P. i.c. the second day after Christmas; it is veiled during the evening of the following day when the public is present. [Giuseppe Sigismondo, *Descrizione della città di Napoli e suoi borghi*. Naples: Fratelli Terres, 1766–69, 2:163. (Trans. L.N.)]

THE CERTOSA DI SAN MARTINO, ART INVENTORY

The church was consecrated in 1368 by Cardinal Gugliemo of Agrisoglio who was nunzio [papal ambassador] in Naples during the time of Archbishop Bernardo di Bosquetto. With a single nave, six chapels, and a choir behind the altar, it was rebuilt in its major parts during the past century when P.D. Severo Turboli arranged it in better form with the tribune (apse) cut in half as it appears today.

The atrium of this monument was painted all over in fresco by Luigi Siciliano. The choir [should be vault of the nave] of the church, with Our Lord who rises up toward heaven, the lunette(s) of the apse, and the apostles who are standing between the windows (of the nave), are among the best works of [Giovanni] Lanfranco [of Parma]. The ornaments of joined marble, with which the entire church (interior) is covered, were conceived by Cosimo [Fanzago], and the major portion executed by the same. The church's marble pavement was designed by a lay brother Martiniano called Fra Bonaventura Presti [of Bologna]; that of the choir is by the same Fanzago. The two marble statues above the shells containing holy water were sketched out by the same Cavaliere [Fanzago] and completed then by our own Domenico Antonio Vaccaro: the little marble putti above the chapels for the most part are the work of Alessandro Rondo Romano. The painting which serves as an overdoor along with Our Lord's descent from the cross, with Mary, [and] Saint John [the Evangelist], and two Carthusian saints, is by Cavaliere Massimo [Stanzione]; and the two prophets Moses and Elijah, who are to the sides (of the main entrance), are by the "Little Spaniard" [Ribera], by whom also are the twelve prophets above the lunettes of the chapels; in the first of [the chapels] on the side of the lectern [i.e., on the right as one faces the choir] there is the vault painted in fresco by Corenzio; this painting in which is represented the Blessed Virgin with Saint Hugh and Saint Anselm is by Massimo [Stanzione]; the two side [paintings] are by Andrea Vaccaro.... [Sigismondo, *Descrizione*, 3:108-9. (Trans. J.C.P.)]

Figure 24

PART II:
THE
CULTURE
OF
NAPLES

Figure 25

CHAPTER 3
Art, Architecture, Archaeology

22. GIOVANNI BATTISTA MARINO (1569–1625)

The flamboyant and erudite Marino was undoubtedly the most famous Neapolitan poet of the seventeenth century. His rakish lifestyle echoed that of the sixteenth-century Florentine sculptor Benvenuto Cellini; and although Marino was eventually imprisoned in Naples, he was lauded elsewhere in cities, such as Padua, Siena, Florence, and Rome. He exercised a considerable influence not only upon contemporary poetry but upon painting as well. Artists, such as Caracciolo, Ribera, and Stanzione,[36] were well aware of his literary achievements and incorporated aspects of his poetry into their painting. The latter artist's *Massacre of the Innocents* (Rohrau, Graflich Harrach'sche Gemaldegalerie) was inspired by a poem on the same subject by Marino. This great Neapolitan poet was a friend of the classical French baroque painter Nicolas Poussin, who probably encouraged him to travel to France where he wrote an address to the reigning Marie de' Medici.[37] Although Marino's *Galleria* of 1619 was primarily a collection of poems commemorating the poet's own art collection [**29** and FIGS. **25-26, 34-35**], the following tributes to Caravaggio and Carracci,[38] the two founders of baroque painting in Italy, are from his *Dicerie sacre* of 1614. This volume treats primarily artistic topics but also some that are sacred.[39]

GIOVANNI BATTISTA MARINO, THE FORMAL ELEMENTS OF PAINTING

> There are, in my opinion, two things that make painting admirable: excellence of design and excellence of color. And in both these aspects we can say that the divine painting of this sacred canvas [the Holy Shroud of Turin][40] is most admirable. As for the first [design], it can be considered in two aspects. The one is intellectual and internal, the other is practical and external. Both the one and the other refer only to the form or shape of corporeal things, whether externally or internally, and to the congruence of the whole, that is [so arranged that] each part is placed in its proper

45

position. The internal intellect meditates upon these forms [as they exist] in the concept of the painter, in accordance with his knowledge. The external aspect, that aspect which is put into practice, displays these forms on paper, canvas, or in any other material way, so that they may be judged with the corporeal eye. Then, in accordance with the secret rites [of art], they are refined and corrected to the point of ultimate perfection.

The Christian soul can contemplate this same thing in this marvelous painting of Christ [the Holy Shroud, which contains] internal design and external design, love, and pain. The one is in the spirit, the other in the senses; the one is in the volition, the other in the execution. The one offers, the other suffers. The one chooses to suffer, the other actually suffers. The internal one is content to undergo an ugly and ignominious death for the salvation of mankind. The other submits and subjects himself to all those martyrs and suppliants that the sins of men have earned. And who knows if this mystery is expressed in the duplication of the Holy Shroud itself? In the cloth, both on the one and on the other side, one sees the figure duplicated, almost as if to make reference to these two types of design.

The practice of design, whose function is to put into effect the concepts of the imagination, or objects that are seen, ordinarily operates among earthy painters in three different ways. The one is to make things up out of one's own brain, that is to say, to do it from practice, or from fantasy. Another is to be guided precisely by the rules of perspective. The third is to draw on [examples found in] nature.

The first method, being the most rapid of the three, is also the one most used by the majority of those who paint. Those who use it profit from what, through long practice in drawing, they have stored up in their minds. And this method usually turns out well or less well according to the degree of the painter's talent and application.

The second method, without doubt, is the most certain and secure. That way nothing is done by accident, but instead for good reasons and on the basis of proof and infallible demonstrations. Besides this provides the size, the diminution and the recession of constituted or imagined objects that one wishes to set back in space on a slant, or in reference to the visual pyramid, according to the different horizon lines, views and distances from which they are to be seen [in the painting]. This method teaches how to draw everything, as for example the various angles that apply to the various points of view.[41]

But just as it is easy to draw regularly shaped objects in perspective, so it is difficult and takes a long time to draw the irregularly shaped ones. Thus it is more expedient for painters to use the third method, which is half way between the other two and makes use of both. This method is to copy visually, from nature, the things that are to be painted, or to reproduce them from models made for that purpose, or with the help of some mathematical instruments.

Neither of these last two methods was used by God in his Design. He made use neither of natural objects nor of the geometrician's compass, having no need of them. Being, besides, the Mind Eternal in which all concepts are resplendent, he could find no created thing that could express so lofty an idea. What mathematical measure could circumscribe that love which had no measure?

THE HEAD OF MEDUSA, PAINTED ON A SHIELD BY MICHELANGELO DA CARAVAGGIO[42]
(IN THE GALLERY OF THE GRAND DUKE OF TUSCANY)

What foe will not, Sir, find himself congealed
Into cold stone on seeing on your shield
That Gorgon wild whose plenitude of snakes
So horribly, so very grimly makes
Among her locks a terrifying display?
But why, I pray?
List monsters not nor arms among your needs;
Your true Medusa is your valiant deeds.

ON THE DEATH OF ANNIBALE CARRACCI

He who once gave to naught the power to be
Behold is now himself to naught dissolved;
He who gave canvas life's a lifeless form.
From him who from dead hues so oft evolved

Live colors, death has now all colors shorn:
Well might you find
The way to make equal in kind:
Nature as rich as his, as lush
Had you his brush.

IN MEMORY OF HIS FRIEND, CARAVAGGIO

Nature, who feared to be surpassed
In every image that you made
Has, Michele, now in league with Death,
A cruel plot against you laid;
For Death with indignation burned
To know that many as his scythe
Cut down, still more and usurously
Your brush contrived to make alive.

[From Jonathan Brown and Robert Enggass, *Italian and Spanish Art,
1600–1750: Sources and Documents.* Evanston, IL: Northwestern University Press, 1972, 1:33, 75, 83.]

23. GIAMBATTISTA PASSERI (1610–1679)

Passeri, in his own day, was more an artist than a writer. A student of the Bolognese painter Domenichino[43] and a friend of the sculptor Alessandro Algardi,[44] he reflected their adherence to a classical tradition. His *Lives*, only in manuscript until almost a century after his death, appeared first in an abridged and somewhat distorted version. (The best critical edition is that of Jacob Hess, and it is from this that the following excerpt was selected and translated.) Despite Passeri's classical inclination, he had broad tastes and appreciated artists working in various modes of the Baroque. Proof of this is in his *hommage* to Pietro da Cortona[45] who represented the dramatic High Baroque. The most extreme example of his catholic taste may be his admiration for the romantic, eccentric, and versatile Neapolitan painter Salvator Rosa (1615–1673). [**24, 34, FIG. 27**]

GIAMBATTISTA PASSERI, "THE PAINTER, SALVATOR ROSA"
FROM *Vite de pittori, scultori ed architetti*

Salvator Rosa always loved applause and acclaim and he never wearied of working to achieve this end. He wanted his new work displayed each year at the celebrations at the Pantheon [St. Joseph's Day, March 19] and the church of San Giovanni Decollato[46] [the feast of St. John the Baptist, August 29th]. He imagined himself becoming as important for paintings with large-scale figures as he had become for those with tiny ones. He strained every effort to appear to the public equal to anyone working in monumental proportions. He painted and exhibited a battle scene the size of the Bacchanal done in Volterra. It is a work worthy of admiration for its perfect expression of violent actions, the shouts of the combatants and the wounded, the interwoven masses of foot soldiers and horses, the killed, and the trampled upon, and the dust raised; in addition there are several assaulted encampments, hills covered with small trees, and the confused movement of clouds, coupled with the masterly manner of his brushwork.

Rosa liked to paint canvases from his own imagination, and in this he found more satisfaction than through obedience to a restricted commission wherein his hands were not released to follow the freedom of his imagination. Therefore he gave free play to his inclinations.

With the passage of time his figures grew larger and he painted various compositions with histories, fables, and caprices. He exhibited them among the other pictures on the feast-day of St. John, while his so-called friends milled about, and by their hyperbole did him more harm than good. Since on that day it is customary to exhibit the works of famous painters, these fellows said to everybody: "Have you seen Titian, Correggio, Paolo Veronese, Parmigianino, Carracci, Domenichino, Guido Reni, and Signor Salvator Rosa? Signor Rosa fears neither Titian nor Guido nor Guercino nor anyone else."[47] And they carried on so much about Salvator that honorable men were disgusted and began almost to hate him, as if he had instigated the boasting, of which he was innocent. That then is the good those busybodies bring a poor fellow. However all those acclamations have ended up by putting a price on works by him in the hands of those who had bought them for a crust of bread, and stimulated an infamous traffic at the cost of his other work.

He always fought to maintain that his larger paintings, those with figures approximately life size, were as valuable as the smaller and the tiny ones. He fell into such anxious frenzy because of so much opposition to this point of view that he decided never to paint small pictures again, although he was offered considerable sums to do so. Who knows whether he acted for good or ill, but one thing is certain. His exaggerated stubbornness deprived him of money that would have been sufficient to maintain him in a much more respectable state; and then too he would have given satisfaction to many people who regretted his strange behavior. It was said that when working in large dimensions his paintings were quite lacking both in overall design and in the details, and that his way of using color was neither suitable not natural for that type of painting; that his flesh tones were wooden and bloodless; that the expression on the faces of his figures was displeasing, inappropriately and rustically conceived; that his colors were lifeless; that the garments did not form elegant and well-proportioned folds, and did not cover the nakedness of the figures in a natural way; that the contours of his forms were disorganized and confused; and that he had little understanding of the nude; and that he was quite incapable of bringing his works to that level of perfection to which a well-disciplined painter brings them, and that these failings applied to the whole painting and to the parts. He was tormented when he heard praise that in landscapes he held the first place, that in seascapes he was singularly fine; that in tiny compositions of fanciful invention he excelled all others; that in battle scenes he was unique; that in his caprices and his scenes of the exotic and the recondite he touched the highest level; that he had no equal in mastery of the brush, that he was a true maestro in harmony of color; but that in his paintings with large figures, since he lacked the foundation that comes through study, he lost all those qualities that made his work beautiful.

As admirable as he was in other things so was he in poetry [see 34], which he practiced with much magnificence and singularity, even though many ignorant persons try to degrade their status by calling them satire. However, if they think the term "satire" is pejorative, then they are greatly mistaken. Satire is the most majestic, the most learned, and the most exemplary of all forms. In my opinion it is the terror of the gifted, even the most exalted, in that it greatly resembles a perfect apostolic action, being a severe lash that punishes vice. It is quite true that that makes it very difficult to manage. It is easy for those employing it to stumble into the trap of hitting the corrupt person rather than the vice itself. In that case it changes aspect, becoming a malignance and a particularly evident hatred. But he who is able to use it wisely and to extract from it the fruit of reformation, and who is able to reveal the purity of his heart, which is not directed against the offending individual but acts from a just resentment of the functioning of evil — such a one is worthy of high praise. Certainly it is necessary in order to justify one's zeal that he who wishes to expose himself to these rigors be most pure in habit and blameless in his way of life, since a Zoilus[48] can scarcely act as the castigator of vice. With these his literary works Rosa makes for himself a broad road to glory. If they could be published so that the world was able to enjoy them he would be largely satisfied. But God knows what will become of them. [From Brown and Enggass, *Italian and Spanish Art, 1600–1750,* 1:128-30.]

24. SALVATOR ROSA (1615–1673)

This famous Neapolitan painter was known for his dramatic and eccentric depictions, sometimes referred to as "caprices" by his contemporaries. These portrayed romantic landscapes, battles, philosophers, and scenes of witchcraft. With a thirst for culture and erudition, Rosa sought recognition as a painter of historical and biblical subjects. Although born in Naples, in around 1635 he left for Rome and a few years later, c.1640–1649, resided at the Medici court in Florence. Rosa was known also as a writer whose poetic and personal satire was directed against the famous baroque sculptor-architect Gianlorenzo Bernini,[49] as well as

Figure 27

the painter-architect Pietro da Cortona. His acerbic wit attacked the Roman curia, and even the papacy, while his international reputation produced invitations from the royal courts of Sweden and France. One of his self-portraits bears the cryptic inscription: "Be silent unless you have something to say that is better than silence." Rosa's emotional and fretful letter of 1656 to his friend, Giovanni Battista Ricciardi, is hardly taciturn and seems to contradict such a declaration.[50]

SALVATOR ROSA, "LETTER TO GIOVANNI BATTISTA RICCIARDI"

From Salvator Rosa, 1656
Dear Friend,
For twenty-two days I have known no rest in body or mind. As soon as I eat enough to keep alive I howl, weep, and cannot stand the sight of a paintbrush. Now I really know that the errors of the wise are always greater than those of ordinary men. How stupid I

was to agree that Signora Lucrezia should leave me. What a pig's ass I was, more beastly, more perverse than the greatest clown in the world. I swear to you by the little sense I have left that every time I think of it my head bursts, my bile boils, and I injure myself to pay with blood for my terrible stupidity, for such an ill-advised career. Oh shame! Am I he who began by intending to be the greatest man of the century? With the finest genius, with extraordinary prudence, with a plan of action? Oh shame! I am an idiot, an ass, a fool.

Yesterday Father Cavalli, in order to console me, tried his hand at spirituality to the detriment of his art. But my need and pain must be borne in my heart, since the liability I have brought on myself is so extreme. I deluded myself with the thought that going out more frequently and talking more often with friends would bring me relief. But fantastic as it seems, the minute Lucrezia set foot outside the house to leave for Naples with Rosalvo I was filled with hatred for my friends, for the light of day, and even for myself. Oh God! As soon as I began to kick myself for my stupidity, for my buffoonery, they quickly began to spread the rumor that mother and son left for no other reason than for me to marry that singing strumpet....

And now I am alone, without maid, without servants, with no other companion except a cat, who to compound my misfortune turns out to be a tabby, that is to say, undomesticated....

For the love of Christ, for the love of God, in your goodness console me, advise me!... [From Brown and Enggass, *Italian and Spanish Art, 1600–1750*, 1:132–33.]

25. BERNARDO DE DOMINICI (1683–1759)

Born in Naples, De Dominici spent his life in Naples and has always been associated with that city. The birth and death dates included here replace those that scholars once accepted and that indicated that he had lived to be 102 years old. An insignificant artist himself, De Dominici's major achievement was as a biographer of Neapolitan painters, sculptors, and architects. His account, which appeared in three volumes, was published in Naples between 1742 and 1745. De Dominici wrote in the tradition of the sixteenth-century Florentine biographer Giorgio Vasari,[51] whom he praises in his introduction to the third volume. De Dominici's eighteenth-century accounts of the primarily seventeenth-century Golden Age of Neapolitan art, renders him a latter-day Vasari who knew some but not all of the artists he mentioned. While he continues and corrects the tradition of both Vasari and the seventeenth-century biographer Filippo Baldinucci,[52] he models his accounts on yet another literary precedent, the lives of the saints. De

Dominici claims that the motivation for his biographies arose from a sense of honor to the country, love of virtue, and a zeal for truth. Although such biographies of artists are more common in Rome and Bologna, De Dominici's remains the predominant one for Naples. Our first passage is a commemoration of the seventeenth-century architect, Cosimo Fanzago of Clusone, near Bergamo in Lombardy (1593–1678), who designed and decorated much of the famous Certosa di San Martino. The second is from the biography of Jusepe de Ribera (1591–1652), who painted for that same Carthusian church as well as the cathedral of Naples. Ribera's paintings for both monuments are still in situ.

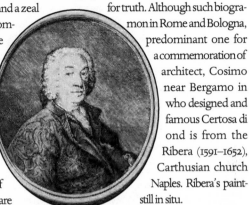

Figure 28

BERNARDO DE DOMINICI, "THE ARCHITECT, COSIMO FANZAGO"
FROM *Vite dei pittori, scultori ed architetti napoletani*

Finally he died in his eighty-seventh year, saddening the entire community who had admired him for his rare talents; not many artists can be compared to him, since he was both a truly excellent architect and quite outstanding as a sculptor. His corpse, escorted by a host of mourners, was taken for burial in the vault of the Servite fathers' church of Santa Maria d'Ognibene, near where he used to live, and interred there with much honor and everyone's tears on the 13th February in the year 1678. In countenance Cosimo was striking, white-skinned but high-colored, wearing huge mustaches, with fine features and a noble forehead and a jovial expression, very impressive to behold. He had been well paid for his labors yet left little on account of entertaining his friends far too generously. A sincere man, he has since been greatly maligned. He bequeathed a good name to his profession, doing much to bring his art to a high degree of perfection and towards elevating it to an honored place. [From Seward, *Naples: A Traveller's Companion*, pp. 119-20.]

BERNARDO DE DOMINICI, "JUSEPE DE RIBERA, 'SPAGNOLETTO,' AND HIS FOLLOWERS"
FROM *Vite dei pittori, scultori ed architetti napoletani*

The Decoration of the Naples Cathedral's Chapel of San Gennaro

During that great period there was a competition among the most renowned painters to determine who would decorate the large, elaborate and magnificent chapel of San Gennaro, commonly called the Treasury. "The Little Spaniard" understandably was one of those who strove to obtain the commission for these large altarpieces, which were elaborately framed, as were the other minor ones on small altars placed on the piers of the dome; as a result, the effect of the great chapel was that of a Greek Cross [with four equal arms]: and Belisario [Corenzio] wanted to paint the dome in fresco as were the vaults and lunettes in which were represented the story of our own protector saint [San Gennaro]. But the nobles in charge had decided upon one single, famous artist to execute the stories in fresco to be in harmony with the paintings in the cupola, and the pendentives were to be like oil paintings: and having heard of the prowess of the outstanding Guido Reni, the Cavaliere d'Arpino being no longer around, they called him for this purpose. Guido arrived, but Belisario, who had long favored Ribera, was angry over this invitation and had one of Reni's servants beaten, causing the terrified man [Reni] to flee. The same thing happened later to his follower, Francesco Gessi.

Then Domenichino came [to Naples], determined to have peace and safety. According to Belisario's account this aggravated Ribera's proud spirit, further agitated by Corenzio himself who called attention to the great importance of these works. There was not only honor at stake but money, which the Bolognese painter [Domenichino] deprived him of. There was no hope of changing the rigid orders from the viceroy, via the request of Cardinal Buoncompagno, then archbishop of the church in Naples, who strove to protect his [Emilian] compatriot painter. These thoughts brewed

Figure 29

in Ribera's mind and out of a healthy pride he developed a permanent dislike for Domenichino; it affected his behavior and he became moody and depressed as he could see what was to follow.

At the same time the viceroy, who was fascinated by all painting and hoped to commission not just those of Ribera, ordered frescoes from Belisario and others for the rooms of the Royal Palace. He had noted the fact that Ribera never painted in fresco [direct or glued to the wall]. Now Ribera, who was turning out various paintings to send to Spain, very delicately proposed to the viceroy that a portion of these be done by Domenichino, and others by Belisario, or [Giovanni Battista] Caracciolo, as quickly as possible in order that they could be sent to Spain. Thus Ribera fervently hid his dislike of the poor Domenichino. By applying himself to other work Domenichino was working half-time on the agreed contract for the patron. And although Domenichino had prudently requested from the viceroy [the duke of Alcala or count of Monterey, see Appendix] a time extension for the works of the Treasury, the Spaniard nevertheless still had hopes of drawing it out so that with these troublesome lords, Domenichino's natural slowness, and the oppressive delay in general, it finally caused Domenichino to be given the contract but the altarpieces at least to be allocated to Ribera. Great was the obvious resentment and sadness that Domenichino suffered....

Ribera represented in his great painting [for the chapel] the torture that the bishop San Gennaro suffered in the furnace: here he is seen standing surrounded on all sides by ropes, with hands on his breast, eyes and head raised toward heaven and offering everything in thankfulness for the miracle that took place; thus seeing the furnace's fire engulf the infidels and cruel officials.... [Bernardo De Dominici, *Vite dei pittori, scultori ed architetti napoletani*. Naples, 1844, 3:118-21. (Trans. J.C.P.)]

26. OCTAVIO ANTONIO BAYARDI (1649–1764)

Bayardi was titular archbishop of Tyre. His literary contribution consisted of his catalogues, containing descriptions, measurements, and illustrations of the ancient paintings of Herculaneum, one of the nearby towns destroyed by the eruption of Vesuvius in 79 C.E. These ten volumes with engravings by Nicola Vanni[33] were published by the Royal Press in 1755. Volume 4, an excerpt of which appears below, presents the paintings of Herculaneum. Other volumes include records of

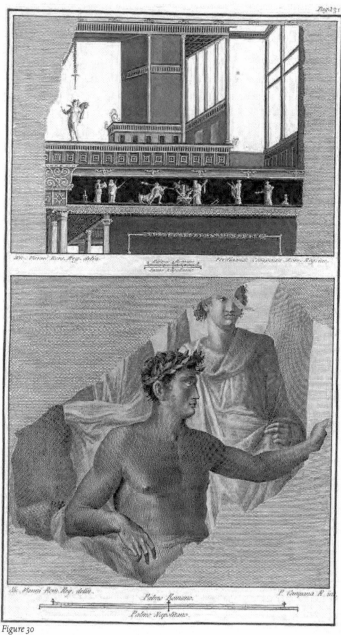

Figure 30

candelabra, bronzes, and examples of the minor arts. Such recording of the treasures of Herculaneum was encouraged by Charles III, who had been king of the Two Sicilies when the ancient city was rediscovered during the 1740s. This Spanish Bourbon monarch had a royal residence at Portici where he created a legendary secret museum that housed the spoils. Although tightly controlled initially and open to few visitors, the Portici[54] collection became widely known in 1757 with the first of these enormous volumes of the antiquities of Herculaneum. When in 1759 Charles left Naples to become king of Spain, he took the Capodimonte porcelain factory with him to Madrid but left the contents of Portici behind on the condition that he be sent drawings of all future excavations. The excerpt below describes two of the newly-discovered paintings from Herculaneum. [See FIGS. 30 (especially left portion of top) and 31.]

OCTAVIO ANTONIO BAYARDI, "THE PAINTINGS OF HERCULANEUM"

This engraved illustration contains two different sections: the first is part of the wall painting already described in the preceding illustration; and this portion corresponds in every way, whereas in the preceding print a portion of the figure is seen on the platform, which is here whole and better preserved. The complexion is delicate, the hair blond, and surrounded by a wreath crown. The wings are of turquoise color; the ribbon that falls from the shoulders and crosses the breast is yellow; and yellow also are the rings that are worn on the wrists and legs. And likewise the scepter that he holds on the left side is yellow; and on the right there is a staff or such, also yellow. Better preserved still, and more complete is the building [in the painting] of which the colors match those of the preceding illustration. The ceiling seen here and missing there, is yellow and supported by four green columns with white molding. The other ceiling, from which hangs a green festoon with red ribbon, is yellow as well. The molding on the right, supported by two green columns with two yellow partitions, has a red background and white ornaments. Underneath, where the columns rest and many gaps in perspective are seen, is a dark color that appears reddish.

The other piece is rather lost in the field. The young man seated has a strong complexion. He has a little beard or down, and short, curly chestnut hair, and a laurel crown. The cloth that is under his right arm is lacquer-colored. Behind, one can see a rock and parts of a tree trunk. Next to this, one can see a part of a figure whose dress is lacquer-colored. The other figure with a warm complexion has curly blond hair and a yellow dress. It seems that he is holding something, that can no longer be distinguished, with his left hand. Next to this figure one can see another tree trunk. [Octavio Antonio Bayardi, *Le pitture antiche d'Ercolano....* Naples: Regia Stamperia, 1765, 4:229-30. (Trans. L.N. and J.C.P.)]

Figure 31

27. LUIGI VANVITELLI (1700–1773)

The son of a Dutch painter who resided in Italy, Vanvitelli was born in Rome. With an international reputation, he studied with the architect Filippo Juvarra and established his own artistic reputation at an early age. In 1725 Vanvitelli became supervising architect of St. Peter's. He was responsible also for the design of such famous monuments as the harbor of Ancona, the campanile of La Casa Santa at Loreto, the convent of St. Agostino in Rome, the chapel of the church of the Jesuits at Lisbon, and the archducal palace in Milan. His crowning achievement was, however, the Palace of Caserta, "Italy's Versailles," about twenty-eight kilometers north of Naples. Modified by his son Carlo in 1773, it was imbued with loveliness and grandeur exemplified by its waterfalls, parks, statues, and grottoes.

Vanvitelli's huge folio description of Caserta, published in 1734, had been recommended by Giuseppe Sigismondo [21] in the third volume of his description of the city of Naples. By 1789, Sigismondo indicates that the book was difficult to find and in need of reprinting. Published by the Regia Stamperia, this tome contains fourteen double-page engraved plates by Carlo Nolli, Nicola d'Orazi, and Roccus Pozzi[55] after the designs of Vanvitelli. There are accompanying descriptions and plans of the magnificent palace designed by Vanvitelli at the request of Charles III and intended for Charles' son, Ferdinando IV [FIG. 47]. Although construction had begun in 1752, it was not finished until 1774. Here Vanvitelli describes the site and beginning of the project. [See FIGS. 32, 33.]

LUIGI VANVITELLI, "THE PALACE OF CASERTA"

The remains of this hillside of Tifata[56] and the plain below, although being the prettiest section of the Campania region, were never occupied by the Ancients' munificence, perhaps because being so fertile, they had to be used as pastures, for they were the nearest to the destroyed bay of Galazia and to Capua,[57] which was two miles closer from its present-day location. Therefore, these lands being empty and open were sometimes used as army campsites. Consequently, there encamped Titus Veturius Calvinus and Spurius Postumius,[58] Roman consuls, who were taken into the insidious Caudine Forks[59] after being deceived by the Samnites.[60] Similarly in this vicinity, Hannibal set up his tents when he was expelled from the Latin garrison, Galazia. He stopped to wait for the opportunity to liberate Capua from the Roman siege. Therefore, the first population that received this side of Tifata looking to the south, was the city of Caserta. However, because its construction was made in chaotic fashion by the Lombards in rough and difficult times, it had no splendor until the eleventh century of our salvation, when [building materials from] the ruins of Capua and Galazia contributed little by little to its increase of buildings, people, and the bishop's residence. Finally, the first destination of such a pleasant and delightful site for use as a wonderful splendor was due to the acumen of Charles, the very wise king, and Maria Amalia,[61] magnanimous queen, who were infatuated by the healthiness of the air, the proximity to the metropolis [Naples], the spaciousness of the view, the fertility of the land, the charming arrangement of the hills, and the abundance of water. They decided to build here a

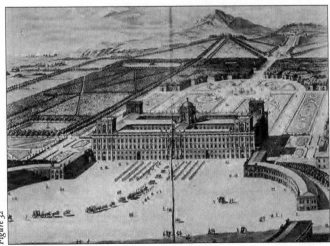

Figure 32

beautiful royal palace on the extensive plain. Thus from [their] unique benignity I was called from Rome to Naples to listen to the high ideas of their majesties and to express my limited talent in the following engraved drawings. With the sovereign's approval, it was decided not to delay work. [Luigi Vanvitelli, *Dichiarazione del disegno del Reale Palazzo di Caserta....* Naples: Regia Stamperia, 1756, pp. II-III. (Trans. L.N.)]

Figure 33

CHAPTER 4
Literature

28. GIULIO CESARE CORTESE (1575–1621/27)

Known as *"l'attonito"* (the amazed) and often considered the father of dialect literature, Cortese, who referred to himself as "Pastor Sebeto," wrote lengthy poems as well as satires in which he displayed his love of his birthplace, Naples. Cortese was a friend of, and inspiration for, his contemporary, Basile [30], another famous writer in dialect. Although Cortese's youthful rhymes and prose had been published in Naples in 1592, three years later, at the age of twenty, he turned to jurisprudence, as did so many Neapolitans. He traveled to Spain in 1600 and was subsequently at the court of Ferdinand de' Medici in Florence where he experienced many amorous misadventures. From 1604 he resided once again in Naples where he campaigned against the official poetry of Tuscany. His major interest lay in the legends, fables, and songs of his native city. A portion of his most famous poem, "La Vaiasseide o Poema delle serve" of 1615, which has not hitherto been translated into English and which consists of five canti in octave rhymes, appears below. In it he describes scenes of love, jealousy, celebration, and marriage among the common folk of Naples. In 1621 he wrote "Micco (Domenico) Passaro 'nnamorato," a little poem in ten canti of octave rhymes that portrays an enamored *"guappo"* (Neapolitan "bravo" or rogue). His last work, "Lo Cerriglio 'ncantato," was published posthumously in 1628. In it the author exhibits his romantic sensibilities by assigning fabulous sources to small-town monuments. Cortese died in Naples some time between 1621 and 1627.

Giulio Cesare Cortese, "The Common Folk of Naples"
"La Vaiasseide," Canto iii, *verses 20-24*

Then, after him, came Pacione,
who was wearing a suit made of rough cloth,
and who held a ball on which was written:
"the love that swells me is of a lustful kind."
And after him, came Menecone [big Domenico]

61

and right in the middle of the bottom of a tub
he had a golden purse of white silk
and written on it a Spanish saying "I'm broke!"

Then came Tonno who was wearing
a big leather jacket embroidered in the style of Cordova
and quilted, rust, whoved linen pants
and who brought with him a special carding comb
with this saying on it:
"Love has carded me"
and it went on the top of a load
so that anyone could see it as if it were
a small votive figure made of wax.

After him, came Mase, all dressed up
in fabric made of hemp, sewn together in circles,
and on the very bottom of a lute
he had painted both a curved piece of wood and a wine carafe
and a very knowledgeable school teacher
had found the following saying for him:
"If you have a beautiful wife at your side,
She will be of no use without bread or wine."

Then came Titta, a man of utmost polished style
He had to be, for sure; the honour of the feast day
because he wore a pair of gloves, suitable for a simpleton
together with a poor pair of boots and a rough woolen
cloak over his head.
And his coat of arms was truly that of the lover:
a life, little bit of beard, radish
with these letters written on a wicker basket
"Please open this life of mine, heart of a dog."[62]

Even others came around: Ciullo, Masillo,
Pizio, Meo, Peppo, Tonno, Cicco, Nato
Cola, Nardo, Pione, Lello and Millo —
Together with all the riffraff hanging around
the Port and the Market Square.

[Giulio Cesare Cortese, *Opere poetiche,* In appendix to *La Tiorba a Taccone de Felippo Sgruttendio de Scafato,* ed. Enrico Malato. Rome: Edizioni dell'Ateneo, 1967, 1:62-63. (Trans. M. R-D.)]

CHAPTER 4. LITERATURE

29. GIOVANNI BATTISTA MARINO (1569–1625)

Figure 34

As a poet, Marino [**22** and FIG. **34**] can be considered as a younger contemporary of Torquato Tasso (1544–1595). It was in 1602 that he produced his major collection of poems. George R. Kay (see Bibliography) refers not only to the musicality of Marino's "conceits," but to their caressing pleasure. The first passage on "how to steal" is from a letter to Marino's associate, Claudio Achillini, and dates from 1620, the same year in which his *Galeria* was published. The *Sospetto d'Herode*, from which the final verses are derived, was planned in 1605 but published posthumously in 1632. For a sample of the numerous so-called Marinisti, imitators of Marino's poetry, see **33**.

GIOVANNI BATTISTA MARINO, "WOMAN WASHING HER LEGS"

In a shell of gold upon silver base I saw two columns of alabaster amid perfumed and crystal currents breaking a white treasure of pearls. Ah (I said), resting-place and balm of my suffering, divine ends of Nature and Love, set as the utmost bounds in the Ocean of their own delights,

Might I be a new Alcides,[63] for, taking you up in my arms, I would raise my trophies where human desire had never reached. Or might I crush you together, like Samson, for I would give death a tomb with your sweet fall and death to my grief.

"DAPHNE INTO LAUREL"

O why do you flee, O Daphne, from him who follows and loves you, and desires nothing other than your lovely eyes? Are you a soft nymph? or perhaps a hard tree-trunk of this flinty mountainside, unbending and deaf to him who begs and calls you? But if you are a trunk, why are your feet so ready to flee? How can you not stay for my entreaties? So Apollo was speaking, but he was then the lovely fugitive, changed into a real trunk, stay unmovingly upon the bank.

"BROKEN VOWS"

On the damp sands of the Italian shore, I saw Tirrena with her own hand writing these words one day: Mirtius is my only love.

Ah, cruel fair, the sand alone was fit for words so frail; since the waves of the Tiber and forgetfulness at the one instant erased Mirtius, who was your love, from the beach and from your heart.

"Beautiful Slave"

Black, yes, but you are beautiful, or a graceful monster of Nature's among Love's beauties. The dawn is gloomy where you are; ivory and hue of rose fade and are darkened beside your ebony. When or where did the ancient world, or ours, see so living, feel so pure a light come from shady ink, or burning spring from burnt-out coal?

Slave of her who is slave to me, look, I bear a dusky noose round my heart that will never be loosed by white hand. Where you most burn, o Sun, a sun has been born for your sole shaming; a sun that wears night upon her face, and in her eyes has day.

"Leave-taking"

Already the sun whips his coursers from the waves, and now the hour of my leave-taking arrives; Lilla, the while, if Love warms and pricks us on, let our faithful sighs be our messengers. And as by unknown ways Alpheus[64] joins himself with Arethusa[65] again, so while our bodies live far apart, let our thoughts come back to visit one another.

Often two stars, nimble and happy in heaven, even though they take their way through different parts, have met at least with glad and loving look. And two plants often stand separate, but move to find one another again, if not with their branches, still with their roots underground.

"Inconstant Love" (to Signor Marcello Sacchetti)

Whoever cares to see a Proteus[66] of new love, Marcello, a new chameleon, let him turn his eyes on me, for, as my thoughts come back to this subject at all times, so do I embrace different forms and various colours.

I do not in the least dare defend my amorous failing; rather I confess my being wrong, and charge myself with the fault: but who is there who can catch the bridle of the unbridled will as it careers?

Who can circumscribe or bind the wandering desire of a covetous lover which moves and bends lightly as seaweed or leaf trembles on the branch in the breeze, by the seashore in the wave?

My burning affection has not just a single object: I find a hundred causes for torment and a hundred more; as long as I go or look about, I always have new reasons for sighing.

Every beauty I see dominates my heart; I flame and burn instantly at each kind look. Alas! I gradually grow to be unfailing fuel for every fire.

The sudden forms the eye offers to the mind are so many traps and hooks to make me love much more and more: now I languish for one woman, now for another am destroyed and turned to ashes.

Fresh beauty or maturer age inflame and spur and take me: the former sets me on fire with her graces and her eyes, the latter with her stately gestures and her ways.

The first for her pure simple nature, the other for the other endowment of wit and art, — the uncultivated beauty and the wise one please me equally.

Let a woman be in the habit of tricking herself out: who will not appreciate her ornaments? Let her be unsophisticated and negligent, adorned only with herself: I adore that directness, that poverty of hers is my treasure.

Let her be winning and lascivious, or shy and backward, the first makes me hope she will be as she seems, the second gives me the flattering idea that she loves to be loved and pretends.

This one, because she is seen to be of uncommon height; that one because she seems more supple of limb: taken in a double knot, I admire and praise each to myself.

A white and crimson cheek delights me wonderfully; a pale, white face has often claimed my heart: but dusky brow, dark eye and swarthy cheek are also to be loved at times.

Let a carefree hand unbind a head of gleaming fair hair, clustering, smooth, loosed about living flowers, I seem to see in that action the fair portrait of the rose-hued Dawn; or let another show me hair as black as ink, gathered up or falling above two burning stars, I compare her no less to the lovely calm of quiet Night.

If an angelic little creature laughs, that face of hers is an arrow; if she weeps, her weeping is a wound in my life; if she neither weeps nor laughs, without arrow, or wound, she still kills me.

A nymph who looses her soft voice softly, now high, now deep, and utters angelic harmonies, who is there who does not have the desire to kiss that mouth whence she frees her voice?

Where an alluring girl in a gay company strikes the sweet, fine cords with subtle fingers, what soul would not desire to be caught and wounded by so expert a hand?

See a young girl dancing by bank or valley, graceful in a fair dress, who skillfully whirls body and foot; and what rustic heart does she not imprison?

If I meet a beauty that can take her place beside the nine sirens of Pindus and Hippocrene,[67] with her looks and songs she can wound me and, at the same time, heal me.

There is a courteous lady who extols my style to heaven. Her who loves my song I love and desire as much, and I would change my nature to be in her bosom with my poems.

Another, when she reads me, reproves and corrects me. Then must I needs say: 'O might I yet have her as lover, — o happy submission to so lovely a teacher and corrector!'

In short, these ones and those, they are all beautiful to me, my desire burns for them all. Now, Marcello, if I had a thousand souls and a thousand hearts, would I be a nest large enough for so many loves? [From George R. Kay, ed., *The Penguin Book of Italian Verse*. Baltimore: Penguin Books, 1960, pp. 217-27.]

HOW TO STEAL (LETTER TO CLAUDIO ACHILLINI)

...Communion with other writers can occur in two ways: either by chance or by art. By chance it is not only possible, but in fact easily happened to me, not only with Latin and Spanish writers, but also with those of other languages, since whoever writes much cannot avoid using a few commonplaces that have probably been investigated by others. Beautiful things are few, and all acute intellects, when they begin speculating about a subject, seize what is best, so there is no wonder that occasionally they come up with the same result; not does it seem infrequent in recent times, when most of the most beautiful things have been appropriated, to find something extremely refined among many ordinary things.

This communion can be achieved by art and on purpose in one of the three following ways: by translating, by imitating or by stealing. Translating, when not pedantic, deserves more praise than blame. In fact, there are many examples of famous men who practiced it even if they were extremely fruitful creators of their own things. By "translating" I do not mean literal and word-for-word;

but paraphrasing, and changing the details of the hypothesis and altering the episodes without ruining the substance of the original sentiment. Even I have translated to pass the time or to please someone; but my translations were only from Latin or from Greek into Latin and not from any other language and were always under the foregoing conditions.... Borrowing like this cannot incur the accusation of stealing, since certain commonplaces are visible to anyone who can see and are available to whoever finds them first, like gems scattered on the beach. And as Virgil was not ashamed to include whole verses by Ennius[68] and Catullus[69] in his *Aeneid*, so other lyric and epic Tuscan poets were not ashamed to use verses by Dante and Petrarch. Therefore, when anyone borrows from them or from others and translates some longer passage into another language, this is supposed to be known by the experts in poetry and he should not be called an usurper. Among the idylls of my *Sampogna*[70] there is something that at first sight might seem translated from a foreign language; but nevertheless the first and most ancient source from which both of our rivulets originate is Ovid, and perhaps before Ovid, some Greek author....

I pass now from translating to imitating. I am not alluding to that kind of imitation which Aristotle considers characteristic of poetry — that which represents nature and which produces verisimilitude and consequently delight — but that kind of imitation which teaches us to follow the tracks of the most famous masters who have written before us. All men are naturally inclined to imitate; wherefore fertile imaginations and inventive intellects, absorbing the impressions of a joyous reading like seeds, become desirous to develop the concept they learned and immediately start concocting other fantasies that are often, by chance, more beautiful than those suggested by other people's words because they often draw out from a single and concise poet's phrase something that even the poet himself never thought about, although he creates it and is the first initiator. This imitation can be concerned with the universal or the particular. The universal consists in the invention itself and the ideas; the particular consists in the phrases and words. The former is typical of the heroic mood, the latter belongs more properly to the lyrical mood. The former is more poetical and can be hidden more easily than the latter; the latter is more shameless and less commendable. I omit the innumerable ancient examples and mention only the two most prominent epic poets of our time.

Ariosto, according to me, as imitated the Greek and Latin poets and concealed the imitation better than Tasso....

I finally come to the third and last way, which is stealing.... And here what can I or must I say? With all ingenuousness I must admit I am sure I have robbed as much as any other poet. The whole world should know that since I began to study letters, I learned to read with a hook, pulling out the things I found good as I read them and noting them down in my notebook and using them when I needed. Indeed, this is really the way one usually uses one's reading. Everyone who writes does this; and whoever never did, according to me, cannot get very far, because our memories are weak and deficient, and without this aid rarely give us the proper things when we need them. It is true that everyone has to make his own repertory according to his fancy, using a method that will allow him to find his material easily when he goes looking for it. All intellects are different; and the humors of men are even more diverse; so that what pleases one displeases another, and one will choose one phrase that someone else will reject. Ancient statues and relics of destroyed marbles, placed in a good location and with care, give a good measure of majesty to a new building. Similarly, according to the precepts and circumstances in the above discourse, I have pecked with my beak and committed a few little robberies, but I accuse and excuse myself at the same time because my poverty is such that I must grab the riches of whoever is richer than me. [From Dooley, *Italy in the Baroque*, pp. 458-59.]

An English poet known for his piety, wit, and imagination, Richard Crawshaw (c.1613–1649) was the author of *Epigrammatum sacrorum liber*, scriptural verse, and *Steps to the Temple with the Delights of the Muses*. From a Puritan family in England, he graduated from Cambridge University in 1634 and traveled through Europe, finally settling in Italy after converting to Roman Catholicism. Just before his death, he was appointed to a canonry at the cathedral of the Santa Casa at Loreto. His poetry, perfect for the Counter Reformation, was a combination of sensuality and the otherworldly. It reflects as well his ability as a linguist and scholar. One of his most memorable poems was "The Flaming Heart," written as a tribute to St. Theresa of Avila.

Crashaw translated only part (66 stanzas) of Marino's *Sospetto d'Herode*. His *Steps to the Temple* incorporate aspects of Marino's poetry, which may have been known in Cambridge during the 1630s. He may have learned of Marino's writing through Nicholas Ferrar, who traveled to the Continent and collected Italian books.

"THE MASSACRE OF THE INNOCENTS: HEROD'S MISTRUST"

Book One

Argomento

Casting the times with their strong
  signes,
Death's Master his owne death di-
  vines.
Strugling for helpe, his best hope is,
Herod's suspition may heale his.
Therefore he sends a fiend to wake
The sleeping Tyrant's fond mistake;
Who feares (in vaine) that he who
  Birth
Meanes Heav'n, should meddle with
  his Earth.

Muse, now the servant of soft Loves
  no more,
Hate is thy Theame, and Herod, whose
  unblest
Hand (O what dares not jealous Great-
  nesse?) tore

Figure 35

A thousand sweet Babes from their
  Mothers Brest:
The Bloomes of Martyrdome. O be a Dore
Of language to my infant Lips, yee best
Of Confessours: whose Throates answering his swords,
Gave forth your Blood for Breath, spoke soules for words.

Great Anthony! Spains well-beseeming pride,
Thou mighty branch of Emperours and Kings;
The Beauties of whose dawne what eye may bide,
Which with the Sun himselfe weigh's equall wings.
Mappe of Heroick worth! whom farre and wide
To the beleeving world Fame boldly sings:
Deign thou to weare this humble Wreath that bowes,
To be the sacred Honour of thy Browes.

Nor needs my Muse a blush, or these bright Flowers
Other then what their owne blest beauties bring.
They were the smiling sons of those sweet Bowers,

That drinke the deaw of Life, whose deathlesse spring,
Nor Sirian flame, nor Borean frost deflowers:
From whence Heav'n-labouring Bees with busie wing,
Suck hidden sweets, which well digested proves
Immortall Hony for the Hive of Loves....

[From Claes Schaar and Jan Svartvik, eds., *Marino and Crashaw*, Sospetto d'Herode. Lund Studies in English 39. Lund: C.W.K. Gleerup, 1971, pp. 37–39.]

30. GIOVANNI BATTISTA BASILE (1575–1632)

Like Cortese, Basile was one of the first writers to employ the Neapolitan dialect, which became popular during the early seventeenth century. Officially known as the Count of Torone, Basile was born in Naples. He traveled to northern Italy, where he was a soldier in Venice, and for one year visited the court of Ferdinand Gonzaga of Mantua. After having been made a count, he returned to the south where he held office as feudal governor of several lands. There Basile was introduced to the circle of the poet Giovanni Battista Manso, patron of Marino, as well as some of the major Neapolitan painters. His literary works include fanciful stories such as "The Cat Cinderella," a precedent for the modern fairy tale, as well as poems, madrigals, and odes. In 1617 Basile composed an ode to the Neapolitan baroque painter, Massimo Stanzione [note 36], in which he mentions three of his paintings. Basile dedicated a poem to another contemporary painter, Giovanni Battista Caracciolo [note 36], who executed a portrait of the author. This portrayal [above] was later engraved by N. Peray and appears at the front of the 1637 edition of Basile's epic poem *Teagene*, which was published in Rome. These two selections give an introduction not only to the prose of Basile but to the varied translations available of his work: the Victorian style of Burton vs. the more modern presentation of Croce, who published his translation from old Neapolitan dialect into modern Italian in Bari in 1935.

CHAPTER 4. LITERATURE

GIOVANNI BATTISTA BASILE, "TWO CAT TALES"

THE CAT CINDERELLA

Sixth Diversion
On the First Day

Zezolla is taught by her governess to slay her stepmother, and believing that in persuading her father to marry her teacher she would be well treated and held dear, instead is sent into the kitchen: but, by virtue of the fairies, after passing various adventures, gaineth a king for a spouse.

The hearers were silent as statues, listening to the story of the flea, and as soon as it was ended, all declared that the king had behaved like an ass in placing in jeopardy his own flesh and blood and the succession of his realm: and all having said their say, Antonella began to relate as follows:

Envy is ever a sea of malignity, and giveth in exchange for bladders a rupture, and when it desireth to see folk drowned in the sea, findeth itself under water or impelled against a rock, as I am now going to relate.

Once upon a time there lived a prince who was a widower, and he possessed an only daughter, so dear to him that he saw nought but by her eyes: and the princess had a governess, who taught her all kinds of fancy work, and educated her in many other feminine endowments.

Now this woman made a great show of affection for her pupil, more in sooth than can be expressed. The prince took to himself a wife after a little while, and she chanced to be an evilly-disposed woman, who looked with disfavour on her charming stepdaughter, treating her with contempt, and coldness, and spite, so much so that the unhappy child used to complain of the ill-treatment she received to her teacher, saying to her, 'O God, would that thou hadst been my darling mother, thou who lovest me and art always caressing me!' And so long did she continue this song that the governess at last lent a pleased ear to it, and blinded by Satan, spake to the child thus: 'If thou wilt do as I bid thee, I will become thy mother, and thou shalt be dear unto me as my very eyes.' She was going to end her say, when Zezolla (thus was the princess hight), interrupted her, and said, 'Pardon me if I thus stop the words upon thy lips: I ken quite well that thou lovest me: therefore say no more, but teach me only by what art we can come to an end of our desires. Write thou, and I will sign the deed.' The teacher rejoined, 'Open thine ears, and hearken well, and thou shalt have bread as white as snow. When thy sire fareth to the chase, say to thy stepmother that thou wouldest like to wear one of the old raiments which are to be found in the large chest stored away, as it is thy desire to save for high occasions the one thou wearest now. Thy stepmother, who loveth above all things to see thee in rags, will at once consent, and will go and open the chest, and will say to thee, "Hold up the lid," and thou wilt hold it: and when she searcheth therein, thou wilt let it fall, and thus her neck will be broken. And after this thou knowest thy sire will do anything, even to false coinage, to please thee: therefore, when he caresseth thee, beseech thou him to take me to wife: and then wilt thou be blessed and happy, since thou wilt be the mistress of my life.'

Having listened to the bidding of her governess, every hour seemed a thousand years to her until she could execute her teacher's rede. And after a time she did so: and when the mourning for her stepmother's untimely end had passed, she began to speak to her sire, telling him that she would be very happy if he would wed her teacher.

The prince at first heard not; but the daughter kept ever speaking and persuading him, till at last he lent a willing ear to her desires, and took Carmosina (thus was the teacher hight) to wife, and ordered great joyance and feasting in all his realm. Now it so happened that whilst the bride and bridegroom were toying and playing, and spending their time in joyance, Zezolla was looking out of one of the windows in the palace, and beheld a pigeon flying about, which at last settled upon a low wall in front of her, and addressing her in human voice, spake thus: 'When thou desirest to have something, send to the pigeon of the fairies in the island of Sardinia, and thou shalt have thy wish.'

The new stepmother for five or six days caressed and petted the young princess, seating her in the best place at table, giving her the choicest morsels, arraying her in the finest raiment: but having passed a short time, forgetting the deed Zezolla had done to serve her (and sad the soul who hath a bad master), she brought forward six daughters of her own, whom she had kept hidden secretly: and so much art did she use that, having ingratiated her daughters in the stepfather's favour, he lost all love and affection for his own child, so that (argue-to-day and speak to-morrow) Zezolla was sent from the chamber to the kitchen, from the dais to the fireplace, from the silken and golden raiment to the coarse cloth, and from the sceptre to the spit.

And not only did she change her estate, but her name was changed also, and she was hight the Cat Cinderella. So it chanced one day of the days that the prince her sire had to journey to the island of Sardinia on matters concerning his realm; and before departing he asked each one of his stepdaughters — Mmperia, Calamita, Sciorella, Diamante, Colommina, and Pascarella — what they would that he should bring to them on his return. One asked for fine raiment, another jewels for her hair, another cosmetics and pomade for the skin, another divers playthings to pass the time, another fruits, another flowers: and at the last, in contempt for his own daughter, he turned and said to her, 'And thou, what wilt thou?' and she answered, 'I want nought, but I desire that thou recommend me to the pigeon of the fairies, bidding her tell them that they would send me somewhat: and thou shouldest forget to do my bidding, mayest thou not be able to stir forward or backward from thy place. Remember well my saying: thine is the weapon, and thine is the sleeve.' The prince fared to Sardinia, ended all his affairs, bought all the things desired by his stepdaughters, and forgot quite Zezolla's bidding. He took ship for his return: but do as they would, the ship would not move from its place, neither backward nor forward, and it seemed glued to its mooring. The vessel's master was in despair, and in the evening, being very tired, he lay down and slept: and he beheld a fairy in his sleep, who said to him, 'Knowest thou wherefore thy ship cannot sail? 'Tis because the prince thou hast on board hath failed to keep his promise to his daughter, remembering all his stepdaughters, and forgetting his own flesh and blood.' The master awoke from sleep, and related his dream to the prince, who, confessing the fault he had committed, fared at once to the fairies' grotto, and recommending his daughter to them, begged that they would send her somewhat: and at his words out of the cave came a beauteous young lady, who said to him that she thanked his daughter for her kind remembrance, and that she bade her take for love of her these her gifts: and thus saying, she gave him a date-tree, a mattock, a golden bucket, and a silken napkin, the one to transplant, and the others to cultivate the tree. The prince marvelled at the present, took leave of the fairy, and journeyed with the ship towards his country. On his arrival he gave his stepdaughters that which they had bidden him bring, and lastly to his daughter the gifts of the fairy. Zezolla accepted the gift with great joy, and transplanted the date-tree in a larger and finer vase, and watered it, and dug round it morning and evening, and dried it with the silken napkin, and in four days it grew to a woman's stature: and the fairy came out of it one morning, saying, 'What wilt thou?' and the princess answered, 'I would like to fare from this house, but should desire that my stepsisters should not know of it': and the fairy rejoined, 'Each time that thou wouldest fare out and enjoy thyself, come to the date-tree, and say,

"My date-tree tall and golden,
With a golden mattock I dug thee around,
With a golden bucket I watered thee,
With a silken napkin I wiped thee dry:
Undress thyself, and robe thou me."

And when thou wouldst undress, change the last verse, and say "Undress thou me, and robe thyself."'

Now it so chanced that a great festival was held by the king: and the daughters of the teacher went to it in fine raiment, and jewellery, and ribbons, and fine shoes, and flowers, and perfumed, with roses and posies. As soon as they departed, Zezolla ran to the date-tree, and repeated the verse taught her by the fairy: and at once she was arrayed as a queen, and put on a steed, and twelve pages followed her, all dressed with luxury and taste: and she went where her stepsisters had gone before her, who knew her not, and were ready to die with envy. But as fate decreed, came to that same place the king who on beholding Zezolla fell enamoured of her, and desired one of his most trusty followers to learn who was this beauty and where she dwelt. The king's servant at once followed the princess: but Zezolla, perceiving the snare, threw an handful of golden coins to the ground, at the sight of which the man forgot to follow the courser as he stooped to gather the gold, which Zezolla had begged the date-tree to give her for this same purpose. Thus she had time to run into the house, and undress herself as the fairy had taught her. And when those witches, her stepsisters, arrived home, they said many things in praise of the festival, of what they had done and what they had seen, to cause her vexation, as they supposed. In the meanwhile the follower returned to the king, and related to him about the handful of coins and how he had lost sight of her, at which the king waxed wroth, and said to him that for a few dirty pieces of gold he had deprived him of his delight, but that he would forgive him this time, but he must be sure to follow her on the next feast-day, and to discover for him who this beautiful bird was.

The next feast-day the stepsisters went their way all bedecked in finery, and left the despised Zezolla at the fireplace. As soon as they were gone, she ran to the date-tree and said the usual charm: and some young girls came forward, some with the mirror, some with the perfumes, some with the curling tongs, some with the comb, some with the hairpins, and others with the raiment, some with the necklace, and others with flowers: and decking her like a bride, she looked like the sun, and setting her in a carriage, with six horses, with footmen, and servants, and pages in livery, she arrived at the same place where had been held the festival heretofore: and she lit more marvel and envy in her stepsister's breasts, and greater love and fiercer fire in the king's heart. But having departed, the same servant followed her: but she threw at him a handful of jewels, and pearls, and precious stones, and he could not withstand the temptation to gather them, as they were too precious to lose. And the princess had time to reach her home, and to undress as usual. The man returned to the king, who said, 'By the bones of my ancestors, if thou findest not this lovely being for me, I will give thee as many kicks on thy backside as thou hast hairs in thy beard.'

The third festival came: and the stepsisters having departed, Zezolla went to the date-tree, and saying the charmed verse, she was at once apparelled most splendidly, and seated in a golden carriage, followed by many servants, pages, and retainers. And thus she caused more envy in the sisters' breasts: and the king's follower stuck to the carriage. And the princess, sighting him always beside her, said to the coachman, 'Hasten on,' and the horses raced with such speed that nothing could be discerned clearly, and in the fury of the race a slipper of the princess flew out of the carriage. The servant, unable to follow the carriage, which seemed to fly, picked up the slipper and brought it to the king, and related all that had happened; and the king, taking it, said, 'If the foundation is so beautiful, what must be the house? O beauteous candlestick, which holdest the candle that consumeth me! O trivet of the beauteous kettle where boileth my life! O fine cloth, to which is tied the net of love wherewith thou hast caught this soul! I embrace thee and hold thee to my bosom; and if I cannot have the tree, I worship the root; and if I cannot hend the chapiter, I kiss the foundation. Thou wert the covering for a white foot, and now art thou the pulley of this blackened heart; by thee stood thy fellow, an inch tall and more, who is the tyrant of this life of mine; and by thee groweth so much sweetness in my soul, whilst I gaze upon thee and possess thee!' And thus saying, he called his secretary, and commanded him to send the public crier to publish a ban that all the women in the land should be invited to a banquet by the king.

And the day came. O goodness me, what a banquet was that, and what joyance and amusements were there, and what food: pastry, and pies, and roast, and balls of mincemeat, and macaroni, and ravioli, enough to feed an army! All the women came: noble and commoner, rich and poor, old and young, wives and maidens, beautiful and ugly; and the king, arrayed in costly raiment, tried the slipper on each one's foot to see if it would fit one of them, hoping thus to find the one he was seeking: but he found not what he sought, and he came nigh unto despair. At last, commanding perfect silence, he said to them, 'Return to-morrow to do penance with me: but as ye love me, leave not a single female in the house, be she who she may.' Said the prince, 'I have a daughter who sitteth always in the kitchen by the fireplace, because she is not worthy any one's notice, and she deserveth not to sit at thy table.' Said the king, 'Let this be the very one at the head of all: such is my desire.' Therefore all departed, and on the morrow all came again, and with the daughters of Carmosina came also Zezolla, and when the king beheld her he knew her for the one he sought: but he dissembled.

The banquet was more sumptuous than the last, and when all had eaten their fill the king began to try on the slipper: but no sooner came he to Zezolla than the foot was caught by love like steel to the magnet; and the king surprised her by putting his arms around her, and seating her under the dais, and putting the crown on her head, commanded that all should do her obeisance as to their queen. The stepsisters, beholding this sight, full of wrath and envy, and being unable to support this blow without showing their chagrin, departed quite quietly towards their mother's home: confessing, in spite of themselves, that

"'Tis a madman's deed to dispute the stars' decree."

Chapter 4. Literature

[From *Il Pentamerone or The Tale of Tales,* trans. Sir Richard Burton, K.C., M.G. from Giovanni Battista Basile, *Immortal Classics.* New York: Horace Liveright, 1927 (reprint of London 1893), pp. 45-51.]

The Benefactor Cat

Once upon a time in the city of Naples there lived a beggar, who was so penniless, exhausted and desperate, so worn out, destitute and bereft of even the smallest coin in his purse that he went about completely naked. The day came for him to settle his debt with life, and so he called for his two sons, Oraziello and Gagliuso, and spoke the following words to them: "I have been rightly called upon to give account of myself at a higher station, and believe you me, if you're Christians, I shall be only too happy to get away from this rat-hole of weariness, this treadmill, if it were not for the fact that I will be leaving you on this bare earth, as large as the Church of Santa Chiara at the crossroads in Melito,[71] and without a shirt on your backs, as clean as a barber's hand-basin, as quick as sergeants and as dry as plum-stones. You carry as much as can be placed on the foot of a fly, and even if you ran for a hundred miles, you wouldn't lose anything. Destiny has reduced me to such a state that I have nothing but life itself, and as you see me here before you, so you can describe me, because I've always yawned, made my crosses, and gone to bed without candles. Nevertheless, I wish to leave you with some token of my Love. And so, Oraziello, you are the first-born, take that sieve hanging on the wall — it'll help you earn your living; and you, who are more of a stay-at-home type, take the cat, and remember your father." So saying, he burst into tears and shortly afterwards said "Farewell, for it is night-time."

Oraziello set about burying his father with the help of charity, and then took down the sieve and set off in search of his living; the more he sieved, the more he earned. But Gagliuso, who had got the cat, started complaining: "Now look what sort of heirloom my father left me! I can't look after myself and now I've got two mouths to feed. Why this stupid legacy? I could've done without this!" The cat, who had heard these complaints, told him: "You moan too much; you've got more luck than sense!" Gagliuso thanked the cat for this and, stroking him three or four times on his back, entreated him to keep his word. Being compassionate towards him, the cat would go out of the house at that time of the morning when the sun lowers its fishing-line baited with gold into the dark depths of the night, and go to the beach at Chiaia,[72] or the Fish Stone where, having espied some fat mullet or bream would steal off with it and take it to the King. Giving it to him, he would say: "Mr. Gagliuso, Your Majesty's most devoted servant, sends you this fish with deepest reverence and asking for your pardon. A small present for a great lord." And the King, with the best smile that was reserved for those who brought him gifts, answered: "Tell this gentleman, whom I knoweth not, that I thank him with all my heart." Other times, the cat would scamper off to where there was a hunt, the Marshes or the Astroni,[73] and just as the hunters struck down some oriole, chaffinch or blackcap, he would pick it up and take it back to the King with the same words. And he did this so often that one day the King said to him: "I feel so much obliged to this Signor Gagliuso that I should like to meet him, in order to exchange a sign of affection." The cat replied: "It is Mr. Gagliuso's desire that he should put his life and blood at the disposal of the crown; and, tomorrow morning, he will certainly come to visit you at that time when the Sun sets the stubble and the fields of the air alight." But, when morning came, the cat came to the King and said: "My Lord, Mr. Gagliuso has sent me to apologize for not coming: you see last night some of his servants robbed him and he now does not even have a shirt to wear on his back." When the King heard this, he had clothes and linen sent from his own wardrobe to Gagliuso who, two hours later and led by the cat, came to visit the king.

The king complimented him, and bade him sit next to him at a banquet he had prepared in his honor. But while he was eating, Gagliuso turned to the cat every so often and said: "Pussy, my dear, don't forget to look after those rags of mine — I wouldn't want to lose them." And the cat replied: "Be quiet, don't speak of those dreadful things!" And the King, who wished to know if he was in need of something, was informed by the cat, who spoke on Gagliuso's behalf, that he needed a small lemon; and so the King immediately went off to the garden to get one. Gagliuso, a little later, went back to the subject of his dirty rags, and the cat yet again told him to hold his tongue; the King asked what the problem was and the cat, who had another excuse ready, saved Gagliuso's skin once more. After eating and chatting for some time about this and that, Gagliuso bade farewell.

Now that the cat was alone with the King, he set about describing the valor, the servility, wisdom and, above all, the wealth that Gagliuso possessed in the lands of Rome and Lombardy, and that it would be most expedient for him to enter the family of a real king. The King inquired as the extent of this richness, but the cat replied that it was not possible to count the value of all that rich man's property and goods, and that he didn't even know himself what their value was; if the King wanted to find out more, then he would have to send some men with him, the cat, outside the Kingdom, and thereby would learn that there was no wealth that could compare with this.

The King excharged some of his faithful servants to check up on this, and so off they went following the cat. As soon as they had left the Kingdom the cat, with the excuse of going ahead to find out some places of refreshment for the company, ran ahead and when he came across a herd of cows or flock of sheep would tell the farmers who looked after them: "Hey there, be careful, a band of thugs are coming along and they are plundering and stealing everything they find in the countryside: however, if you wish to save yourselves from their fury and destruction, just tell them that it all belongs to Mr. Gagliuso, and you'll see that you will be left unharmed." He said the same to the farmhouses he found along the way. And so, wherever the King's men went, they heard the same old story: it all belonged to Mr. Gagliuso. And, being tired of asking and hearing the same things, they went back to the King to whom they recounted news of all Mr. Gagliuso's riches.

Hearing all this, the King promised the cat a handsome tip, if he were able to arrange the marriage of his daughter to Mr. Gagliuso.

And the cat, busily going backwards and forwards, finally managed to conclude the deal. Gagliuso came and the King handed over his daughter and a handsome dowry; and after a month of celebrations, he announced that he wished to lead his bride back to his own lands; the King accompanied them to the frontier and they set off for Lombardy where, following the cat's advice, he bought territory and became a baron.

Now that Gagliuso was rolling in money, he turned to the cat and thanked him profusely, telling him that it had been due to his good offices that he owed his present good fortune and that the cat's ability had brought him more luck than his father's had. He was now able to do whatever he liked with his things, and so he promised the cat that when he, the cat, died, hopefully in a hundred years time!, he would have him embalmed and placed in a golden cage in his bedroom.

Hardly had three days passed from that promise when the cat, who was pretending to be dead, could be found lying on the ground. Gagliuso's wife saw him and cried: "Dear husband, what a terrible thing! The cat is dead!" "May he take away all evil with him," replied Gagliuso. "Better him than us." "What shall we do?" answered his wife. And he said: "Take him by the feet and throw him out of the window."

The cat, who had heard this reward for his troubles, leapt up onto his four paws and exclaimed: "So this is all the thanks I get for having defleaed you! This is what you meant by the 'thousand times thank you' for the rags I took off you back! This is all I get for having placed you in the position of a spider, for having fed you, you beggar, you tramp! You were in pieces, torn and shredded, flea-ridden and filthy! This is what happens to he who washes a donkey's head! Let everything I did for you be cursed, you don't even deserve to have your throat spat down! What a nice golden cage you have prepared for me! What a nice surprise! You slave away, wear yourself out and sweat — and look what you get in return! Oh woe is he who prepares the saucepan in the hope of others! That philosopher was right: he who goes to bed a fool will wake up a fool! In other words the more you do, the less you get. But fine words and sad deeds deceive both wise men and mad men!"

And thus saying, he went out shaking his head; and as for Gagliuso, although he tried hard to calm him down and get him to come back, it was all in vain. The cat ran off without turning back, muttering to himself: "God preserve us from the impoverished rich man and from the beggar, when he is on the make!" [From Massa Nunzia, ed., *Napoli-Guida, Guide-Naples, Reisefuhrer Neapel*, trans. Benedetto Croce. Naples: Graphotronic Edizioni, 1994, pp. 367-71.]

31. TOMMASO CAMPANELLA (1578–1639)

Relatively little has been written about Campanella's poetry although, evocative and spiritual, it was perhaps the most original in Italy at that time. This famous friar of the Counter Reformation was born to a poor family in Calabria. He came to Naples in order to study law but instead became a Dominican. One of his major goals, which permeates much of his writing, was to reconcile Renaissance naturalism with Catholic orthodoxy. Although associated primarily with a philosophy that he derived from Telesio's naturalism, and to a lesser degree science, the versatile Campanella also wrote poems, madrigals, and sonnets, which he clustered into "psalms." Upon the publication of his *Philosophia sensibus demonstrata* of 1591, he was accused of heresy, and from then on was repeatedly tried and imprisoned. Some of his poetry was confiscated in Bologna. When Campanella was incarcerated in Naples' Castel Sant-Elmo, he was chained and tortured. Eventually he feigned madness in an attempt to be freed. His final imprisonment occurred in 1602 when he was rightly accused of leading a revolutionary plot to reform Calabria as a first step in reforming the world.

Figure 37

To understand his poetry, one must examine Campanella's role as both astrologer and magician. His verse is simultaneously philosophical, spiritual, and highly personal and often contains revelations of previous mystical writers. It is valued as a kind of diary that records his suffering; and this aspect of his poetry, derived ultimately from Tasso, is a tradition shared by several of his contemporaries, including Michelangelo Buonarotti and Gaspara Stampa. George Kay calls Campanella "the friar who could accept prison, torture, oblivion from his church and still write with such feeling." This was possible because of his persistent ideals concerning heroism and universal achievement, themes that he incorporated into his utopian treatise, *City of the Sun.* [See **52, 67,** and FIG. **37** above.]

TOMMASO CAMPANELLA, "THE WAY OF PROGRESSING IN PHILOSOPHY"

The world is the book where eternal Wisdom wrote its own ideas, and the living temple where, depicting its own acts and likeness, it decorated the height and the depth with living statues; so that every spirit, to guard against profanity, should read and contemplate here art and government, and each should say: "I fill the universe, seeing God in all things."

But we, souls bound to books and dead temples, copied with many mistakes from the living, place these things before such instruction. O ills, quarrels, ignorance, labors, pains, make us aware of our falling away: o, let us, in God's name, return to the original! [From Kay, *The Penguin Book of Italian Verse.* pp. 203-4.]

"Men are the Sport of God and His Angels"

Masked upon the stage of the world by bodies and their properties, our souls, prepared by nature, divine art, for their performance before the highest council, go through the actions and pronounce the words which they were born to; from scene to scene, from interlude to interlude, clothe themselves in gladness and suffering, as ordained by the fateful comedy-book.

Nor do they know, nor can they, nor wish to do, or suffer other than what great Wisdom, pleased with all, has written to make all glad; when, at the end of games and disputes, their masks restored to earth, sky, sea, we shall see in God who best wrought and how best spoke. [pp. 204-5]

"Against Cupid"

It is now three thousand years since the world first worshipped Love that is blind, with his arrows and his wings; who now, in addition, has been made deaf, and will not, in his lack of all charity, hear of another's misfortune. He is gluttonous of silver, and accustomed to dress in brown, no longer a plain and loyal naked child, but a cunning old man; and he does not use a golden arrow, since pistols were contrived, but coal, sulfur, flame, thunder, and lead, which infects bodies with hellish wounds, and makes greedy minds deaf and unseeing. Yet I hear an echo to my alarm: "Yield, beast, scarred, deaf, and blind, to the wise Love of innocent souls." [pp. 205-6]

"To His Prison"

As every heavy thing travels from circumference to center, and as, too, the timorous and playful weasel runs into the mouth of the monster that then devours it, so every lover of great knowledge, who boldly passes from the dead pond to the sea of truth, with which he falls in love, fixes his feet at last in our abode.

Which some call Polyphemus's cavern, others, Atlas's palace, and some, the Cretan labyrinth, and some, uttermost hell — I can tell you that here favour, knowledge or piety have no power; for the rest, I tremble utterly, for this is a citadel sacred to hidden tyranny. [pp. 206-7]

CHAPTER 4. LITERATURE

"ON HIMSELF"

Freed and bound, accompanied and alone, quiet and shouting, I confound the savage throng: mad to the mortal eye of this low world, wise to the divine Wisdom of the high pole. With my pinions crushed to earth I fly to heaven, a joyful spirit in sad flesh; and, if at times the heavy burden bows me, my wings still raise me above the hard ground.

Doubtful warfare makes virtues known. Short is every other time before eternity, and nothing is lighter than a pleasing load. I bear the image of my love upon my forehead, sure of arriving happily, in good time, where without speaking I shall be ever understood. [pp. 207-8]

"HIS ESTIMATE OF DANTE, TASSO, AND PETRARCH"

Tasso, the graceful and easy expressions of the two greatest of the Tuscan tongue give much delight, because the garment is fair and does honor to the high, exquisite thoughts; but far more profitable is the fire in their bosoms, from which springs, in the soul not hostile to virtue, that spark and sweet burning which is proper to well-born, chosen spirits.

You equal and surpass them in expression, but the heart does not yet feel itself lifted to heaven on your wings, nor pricked with righteous anger. Oh! when will we feel ourselves snatched by your art from the erring throng to humankind's worthy end? [pp. 208-9]

FROM "THREE PRAYERS IN METAPHYSICAL PSALM-FORM JOINED TOGETHER"

Almighty God, although the unconquerable law of fate, and long experience not simply of my prayers' being poured forth in vain, but of their being taken in contrary sense, banish me from your sight, I still return obstinately, since all other remedies are not enough for me. For if there were, say, another God, certainly I would go to him for help. Nor could anyone ever say I was wicked, if I turned from you who thrust me into such destruction to one who welcomes me. O, Lord, I wander; help! help! before the temple of Wisdom becomes a mosque of foolishness.

Well do I know that no words are to be found that will move you to benevolence towards one whom you did not destine for your love from all eternity; for your counsel is without remorse, nor can the eloquence of worldly assemblies bend you to pitying, if you decreed that my mixed being is to be unmade and to waste among the many miseries I suffer. And if the whole world knows of my martyrdom, heaven, earth, and all their children; why do I rehearse the tale to you who have caused this? And if every change is something of a death, You, immortal God whom I adore, how will you change so as to alter my fate?

Still I come back to ask for mercy, where need and great grief hunts me. But I have not the eloquence or voice that would be fitting then for such a jury. Nor is it little charity, nor little faith, nor little hope that obstructs me. And if, as some teach, there is unspeakable pain in the world which cleanses the soul and makes it worthy of your grace, the Alps have not crystal so clean as would be needed for my purifying. Fifty prisons, seven torturings, have I passed through and still am I in the depths; after twelve years of humiliations and sufferings.

I still excuse you constantly with friends, saying that you keep another world for your own, and that the wicked are unhappy in themselves, as disdain, ignorance, and close-kept suspicion continually afflict proud minds; and they are always overwhelmed in the end by their own treacherous fortune. But my friends ask why, if we are all miserable, those others inwardly, we in an outward way, your good designs should be effected through our wickedness; for if other creatures and we, children of Adam, must be transformed from stage to stage for the good of all, why do you not bring about such change without our lamenting?

If you free me, I promise to make all nations into a school for true and living God the liberator, if so daring a thought is not to be denied the fulfillment to which you spur me; to throw down the idols, deprive every imaginary god of worship and him who makes God serve his own purposes, and is of no service to God; raise the seat and banner of reason against cowardly vice; call enslaved souls to freedom, humble the forward. Nor sing new psalms, for which Sion is faint, under roofs that lightning or beast may spoil. But I shall make the heavens your temple, your altar the stars. [pp. 210-11]

FROM "PROPHETIC PRAYER OF LAMENT FROM THE DEPTH OF THE PIT IN WHICH HE WAS IMPRISONED"

It is for you, O Lord, if you have not created me in vain, to prove my savior. For this I weep and cry to you night and day. When will it seem good to you that I should be heard? I do not trust myself to say more, for the irons I have about me laugh and mock me for praying in vain, for my dried-up eyes and hoarse exclaiming. [p. 209]

Chapter 4. Literature

"Scorn at Death"

How much sweetness and wonder seizes on the soul, when it comes out from this heavy, blinded cave of ours! Clean and glad it flies through all the universe, recognizes the essences of things, and sees by its side the orders of saints and the heroic family, which guide and counsel it, and how first Love comforts all, and how many spirits a single star holds.

Looking on the universe and its holy joys and how many tributes the benign spirits pay to God, you will begin to be amazed that He can look on our little, black, ugly earth, and — I shall say more to you — in which there are so many terrifying and bitter evils, that it seems to lose all sacredness; where hate, death, and war are found, and ignorance, infinitely greater, grips it. [p. 214]

"Song of Repentance for Beryl with the Desire to be Confessed, etc. Composed in the 'Caucasus'"

Lord, too much I sinned, too much, I know; Lord, I no longer wonder at my appalling torment. Nor were my loathsome prayers worthy of balm, but of deadly poison. Ah! foolish and darkened! I said: Judge, God, — not — Have mercy. But your high kindly patience, thanks to which, many times, you have not blasted me, gives me some assurance that you have reserved pardon for me at the last.

I believed I held God in my hand, though not following God, but the subtle reasonings of my intellect, that to me and so many have dealt death. Although wise and pious, human wit becomes blind and profane, if it thinks to better the common fate before you true God, see fit to reveal yourself to its faculties, and send it and arm it as your messenger, with miracles and proofs and signs.

Late, father, I come back for your counsel, late I summon the doctor; so worsened the disease that it does not yield. The more I wish to raise my eyes to your brightness, the more I feel dazzled, my eyelids weighing. Then, to my fierce danger, I try to get out of the bottommost lake with those powers that, wretch, I do not possess. Wretch that I am, lost thanks to myself, since I desire and refuse the divine aid which alone can save me!

I have no merit, thanks to those great sins which I have committed against you, Mother of Christ, and you who are near her, blessed spirits, inhabitants of the light which fills the world, and has not cleansed the ungrateful earth alone; I pray unreasonably, against use, for you to beg some pardon for your fierce major enemy from him who was the friend of sinners; because among the wicked, the greatest one am I. [pp. 215-17]

32. GIOVANNI BATTISTA MANSO (MARCHESE DE VILLA) (1561–1645)

Figure 38

Manso, who bore the title of the Marchese de Villa, was a man of letters and a poet as well as a friend and patron of Giovanni Battista Marino [see **22, 29**]. In 1588 he had befriended Torquato Tasso, who was still in Naples. Manso founded one of the many Neapolitan academies, that of the Oziosi (Idlers),[71] of which the writer of guidebooks Giulio Cesare Capaccio [**14**] was also a member, in order to bring literary men of two nations (Italy and Spain) together. The artists' biographer, Bernardo De Dominici [**25**], relates that, like Basile [**30**], Manso was a friend of the contemporary painter, Giovanni Battista Caracciolo. His literary efforts include his *Poesie nomiche* of 1635 [FIGS. **38, 39**] from which the following excerpts are derived. Manso produced poems which, according to the frontispiece, are "amorous, sacred, and moral." He is known also for his madrigals.

GIOVANNI BATTISTA MANSO, "CONFESSION'S CONFUSION"

When the soul is tempted, pain increases
Discovering its guilt at the last desperate
  moment,
And as pain increases, hope increases
Eclipsing its sins;
  As the soul turns upwards
And aspires to the heavens; by now not
  fearing hell
Pain increases by the hour and the soul cries
  and moans;
Inducing weeping and welcome grumbling.

What the world can give, magnificence, gold
  and purple,

Figure 39

It despises, itself a lonely hermit already at your mercy,
Recalling with sadness every stupid mistake;

Correct the uncertain sentence of supreme isolation
Wet the eyes, as all disdain (yes, true Love
Lightens it) this boring life.

[*Poesie nomiche di Gio. Battista Manso, Marchese de Villa.* Venice: Francesco Baba, 1635, p. 147. (Trans. I.I-D.)]

33. THE NEAPOLITAN "MARINISTI"

In the generations after Marino there followed a group of poets who, though not necessarily Neapolitan, continued Marino's flamboyant style of device and hyperbole. Not really a school of poetry, these writers often owed as much to their native traditions as to any Neapolitan influence. What does characterize them, however, is a common tendency toward linguistic experimentation, toward the "marvelous" and the virtuosic.

GIROLAMO FONTANELLA (1612–1643/4)

Although Fontanella was a native of Reggio in Emilia, he was always considered a Neapolitan as well as one of the "Marinisti," or followers of Giovanni Battista Marino. All of his literary works were composed in Naples after 1632 towards the end of his short life. Fontanella wrote volumes of rhymes including "New Skies," odes, and elegies. According to Giuseppe Ferrero, a modern authority on Marino and the Marinisti (see Bibliography), Fontanella's poetry presents "fresh and vivacious impressionism." With a rich and colorful imagination the poet refers to nature by focusing upon images, such as the rose, moon, coral, pearl, and carnation. Fontanella is concerned also with such melancholy themes as distress, pathos, and death. The lingering effect of Fontanella's poetry, according to Ferrero, is not unlike a "poetic stupor."

GIROLAMO FONTANELLA, "TO TEARS"

Are there only tears, bright tears,
Which the pale Dawn sheds?
More than heavy rains and freezing cold,
Soft frosts and dew.
Tears, those falling drops that emerge
From seeing crevices,
Which trickle down distilling every hour,
Cease to be tears and become rivers and streams.
Who does not bathe his face in tears,

If all the sky brings forth from under its most lovely mantle,
Is not seen in tears?
Grant all praise to these most beautiful things,
The smile is embellished by white pearls.
But tears, by gems that are even more beautiful.

[From Giuseppe Guido Ferrero, *Marino e i Marinisti*. Milan and Naples: Riccardo Riccardi Editore, 1954, p. 849. (Trans. I.I.-D.)]

TOMMASO STIGLIANI (1573–1651)

Born in Matera, Stigliani spent his early years in Naples where he got to know the poet Marino. Later he traveled to Rome, Milan, Turin, and even to Parma, where he was at the court of Ranuccio Farnese. According to Giuseppe Ferrero, Stigliani is known as one of the moderate or "tempered Marinisti" who deals with subjects heroic, moral, and commemorative. In 1617 he wrote his *Mondo nuovo*, an epic poem recounting Columbus's rediscovery of America. His satirical allusions to Marino in the sixteenth canto of this poem led to enmity between the two writers. The poetry of Stigliani has been interpreted by his literary friend, Francesco Balducci. Stigliani's last years were spent in Rome. At times the poet's presentation is pastoral; at others, playful. The passages here were chosen because, in their original Italian, they were most like those of Marino in their preference for rhyme.

Tommaso Stigliani, "Gift from a Flower"

From a high window shone her beautiful fresh face,
One in which nature had placed all its grace;
And wearing a crown of celestial roses
Dawn appeared at that special balcony.
I, who always wander around that favorite house
Surrounded by urns of sorrowful shadows,
Stood still, and seeing me she hid,
Blushing with amorous embarrassment.
And drawing back she threw me down a flower from her breast,
In a curious and awkward manner;
This I happily took as a good omen
Since one day perhaps she will repeat it with ease,
This tiny favor,
Like a perfect fruit accompanied by a sweet flower.

[From Ferrero, *Marino e i Marinisti*, p. 645. (Trans. I.I.-D.)]

CHAPTER 4. LITERATURE

TOMMASO GAUDIOSI (17TH C.)

Beyond the fact that Gaudiosi was born in Cava de' Tirreni, near Salerno, probably during the first half of the seventeenth century, little is known of his life. He is one of the most obscure of the imitators of the poetry of Marino. In addition to verse, he composed a tragedy, *La Sofia, overo l'innocenza ferita*, in 1640. His writing contains numerous historical-political references, and his sacred and moral verse is frequently moving and thoughtful.

TOMMASO GAUDIOSI, "WOMAN POSSESSED"

What agitates the body of my beautiful Clori
Is an infernal army of unclean spirits,
Which torment her in many ways
Since she, in so many ways, torments hearts.
Twisted by Furies and rages
She writhes, shakes, howls, and cries;
Curses, swears, and pulls her hair,
Striking black bursts from her breast.
The priest watches astonished;
Then challenges these monsters to an amazing struggle
Muttering sacred verse and prayer.
But it isn't so difficult to overcome such tortures:
For he who knows that he can't ascend,
Learns how to revel in earthly life.

[From Ferrero, *Marino e i Marinisti*, p. 1084. (Trans. I.I.-D.)]

GIUSEPPE BATTISTA (1610–1675)

Yet another of the Marinisti, Battista was known most of all for his stylistic cleverness. Born in Grottaglie in Cecce, he lived for many years in Naples where he was befriended and protected by Giovanni Battista Manso [32], Marino's patron. Battista traveled to other cities but, during his last years, lived in southern Italy and his native Cecce. His poems include the lyrical *Poesie meliche, Epigramata, Lettere,* and *Poetica,* the latter actually written in prose. Giuseppe Ferrero calls attention to Battista's acute rhymes, his sullen and serious moralizing, and his use of hyperbole.

GIUSEPPE BATTISTA, "BEAUTIFUL EYES"

Let them emerge daily from their cradle
And bring back the sun by their own light;
Let the night close its wings and open them

Around these flickering torches on an ethereal realm;
With the tiny ray of a distant star
May Diana as moon, decorate herself with the bright gleam:
She who gathers all beauty
In her eyes, puts all splendor to shame.
Oh that these two beacons last!
At times she opens them, revealing all of the graces,
At times she closes them, uniting with love.
She places them in the sea and makes it calm,
She lays them on the ground and flowers arise,
She lifts them to the sky and it opens up with stars.

[From Ferrero, *Marino e i Marinisti*, p. 1005. (Trans. I.I.-D.)]

34. SALVATOR ROSA (1615–1673)

It is appropriate that the passage chosen here to represent the poetic efforts of Rosa is entitled "The Witch"[75] as the painter often represented scenes of witchcraft, a subject that had been popular throughout the Renaissance and is referred to specifically in the sixteenth century in literature, such as the autobiography of the Florentine sculptor, Benvenuto Cellini, and prints of Agostino Veneziano. This type of subject, as well as bandits in rugged landscapes, appealed to Rosa's romantic sensibility, which characterizes his individual interpretation of the Baroque. [See 23, 24, and FIG. 27.]

SALVATOR ROSA, "THE WITCH"

Since love does not succeed,
She said, filled full of rage,
To make faithful a traitor,
I will swing this foot,
I will open these lips,
I will cry from the depths
The forbidden incantations,
The deadly fatal art
With the force that will invoke
The very god of hell.
May the god's wrath avenge,
May the god toss and stir.
In the dark realms
May the god strike
The evil, the accursed one

By whom I was betrayed.
Since the cruel one does not hear me,
Since lamentation has no value,
To deception, to deception,
To dishonor, to dishonor,
To enchantment, to enchantment,
And he whom heaven moves not,
Moves hell.

No tempt I need
Magic means
Profane signs,
Diverse herbs and knots
That can arrest the turns
Even of heavenly spheres;
Magic circles,
Icy waves,
Diverse fish,
Chemic waters,
Black balsams,
Blended powders,
Mystic stones,
Snakes and bats,
Putrid blood,
Slimy entrails,
Withered mummies,
Bones and worms,
Exhalations
That will blacken,
wounds of horror
That bring terror,
Turbid waters
That will poison,
Fetid ooze
That corrupts,
That will darken,
That will chill,
That despoils,
That destroys,
That will vanquish

Stygian waves.

Within this fearful cavern
Where sunlight never enters
I'll raise an infernal tumult;
I'll make a spirit of darkness;
I'll burn cypress and myrtle;
While slowly, oh so slowly
I crush his waxen image
And cause his living being
To die by secret fire.

[From Brown and Enggass, *Italian and Spanish Art, 1600-1750*, 1:134-35.]

35. FILIPPO SGRUTTENDIO (?–BEFORE 1678)

Sgruttendio may well be a pseudonym for the dialect poet Cortese [28]. In 1646 the Neapolitan printer Camillo Cavallo published a songbook in dialect. Primarily a burlesque production, its frontispiece bore the inscription *"La tiorba a taccone'* of Felippo Sgruttendio de Scafato." The title, probably a parody of *La lira* of Marino, is derived from the popular musical instrument called the *tiorba* and from *taccone,* or piece of sole with which one picked the ten strings. The writing displays an intelligent and conscious imitation of both Cortese and Basile. It is not known which person wrote under the pseudonym, "Sgruttendio," but it was certainly a young writer of dialect still being formed stylistically. Giulio Cesare Cortese is the most likely choice. These poems, which have never before been published in English, reflect the passion and sensuality of Sgruttendio.

FILIPPO SGRUTTENDIO, "THE PLACE AND MANNER OF FALLING IN LOVE"

I used to roam the world, single and free,
Solid and sturdy like an oak
And I would go here and there, with Girolamo, with Pietro,
Playing hide-and-seek in the market square.

One day cupid took me aside and, as in the nursery rhyme, said to me
"Bird, oh bird, the iron grip has caught you."[76]

There, handsome and charming,
I was sitting in the alley when
All of a sudden sexy Ceccarella passed by.[77]
Alas, what a marvel! She struck me
As so beautiful
Even when she's not in sight, I desire her.

CHAPTER 4. LITERATURE

FILIPPO SGRUTTENDIO, "WOUNDED BY LOVE"

Ceccarella wore elegant boots
Over soft-soled shoes:
With which she trampled over many twigs and thorns
But by her mere strolling brought forth violets.

May I lose my teeth
And eat coarse vegetables no more
If — with such affectation —
She didn't appear beautiful, like a banner of the sun.

I swear that every thump of her boot
Which I heard
Seemed to my spirit like the blast of a gun.

All should realize this fact:
I was smitten not by arrow
But a bold footstep.

[From Cortese, *Opere poetiche*, pp. 517-18. (Trans. M. R.-D.)]

36. "METASTASIO" (PIETRO TRAPASSI) (1698–1782)

Metastasio remains the most celebrated poet and librettist in eighteenth-century Europe. Although his father was from Assisi, he was born in Rome and educated by the learned man of letters, Gian Vincenzo Gravina, who Hellenized his pupil's name. Metastasio was taken to Scalea in Calabria where he studied with the Cartesian

Figure 40

philosopher Gregorio Caloprese. He had started writing at an early age and at fourteen produced a tragedy in verse entitled *Giustino*. In 1718 Metastasio entered the Accademia degli Arcadi[78] (Arcadians) and the following year left Rome for Naples where he was employed in a law office and became introduced to aristocratic circles. With his polished facility in verse, his favorite form became the "canzonetta," and he favored the reinterpretation of classical themes via romance, intrigue, passion, and sentiment. His cantatas, oratorios, and melodramas were extremely popular. Among the most famous texts by Metastasio was his *Didone abbandonata*, first performed in 1724, and used for almost forty settings by different composers, and the *Clemenza di Tito,* Mozart's last opera, but associated in all with nearly fifty settings. His lyrics were put to music by Niccolo Porpora, Domenico Sarro, and composers as famous as Pergolesi and Mozart. In 1729 the patronage of Marianna Pignatelli, countess of Althann, was eclipsed by that of the Austrian emperor who invited Metastasio to Vienna. It was there that he spent his last years. [See FIG. 40.]

Metastasio, "Liberty"

Thanks to your deceits, at last I can breathe, O Nice; at last the gods have had pity upon an unfortunate man: I feel that my soul is freed from its snares; I am not dreaming this time, I am not dreaming of liberty.

The old ardor has failed, and I am so calm that love does not find any scorn in me to mask itself with. I no longer change color when I hear your name; when I look you in the face, my heart no longer quickens.

I dream but I do not see you constantly in my dreams; I wake, and you are not my first thought. I go about in places far removed from you without ever wishing for you; I am with you, and it gives me neither pain nor joy.

I speak of your beauty, nor feel myself melting; I recall my misfortunes, and cannot be offended. I am no longer confused when you approach me; I can talk of you to my rival himself.

Turn your haughty look on me, speak to me with kind face; your contempt is vain, and vain, your favour, for those lips no longer have their accustomed sway over me; those eyes no longer know the way to this heart.

What delights or displeases me, if I am merry or sad, is no longer your gift, nor your fault: for without you I take pleasure in wood and hill and meadow; even with you every joyless place is tedious.

Listen, to judge if I am sincere: you still strike me as beautiful, but you do not seem the woman who has no equal: and (do not be offended by the truth) I now see in your glad face some blemishes which I once took for beauties.

When I broke off the arrow, I felt my heart breaking, (I confess my blushes), I seemed to be dying. But we can suffer anything to free ourselves from woes, to see ourselves no longer tyrannized, to repossess ourselves.

In the lime where it has chanced to come, the little bird sometimes leaves even feathers, but returns to liberty: then grows its lost feathers again in a few days: becomes wary from experience, and does not let itself be betrayed another time.

I know you do not think the old flame dead in me, because I say it so often, because I do no know how to keep silent. The natural instinct which makes every one dwell on risks they have escaped — that, Nice, spurs me to talk.

After the cruel danger we tell of threats that are past, the warrior in this way shows the marks of his wounds. In this way the slave, who has escaped from pain, happily shows the barbarous chain which he once dragged.

I speak, but in speaking have satisfaction myself alone: I speak, but do not in the least care that you should credit what I say; I speak, but do not ask if you approve my words, nor if you are calm in talking of me.

I leave an inconstant heart, you lose a sincere one: I do not know which of us will be first to be consoled. I know that Nice will never again find so faithful a lover; that it is easy to find another deceiving woman.

METASTASIO, "WHILE WRITING OLYMPIAD"

Dreams and fables I fashion; and even while I sketch and elaborate fables and dreams upon paper, fond as I am, I so enter into them that I weep and am offended at ills I invent. But am I wiser when art does not deceive me? Is my disturbed mind perhaps calmer then? Or does love and scorn perhaps spring from firmer cause?

Ah, not only what I sing and write are fables; but what I fear and hope for, all is falsehood, and I live in a feverishness. The whole course of my life has been dream. O Lord, let me find rest in the bosom of truth, when finally I come to wake. [From Kay, *Penguin Book of Italian Verse*, pp. 228-33.]

37. RANIERI DE CALZABIGI (1714–1795)

Born in Livorno, this famous librettist, adventurer, friend of Casanova, and cultured man of letters is associated with the elite who controlled the cultivation of opera. An admirer of some aspects of the "lyric tragedy," Calzabigi represents a severity of style typical of the period of post mid-century intellectualism that directed the arts toward a new natural, direct, and simple mode of expression and away from both Rococo artificiality and classical grandeur. He was in Paris during the 1750s where, through the press, he saw a complete edition of Metastasio's works and, early on, became an admirer. In Paris Calzabigi edited and published Metastasio's works in 1755. In 1761 Calzabigi settled in Vienna. Later he collaborated with Gluck, although not always successfully, as demonstrated by the uneven and eccentric *Paride e Elena* of 1770. His *Poesie* of 1774, published in two volumes, contains not only his *Orfeo ed Euridice* and *Alcesta* but analytical commentary on the dramatic poetry of Metastasio [36]. It is from the latter work that the following passage was selected. Calzabigi died in Naples.

Ranieri de Calzabigi, "Metastasio's Dramatic Poetry"

The old masters decided and the modern ones agree that, except for verisimilitude, interest cannot be sustained. Thus, like vibrations from the blow of a tight cord, whole action will occur little by little. Aristotle observes that those events, which the spectator cannot imagine befalling him, are not interesting nor exciting. Reasoning based upon these principles, apart from realizing that usually poetry of the French lyrical theater is unsuitable for music, would imply that all their lyrical tragedies can never be of interest and thus we would have two valid reasons to support the great elegance and lively expression of Italian music. In our dramatic poetry, be it in those by the poet of whom we speak [Metastasio] or in those by Zeno and his ancestors, both verisimilitude and truth shine everywhere. One sees famous names, historical events, recognized actions, altered little for predominant taste. The passions reign. The affections are manipulated. Tumultuous events — sometimes real, sometimes imagined — are introduced, but none far from truth. Hence, the spectator can easily imagine finding himself in such situations and is easily convinced to either deplore, abhor, sympathize or fear fake characters just in the way he reacts to such characteristics in real people and even himself. The great poet cannot create such songs without feeling first that reality. The composer cannot adapt music without having similar ability. And with the power of the composer's words and with the strength of the harmony, as opposed to what happens when we depend upon a mere reading, affection is stirred in our hearts, frequently moving us to tears.

But in the French lyrical tragedies it is a different case. They often go beyond the fantastic; they give us fantasy that one wouldn't experience even in the wildest dream. Usually any unity of time and place is ignored. The same tragedy can be in a city, heaven, or hell. Magicians, genies, sylphs are all mixed up with deities and demons. Rivers, winds, nymphs, flying dragons, pegasi, hippogryphs — all things mocked nowadays even among children — appear. In such a strange jumble, the poet tries in vain to hold interest, and if he has any sense, he is the first to laugh at such foolish productions. Interest can not be inserted by the musician because he does not discover the action, and the spectator, won over by the falseness before him, does not experience it either. Even when there is a chance moment of passion or tenderness, there is a sun dancing or a fury who jumps suddenly interrupting the continuity; a machine lifts and carries the sun through the air, such false effects leading to no effect. Therefore the spectator, tired of long journeys and foolishness, hates the whole spectacle. [Ranieri de Calzabigi, *Poesie di Ranieri de'Calsabigi*. Livorno: Stamperia dell'Enciclopedia, 1774, 2:273-74. (Trans. L.N.)]

38. MICHELE TORCIA (1736–1808)

Not to be confused with the seventeenth-century economic theoretician of the same name who wrote a discourse on finance in Naples in 1622, which was published seven years later, this eighteenth-century Michele Torcia, a somewhat elusive and allusive man of letters, demonstrates remarkable versatility. In addition to the following eulogy of the "poet laureate" Metastasio [36], which dates from 1771–1772, Torcia was something of an authority on volcanoes in southern Italy and in 1795 wrote a brief account of his excursion through some Neapolitan provinces. At the turn of the century he recorded his observations concerning the latest eruption of Vesuvius in 1799. The following is, in the words of Torcia, a eulogy, rather than a life of Metastasio, and prepares us for the greatness of the poet by first disparaging the literature of the past.

MICHELE TORCIA, "A TRIBUTE TO METASTASIO"

> It would be impossible, even useless, to try here to consider every aspect of Metastasio's life from the death of Abbot Gravina until the time when he held a position at the Viennese court. Very few, except for his friends, were familiar with the minute details of that period. A similar anecdote would not coincide with the historic report that we promised to give here in this brief outline. We would therefore consider Metastasio as author and poet. We are writing a eulogy, not a biography.
>
> In Italy good taste had languished for a long time under a heavy burden, and two contemporary events — the founding of the Accademia della Crusca (academic "high-brows") and the intrusion of "foreign domination" in that noble region — had fatally contributed to make things even worse. Poetry, above all, was

mortally wounded by those occurrences and continued to decline until the beginning of the last century when it was almost dead. Genius languished, already oppressed by the unbearable yoke of the Inquisition. Truth could not raise its head unless jokingly under the mask of burlesque style. The language of the gods became a jargon, execrable in the mouths of hypocrites, charlatans, and harlequins. [From *Elogio di Metastasio, poeta cesareo,* Naples: s.n., 1771, pp. 18-20. (Trans. L.N.)]

CHAPTER 5
Theater and Music

39. GIOVANNI BATTISTA DELLA PORTA (1535–1615)

With his *Magiae naturalis (Natural Magic, or The Secrets and Miracles of Nature)* of 1589, the versatile Della Porta bridges the sixteenth and seventeenth centuries. This text, founded upon both subjective selection and objective observation, deals with basic scientific phenomena associated with plants, medicines, metals, sounds, and candlelight as well as several unexplained mysteries of the physical world. Della Porta was a mathematician as well as a specialist in optics and the probable inventor of the camera obscura, an optical device for achieving three-dimensional perspective, and later used by painters such as Vermeer and Canaletto. In Naples he founded the first scientific society, the Accademia de' Secreti[79] in 1560, an institution which was later dissolved by the Inquisition.

Figure 41

In addition to his scientific contributions, Della Porta was a playwright whose first dramatic effort was published in 1589. More or less a contemporary of Shakespeare and often associated with the tradition of Italian Renaissance literature, Della Porta wrote several plays that date from the early seventeenth century. An example would be his tragedy in verse, *Ulysse*, probably of 1612. Among his fourteen extant comedies is *Gli Duoi Fratelli Rivali* (The Two Rival Brothers), composed during the decade before 1601 as an analogue to Shakespeare's *Much Ado About Nothing*. This brought him international fame. Della Porta's comedy, *Albumazar*, published in Venice in 1606, was well received all over Europe and particularly in England where adaptations were written by authors including Thomas Tomkis, whose own version was performed in 1614/5 for the court of James I. Tomkis's characters, scenes, and plot are the same as those of Della Porta, and he undoubtedly had the Italian play before him when he composed

99

his own version. There was speculation that Shakespeare himself might have been the author of this English version that is presented here.

GIOVANNI BATTISTA DELLA PORTA, "THE COMEDY 'ALBUMAZAR'"

Act I, Scene 2

RONCA, PANDOLFO, CRICCA

RONCA: There's old Pandolfo, amorous as youthfull May,
And gray as Ianuary. I'le attend him here.

PANDOLFO: Cricca, I seeke thy aide, not thy crosse counsell,
I am mad in love with Flavia, and must have her:
Thou spend'st thy reasons to the contrary,
Like arrowes 'gainst an Anvile: I love Flavia,
And must have Flavia.

CRICCA: Sir you have no reason,
Shee's a yong girle of sixteene, you of fifty.

PANDOLFO: I have no reason, nor spare roome for any,
Love's herbinger hath chalk't upon my heart,
And with a coale writ on my braine, for Flavia;
This house is wholy taken up for Flavia.
Let reason get a lodging with her wit:
Vex me no more, I must have Flavia.

CRICCA: But sir, her brother Lelio, under whose charge
Shee's now, after her father's death, sware boldly
Pandolfo never shall have Flavia.

PANDOLFO: His father, ere hee went to Barbary,
Promis'd her me: who be he live or dead,
Spight of a Last of Lelio's, Pandolfo
Shall enjoy Flavia.

CRICCA: Sir y'are too old.

PANDOLFO: I must confesse in yeares about three score,
But in tuffe strength of body, foure and twenty,
Or two monthes lesse. Love of young Flavia,
More powerfull then Medea's drugges, renew's
All decay'd parts of man: my Arteryes
Blowne full with youthfull spirits, move the bloud
To a new businesse: my withered Nerv's grow plumpe

And strong, longing for action. Hence thou poore prop
Of feeblenesse and age: walke with such fires
As with cold palsies shake away their strength,
And loose their legges with curelesse gouts. Pandolfo
New moulded is for Revels, Masks, and Musick. Cricca
String my neglected Lute, and from my Armory
Skowre my best sword, companion of my youth,
Without which I seeme naked.

CRICCA: Your love, sir, like strong water
To a deplor'd sicke man, quick's your feeble limbs
For a poore moment. But after one night's lodging
You'l fall so dull and cold, that Flavia
Will shrike and leape from bed as from a Sepulchre.
Shall I speake plainer, sir? Shee'l Cuckold you:
Alas shee'le Cuckold you.

PANDOLFO: What mee? a man of knowne discretion,
Of riches, yeares, and this gray gravity?
I'le satisfy'r with gold, rich cloathes and jewels.

CRICCA: Wer't not farre fitter urge your son Eugenio
To wooe her for himselfe?

PANDOLFO: Cricca bee gone,
Touch no more there: I will and must have Flavia.
Tell Lelio, if hee grant m'his sister Flavia,
I'le give my daughter to him in exchange.
Be gone, and finde mee heere within this halfe houre.

[From Thomas Tomkis, *Albumazar: A Comedy (1615)*, ed. Hugh G. Dick.
Berkeley: University of California Press, 1944, pp. 78-79.]

40. ANDREA PERRUCCI (1651–1704)

Perrucci was a Sicilian lawyer who resided in Naples. Although he always referred to himself as a dilettante, he was artistic director of the Teatro San Bartolomeo. By Perrucci's time, the Commedia dell'arte, the famous comic improvisational theater that dated from the sixteenth century and perhaps even earlier, was in popular demand. His treatise, *Dell'arte rappresentiva (The Art of Staging Plays, Premeditated and Improvised)*, an excerpt of which appears below, was published in Naples in 1699. Its content emphasizes the preferability of improvisation over other acting techniques. The text evaluates various types and dialogues as well as specific language and dialectal patterns employed for playing the various stock roles in both solo and ensemble scenes. For an example, Perrucci makes use of an entire scenario, "La Trapolaria," (Trapola the Trapper), extrapolated in part from Della Porta's sixteenth-century comedy [see **39**].

ANDREA PERRUCCI, "THE CHOOSING OF COSTUMES:
ON THE COSTUMES IN TRAGEDY, SATYRIC DRAMA, ETC."

> Costumes are also a necessary component part of decorum in the theater, because they cause a man to be respected and considered as something more than what he is, so it is well said: "Men revere him whom clothing adorns." Costumes make a person seem to be a character he is not; and to persuade others he is a king he must dress that way. Julius Pollux[80] explains how to do this, referring to the authority of the ancients, who, according to the above-cited Aelius Donatus, dressed the aged in white, the young in iridescent colors, the servants in tight costumes, the parasites with crumpled cloaks, the happy ones in white costumes, the unfortunate in dark costumes, the wealthy in purple, and the soldiers in reddish or purple military mantles, with capes of different colors, the ruffians in yellow, that is, golden yellow, and the courtesans wore dresses with a train, just as today. Royal clothing was of gold for tragical characters; today however modern dress is appropriate, since Minturno says whatever clothing is in use today must be adopted, accommodated to the customs of the particular country.
>
> Therefore also in operas, in other words, musical dramas, that have something of the tragic, as has been said, and in tragedies, royal characters are dressed in purple[81] and in clothing embroidered with gold, such as the imperial vestments described in Roman Law. As far as the theater is concerned, Aeschylus was the inventor of this practice, and he brought in clothing made of rich ankle-length skins. To make costumes more majestic, the ancient usage must be followed of adding armor, crests and crowns, and dressing the happy characters in purple and gold costumes, the unhappy in dark, dark blue, or in soiled white costumes, the hunters and combatants in short and tight costumes of scarlet. The costume of Tiresias was of wool; of Philoctetes and Telephus,[82] vile and torn. Heroes wore clothing of different color or else embroidered with stars, and wore crowns or miters and carried scepters, lances, swords, quivers and arrows, staffs, rods, and every sort of armament....

The ideal characters for *hypotyposis* or *prosopopoeia*,[83] introduced either in the prologues or in the opera itself for the resolution, for the machines or for the plot, must also dress in the proper expressive colors — for example, white for faith, green for hope, dark blue for jealousy, iridescent colors for inconstancy — with crowns or hieroglyphics showing the listeners what they represent, as in Cesare Ripa's *Iconology*, Piero Valeriani's *Hieroglyphics*,[84] and elsewhere; and if no standard way can be found of expressing a particular character, one might have an ingenious poet or scholar invent a new way. For examples, supposing one wishes to show a city not mentioned in any of the iconologies, one might look into ancient medallions for a coat of arms that was used as its emblem, or else one might adopt its most famous activities.

Cross-dressing is necessary to tragedy and frequently necessary in comedy, although this is prohibited in Deuteronomy ("A woman shall not be clothed with man's apparel, neither shall a man use woman's apparel"),[85] as well as in the civil laws and in the canons. But the Gentiles, as Laertius said in Plutarch and as Gesner proves,[86] had no scruples about admitting cross-dressing in theaters, as they thought it was necessary. In any case, especially when women cross dress, decorum and modesty must be observed, and the precepts of Lope de Vega in the above-mentioned *Art of Comedy*[87] must be observed: And if the tragedians change their dress, let it be as may be pardoned, because....

Neither men nor women must ever appear nude or seminude, since this is against the laws of modesty, as Samuel Pufendorf says.[88] Although the ancient actors observed the evil custom of showing nude women on stage, they were criticized by pagans such as Seneca and Valerius Maximus no less than by a Christian saint like St. Cyprian....[89]

I would entirely ban, as the Spanish do with great judiciousness, the clown mask. This was introduced by Aeschylus, before whom acting was done with faces colored by dirt, as Magnes the Athenian[90] did when reciting satyric dramas in order not to be recognized. According to Suidas[91] and as Giraldi[92] attests, however, it was introduced by Lyko Scarpheus, in order to cause laughter by imitating the grotesque faces in nature, with a huge nose, bleary eyes, large mouth, pointed forehead, and hollow temples, demonstrating the stupidity or the cunning of the character they represented, by monstrous physiognomies taken from animals, as Giambattista Della Porta reports,[93] to signify the cunning of the fox, the rapacity of the wolf, the silliness and agility of the bear, the fearsomeness of the lion, the laziness of the ox, and so on.

[From Dooley, *Italy in the Baroque*, pp. 500-504.]

41. FRANCESCO CERLONE (1750–1800/15?)

The prolific but elusive Cerlone wrote many plays of the type performed by the Commedia dell'arte. Although with a plot rather than the improvisation for which the comic theater in Italy was famous, his scripts relied upon unsubtle and humorous gags and speeches. Vincenzo Flauto was the initial publisher of Cerlone's comedies from 1771 to 1782. His plays were appreciated outside Naples and were later published as a collection in Bologna in 1787 and again, in twenty-two volumes, in Naples in 1825–1829. They include *Le trame per amore (Love Plots)*, a musical comedy performed in the Theater of Santa Cecilia in Este in 1773; *La Bellinda*, another musical comedy, which was presented during the carnival season of 1781 at the Teatro Nuovo above the Via Toledo; and *Pulcinella's Duel*, an excerpt of which appears below. English translations of Cerlone are practically nonexistent.

FRANCESCO CERLONE, "PULCINELLA'S DUEL"

> COLBRAND *(muttering to himself)*: We shall soon see if it is possible or not for that idiot, Pulcinella, to take Nanon away from me. I'll ornament his face for him! If he is a man of his word and keeps his appointment, too bad for him!

Pulliciniello.   Sig.ª Lucretia

Figure 42

PULCINELLA: You are here! I thought, perhaps, you might not....

COLBRAND: Oh! Bravo! You kept your word this time. You came.

PULCINELLA: Listen, Colbrand, if you want to fight, I'm quite ready. But tell me, first, how long it has been since you learned fencing?

COLBRAND: Why? What does that matter?

PULCINELLA: It matters to me.

COLBRAND: Five years.

PULCINELLA: I've been learning for ten. I don't want to take advantage of you. Go home and take lessons for five more years, and then I'll give you satisfaction.

COLBRAND: Oh, you coward! You won't get away. You're caught! Only one of us will remain here on the field of honor.

PULCINELLA: Very well. You remain and I'll leave.

COLBRAND: You needn't pretend you don't understand me. I mean that one of us has to remain here dead.

PULCINELLA: Dead? Is that what you said? Dead!

COLBRAND: That is precisely what I said. Dead!

PULCINELLA: Well, have it your way. You remain here dead, and everything will be all right.

COLBRAND: And who will kill me, may I ask!

PULCINELLA: I will, if you wish.

COLBRAND: I wish nothing of the kind. I intend to defend myself to the utmost.

PULCINELLA: Now look here, let's say no more about it. Is it reasonable to kill a man for the sake of a woman?

COLBRAND: Draw your sword, coward, or I will strike!

PULCINELLA *(under his breath)*: Oh, I'm dead! *(aloud)* Listen to me. The first time I ever wore my sword I made a vow that it would never be stained with blood.

COLBRAND: You ass in clothes! You will either give up Nanon, or I'll rid the world of you.

Pulcinella: Now look here! You have a quarrel with Me out of jealousy, because I took your sweetheart from you. But, on the other hand, I have no quarrel with You. You didn't take My sweetheart from Me. I would really regret killing you when I'm not even mad at you.

Colbrand: I'm not listening. This blade will be your answer. Get ready for some cold steel. Defend yourself!

Pulcinella: No! I have no quarrel with you. How many times must I repeat that, my good man?

Colbrand: What must a man do to make you fight?

Pulcinella: Let's see now. How about calling me some vile names? Then I'll get angry and draw my sword against you. After all, a man must defend his honor.

Colbrand: An excellent idea! Very well; you are a scoundrel, a ruffian, a cowardly knave.

Pulcinella: Supposing what you say is the truth. What reason would I have to be angry?

Colbrand: You are a dissolute wretch, a bastard, a son of a bitch!

Pulcinella: You must be a gypsy fortune-teller to know that. You are saying nothing but the truth.

Colbrand: We'll never get around to fighting this way. Coward! You deliberately misled me.

Pulcinella: Coward, am I? You just try telling me things about myself that are Not true. Then, by God, you'll set me afire. I know my nature.

Colbrand: Very well. You are a gentleman.

Pulcinella: A gentleman! I? When was I ever that?

Colbrand: Always. Yes, a valiant and honorable gentleman.

Pulcinella: And do you expect a valiant and honorable gentleman like me to fight with a dirty blackguard of a pig like you?

Colbrand: What! You say this to Me? By the powers that be, draw your sword this moment, or I'll strike!

Pulcinella: Steady now, steady. Whoa! Wait a minute! Can't you see I haven't got it drawn?

COLBRAND: Well, go ahead them. I'm waiting. If you don't draw, I can't strike.

PULCINELLA: Pardon me, but did I understand you to say that you won't strike unless I draw?

COLBRAND: You understand correctly! Draw!

PULCINELLA: My dear fellow, I am not going to draw for at least ten years. Oh, very well, if you insist. *(Draws his sword.)* Here, I'm ready. *(He strikes at Colbrand, standing as far away from him as he can, meanwhile shouting at the top of his voice.)*

COLBRAND: Hold on, Pulcinella. Stop! Now see here; how can a man fight a respectable duel with all that noise? Be quiet, will you! You'll only attract someone's attention and our fight will be interrupted.

(PULCINELLA, seeing MASTRO LOGMAN approaching, makes more noise than ever. When Logman arrives on the scene, he demands an explanation of the quarrel. The presence of a third party revives Pulcinella's courage, and he loudly declares his intention of running Colbrand through and through till his person is like a sieve. He then starts to scold Colbrand, who loses his temper and finally walks away.)

PULCINELLA *(leaving the stage, asks):* You think I am leaving because I'm afraid, don't you? Well, I'll have you know that you are right — I am Afraid!"

COLBRAND, *(seeing that he is now out of harm's reach, remarks to LOGMAN):* For your sake, and your sake alone, I won't attack. But at another time...."

(He leaves the terrible threat incompleted.)

[From Henry D. Spalding, *A Treasury of Italian Folklore and Humor.* Middle Village, NY: Jonathan David Publishers, 1980, pp. 171-73.]

42. JOSEPH-JEROME LEFRANÇAIS DE LALANDE (CHEVALIER) (1732–1807)

LaLande was known primarily as a French astronomer of the eighteenth century who popularized his science. After studying law in Paris, he was drawn to astronomy when he met J.N. Delisle.[94] Later in Berlin he joined the academy of astronomy. He was concerned primarily with the improvement of planetary theory and in 1759 published a corrected edition of Edmond Halley's tables. At the age of forty-six he replaced Delisle at the College de France. His *Voyage d'un François en Italie*, written during the 1760s and published in either 1765 or 1769, is probably the most internationally known of all the eighteenth-century guidebooks. A considerable portion of it is devoted to Naples. The selection provided below includes his observations of music, often considered to be Naples' crowning achievement, as performed at the city's famous Teatro di San Carlo [FIG. 43 below].

JOSEPH-JEROME LEFRANÇAIS DE LALANDE, "NEAPOLITAN THEATER"

> Music is the Neapolitans' triumph. Apparently eardrums are more sensitive, more attuned to harmony, more sonorous, in this country than in the rest of Europe; the entire nation sings; gestures, inflections of voice, the way each syllable is emphasized, conversation

Figure 43

> itself, all show and manifest a sense of harmony and music. Naples is the principal source of Italian music, of great composers, and of excellent operas....
>
> There are five theatres at Naples; the San Carlo, the Fiorentini, the Teatro Nuovo, the San Carlino — which is where the Opera Buffa is performed — and the Teatro del Fondo.
>
> The San Carlo theatre adjoins the palace and is outstanding for its size among all modern Italian theatres; it has been built more or less in the taste of Turin, with Medrano[95] as architect and Carasale[96] as contractor.... There is a passage to the royal palace, so that the king may go there under cover. The public reach it by large and most

convenient staircases and along fine corridors.... There are six rows of boxes which are big enough to play cards and receive visits in; there are twenty-four boxes in the first row and twenty-six in the ones above. The auditorium is so large and so high that one cannot hear some of the music.... The theatre was beautifully decorated for the King's marriage; besides gilding and painting, the front of each box has been embellished with a looking-glass of about two feet by five. Before each of these are two candlesticks, and the candles are

lit when the King is present on gala days. The partitions separating the boxes have on them mirrors four feet tall and eighteen inches wide — when it is illuminated, the room astonishes one by its magnificence....

Figure 44

In my time the leading composers at Naples were Piccinni, Sacchini, Francesco di Maio, Traetta, Guglielmi, Caffaro, Ferradini, Jomelli.[97] The dramatic side of Italian operas accords very well with the beauty of the music, especially in the verses of Apostolo Zeno[98] and Metastasio [see 36]; the latter is the most sought-after, and no year goes by without his setting a poem to some new music, since musicians are far commoner in Italy than great poets and one may have whatever one wants in the way of music....

La Gabrielli,[99] who shone at

Figure 45

Naples in 1765, was supposed to have the finest voice in Italy. She had been at Vienna for some time, but was obliged to leave; in 1765 she was invited to Petersburg, Berlin, Genoa, Parma, and Florence, but her fees were so exorbitant and she made herself so difficult that in the end she stayed in Naples, where in any case she wanted to spend the year. She was accustomed to wear on her bosom, like some order of chivalry, the monogram in diamonds of a young nobleman with whom she was having an affair, and whom she loved to distraction. (Incidentally, at Naples one is not allowed to maintain an actress openly, nor even to go to the theatre when she is performing; if one keeps a mistress, it costs far less than it does at Paris.) At the moment La Balducci is supposed to have the finest voice, as Marchesini is among the Castrati. [From Seward, *Naples: A Traveller's Companion*, pp. 168-69.]

Figure 46

PART III:
THEORY
AND
INTERACTION

Figure 47

CHAPTER 6
Economics and Social Sciences

43. ANTONIO SERRA (c.1550–c.1625)

A lawyer in Cosenza, Serra evaluated the economic crisis in his *Breve trattato*, a brief memoir submitted in 1613 to the viceroy, Don Pedro Fernandez de Castro, count of Lemos [1 and FIG. 3]. His was a proposal for mercantilism which, although practiced since the fourteenth and fifteenth centuries, had become increasingly popular with its successful use by Charles v and Henry vIII. This economic theory was the same as that promoted in England by writers such as Raleigh, Mun, Child, and Temple[100] and put to its most effective use by Cromwell and Colbert. Serra chides Naples for its dearth of industry and argues that merely raising exchange rates would not be effective in preventing the outflow of currency that curtailed the profit of local merchants. Instead, he proposes a balance of trade whereby industries would transform raw materials into finished products.

ANTONIO SERRA, "VENICE VERSUS NAPLES"

> The kingdom of Naples has food enough not only for its own use but it also exports more than 6,000,000 ducats' worth per year. Venice, on the other hand, does not have nearly enough in its own territories for its own provisioning. It does not export any victuals, and indeed it must spend nearly 8,000,000 ducats per year or more on food.
>
> Gold and silver money in Naples is valued higher than anywhere in Italy, including Venice. Silver brought into Naples from anywhere in Italy earns about 5% or more; and gold, which does not have a fixed price and can be said not to circulate as money, earns much more, according to the usual rate. On the other hand, Neapolitan money brought into any part of Italy loses around 8%. And anyone who does not believe this, let him try to discover his error and learn the truth, as more will be said about this later on.

Gold and silver money is valued at such a low price in Venice compared to Naples that silver, taken from Venice into Naples, earns around 5%, as has been said, and gold earns more, according to the going rate. On the contrary, when money is brought from Naples to Venice one loses, as has been said, according to the conditions of Naples; yet when money is brought from Venice into other parts of Italy or from those into Venice, one pays only the cost of minting.

From Naples no outflow of foreign or local money, of gold or of silver, is allowed, under most heavy penalties and the loss of the said money, and at present the fine is triple.

Any quantity of Venetian money can flow out of Venice, although not foreign money; and every year more than 5,000,000 ducats flow out to the Levant[101] alone.

In Naples, the revenues are priced so low that they yield around 7 ½% or 8%, and even at 10%,[102] and because the [government's] debts are many and money is scarce, any large sum can be employed that way.

In Venice, revenues are so high-priced that their yield is no more than 4% or 5%, so that no one would make much by employing his money in them.

His Catholic Majesty's revenues from the Kingdom of Naples are entirely spent in and die there, because none at all is put away in the treasury and he frequently has to send there as much as millions in cash; and anyway it would be difficult to put any of that revenue away, since they are almost all sold and converted into pay for beneficiaries and militia of the kingdom.

In Venice, all the incomes of the Signoria[103] are not spent, but most are put in the treasury; and after the debt incurred in the year 1570–71 for the navy was retired by Procurator Priuli, nearly 600,000 ducats are placed in the office of the depository every year besides what is brought into the mint.

Therefore, considering the conditions of both cities, Naples should be in a powerful position to abound in money, whereas Venice ought to have very little. Nonetheless, the opposite actually happens, and Venice abounds in money while Naples lacks it. The causes for these opposite effects must therefore be considered....

Just as the above conditions of Venice affect the outflow of money, and we have explained what causes its inflow, so, by contrast, conditions in Naples favor inflow without outflow. The well-known disappearance of the money flowing into Naples is even more marvelous than Venice's abundance, and an explanation must be sought. One of the two propositions must be false: either the supposed outflow must not exist in reality, or else the supposed inflow must not exist, because otherwise there would be a contradiction. This difficulty amazes everyone, and De Santis,[104] unable to find any other solution, blamed the lack of inflow and the excessive outflow on the very high exchange rate. This opinion will be discussed later, and the small or nonexistent inflow into Naples and the destination of the outflow will be explained without taking the high or low exchange rate into any consideration at all.

To discover the truth, both propositions must be evaluated and we must not assume anything unless it is certain and appropriate. Knowing the truth about the inflow of money is essential, and, as we said above, according to the opinion of the said De Santis, this ought to be some 5,000,000 ducats each year, after deducting the outlay for goods that must be imported from outside, which, according to his view, may amount to 600,000 ducats, and the revenues sold to foreigners amounting to the same again. So if the total income from export of goods is circa 6,000,000 ducats or more and we subtract circa 1,200,000 ducats' worth of incomes, some 5,000,000 ducats ought to remain every year. Since the export of commodities worth 6,000,000 ducats is assumed, which ought to bring that much money, there is no need to dispute that point but only to find out whether the income actually comes in, and if it does, where it goes. So the question is: whether there is indeed another outflow of money and whether the money ever actually flows in. In fact, the outflow is far greater than the previously mentioned sum; and the revenues and industries of foreigners, added to the goods imported, amount to far more than the quantity of money [flowing in]; therefore, the opinion [of De Santis] must not be true. And this is why Naples is poor in gold and silver although the value of things exported is circa 6,000,000 ducats per year.

To understand this, it is necessary to keep in mind what goods Naples needs to import, whether they are necessary, convenient or delightful to the persons in the kingdom. Then we must consider how much they are worth and what effect this produces. For they must be considered as an outflow of money; because otherwise the goods exported could not with any consistency be regarded as an inflow of money.

First of all, the kingdom clearly has no artisans making fine woolen clothing: therefore, clothing is imported (as De Santis says in talking about the sixth result which he believes a decree would produce). As a rough approximation, let us consider that the kingdom consists of around a million hearths including freehold and feudal. Counting the persons in each hearth and how many can dress in fine clothes, and keeping in mind that besides all the nobles and merchants and wealthy citizens, every mediocre artisan has clothes made of the cloths in question at least for feast days, and considering the cost of a piece of clothing and how long it lasts, the whole sum will arrive at 3,000,000 ducats. I will be content to place this outflow of money for cloths at less than 2,000,000 ducats. To this must be added priests and friars and monks who all for the most part dress in imported clothing, which amounts to something. So that our estimate can be said to be on the low side rather than in excess of reality.

Besides this, the kingdom needs all the apothecary's products, both simple, such as rhubarb, agaric and others, and compound like theriac and mithridate,[105] almost all of which come from Venice. Likewise, all the spices must be imported, including pepper, cinnamon, cloves, nutmeg, ginger, myrrh, incense, storax, benzuin and infinite others. There are also not enough sugars.

Now, considering the greatness of the kingdom and the number of all such things, especially pepper, of which no family consumes less than a half a ducat, and the same goes for the spicy simples, and counting everything in proportion to the other things, the total will perhaps come to the same amount as the cloths, or a little less.

Furthermore, all drugs, both artificial and natural, are imported, and most of them from Venice, since the kingdom is very lacking in substances such as vitriol, mercury, sublimate, cinnabar, antimony, arsenic, orpiment, verdigris, sal ammoniac,[106] white lead, red lead, tutty, camphor, alum, brazil, and all things for dyeing and coloring, as well as other drugs in great numbers....

Likewise, this kingdom has no mine of metals except iron, and even this is not sufficient for its needs, so a considerable amount must be purchased abroad. All copper, too, comes from abroad, as also all lead and tin. And considering the necessary use of the said metals, particularly copper and tin for artillery and bells, and personal use as well, anyone can imagine the quantity imported. Likewise all brass is imported.

Furthermore, all books on the sciences and the arts must be imported[107]; and although there are printers in Naples, they might as well be nonexistent for this purpose, since they do not print such books but only things of little substance. And likewise everything having to do with glass....

All delicate linen fabrics such as Holland, Orleans and cambrics also are imported, and so is ordinary linen. Likewise all arms. The craft of making arquebuses, morions and corselets[108] has been introduced recently, but it is not extensive. Besides these and other manufactured goods, there are many products of the kingdom which our lazy inhabitants do not know how to craft, so the crafted goods must be imported, at the cost of whatever the goods are worth. For example, the refined sugar called *panetto* [in lumps] comes from Venice. Although sugar is made in the kingdom and there is a sugar-cane business, such is the lack of industry that no one cares to learn the craft of refining it. Instead, it is brought from Venice, paying double. Likewise with the whitening of wax. Occasionally someone has tried one or the other of these trades at the instigation of foreigners, but without success....

But even assuming that it does not (as far as commodity trade is concerned), still one must take into account the revenues accruing to foreigners in the kingdom [from loans] to His Majesty or to private individuals, and their possessions, along with the manufactures they operate in the kingdom, which manufactures are for the most part in the hands of foreigners. The natives, due to their negligence or, one should say, indifference, not only fail to establish industries in foreign countries but cannot do anything with their own products in their own country even though they see foreigners do so.... [From Dooley, *Italy in the Baroque*, pp. 305-6, 308-9, 310.]

44. GIAN DONATO TURBOLO (FL. 1616–1629)

Born at Massa Lubrense near Sorrento, Turbolo (or Turboli) arrived in Naples around the turn of the century, became the director of the mint in Naples and author of various texts on money. His *Discorsi (Discourses on Currency in the Kingdom of Naples)* was published in sections between 1616 and 1629. Turbolo was particularly dedicated to the study of exchange. With regard to mercantilism [see **43**], he opposed vehemently every form of government intervention and maintained that it was irremediable factors that determined the level of exchange; and that legislative remedies were therefore ineffectual.

GIAN DONATO TURBOLO, "DISCOURSES ON CURRENCY"

The kingdom has fallen and deserves every help; I don't want to mention the details and I'll be discrete in saying everything I feel about this subject…so with elevated spirits, shrewd and sharpened, I am not without my wits and, therefore, I am sure my thoughts will not be entirely self-explanatory and accessible. We must admit, to tell the truth, when one considers the condition of other kingdoms and provinces, we should be thankful, first of all, to Her Divine Majesty who grants grace. Then we should be faithful to the discretion and knowledge of she who governs. So, as I look over the matter, I must say that moderate provision will suffice to move us from a state of shortage and scarcity to one of relief and consolation, and it is clear that one and all will thrive.

Those gentlemen in charge and all analytical types, who have the kingdom in their care, will see that for a long time great importance has been given to money: furthermore, prices of some merchandise in this kingdom have to be set in accordance with the currency because of the renewal of certain coins in 1622. In fact, not only have the coins been undervalued, as they should have been, but they have been altered as well, according to the decree of the Regia Camera,[109] by which every ten years new and different merchandise are considered old goods.…

What seems to me to be even more significant is the fact that 12 Castilian reals were equivalent to the gold *scudo*,[110] and now Her Majesty [Isabelle of Bourbon, 1602–1644] has changed the *scudo* to 15 reals. Consequently, we need to believe that she did it for good reasons, although they are to me unknown.…

I repeat, mainly as a reminder, that we must not find a reason to diminish the value of the *scudo* because we may get into a very delicate situation which is out of our reach. Furthermore, we have seen how every theory has been harmful, and hence, I hope we can assign more value to the *scudo*. I dare to insist that we discuss this matter thoroughly and be sure that we do not infringe upon or change previous traditions.…

What we see is that, without doubt, silver and currency produce the best results; that we should change slowly, and adjust the income of the kingdom according to what has been traditional.... In reference to the topics discussed above, the true value of properties, through the purchasing of cities, the court, and other houses, has declined to 58 to 50 to 40 to 35. Ordinary merchandise of the kingdom, as a result of miserable prices, is unequal to our rents paid for furniture and there is evidence of even more damage. The merchants, also victims of bankruptcy, and others are fearful and choose not to trade except when absolutely necessary.... Banks, I'm afraid to say, are reduced by a third of their power, with little money and no buyers....

Quality coins must be made, forged in this Royal Mint of the Kingdom of Naples, as they were in the time of the kings of Aragon and going back to King Charles I.[III] In time, there will be a change of value for this currency.

There should also be a widespread and extensive re-collection of forged coins dating from 1599 to 1628 so that they can be used by the kingdom and also serve as evidence, and so that the ministers can consider all this wisely and advise us cautiously. [Gian Donato Turbolo, *Discorsi sopra le monete del Regno di Napoli*. Naples: s.n., 1629, pp. 25-29. (Trans. I.I.-D.)]

45. FERDINANDO GALIANI (1728–1787)

Figure 48

The Abbot Galiani, a writer and economist, was born at Chieti, near Ancona. From 1759 to 1769 he was in Paris as secretary to the Neapolitan ambassador. There, in the salons, he obtained a reputation as a great wit and befriended the Encyclopedists. His famous treatise on money, *Della moneta*, was published in 1750; that on the grain trade, *Dialogues sur le commerce des blés*, in 1770. With clarity and a methodical approach, Galiani's first study promoted his theory of value based on utility and scarcity, a theory that, although praised for its originality, has its origins in the scholastic tradition. The following passage is from that text. His second book, written in French, emphasizes the necessity of regulation, an approach in opposition to the Physiocrats who advocated unlimited freedom. When Galiani returned to Naples he continued to correspond with Madame d'Epinay and other

Parisian friends. His letters were recognized for their literary and historical value and underscored Galiani's debate with the Abbé Morellet, spokesman of the Physiocrats. Galiani died in Naples.

Ferdinando Galiani, "On Money"

Of the Discovery of Gold and Silver and of Trade in (the) Metals. How and When They Began to be Used as Money. Of Increasing and Decreasing the Quantity of Money. The Present State of Money.

In all nations which avail themselves of its use, money consists of three metals. One is of a high value, another of a middling value, and a third of a low value. Without exception, gold and silver are used for the first and second ranks of value, but the metal used for money of the lowest rank has differed from century to century. Today, Europe uses copper for this purpose, as the ancients did; the Romans sometimes even used yellow copper or brass, and bronze. Lead coins, surely ancient in origin, have also existed and, in Caesar's time, iron money was used in both Greece and Great Britain. In our own day, finally, many use a mixture of two metals for small coins.

In addition to these, there is no lack of nations which use not metals but such things as: bitter almonds, as in Cambay; cocoa and corn, as in some parts of America; or salt, as in Abyssinia; and shells. One many properly ask whether these are indeed money, but such a discussion would be over words and not things. Accordingly, I will turn directly to gold and silver, beginning with their discovery and ancient use, devoting little attention to other metals.

Philosophers have long speculated over the many possible means by which knowledge of the metals might first have been acquired by man. The explanation which seems most plausible to me is that the first metals to become well-known were surely iron and copper, for these are found in ample quantities, in shallow veins which are not difficult to locate. Such ore is often found in great bulk and is usually of almost pure metal....

There is no nation in which these metals are available today, however barbarian, in which women, children, and men are not most eager to adorn their persons, or even their coarse ornaments—when they have any—with gold and silver. The same may be said of earliest man. Everywhere in America, even before its discovery, when money was not used, gold and silver were esteemed over all other things and venerated as sacred and divine. They were only used for the worship of some god and for the adornment of their princes and nobility. Moreover, as we know from the Pentateuch and the poems of Homer,[112] two ancient books still extant, these metals were also held in high esteem and put to the same use in those days. One finds in Homer, for instance, that all ducal military ornaments were garnished with gold and silver and frequently also bestudded with the same metals.

In such works, silver is discussed considerably less frequently than gold. This indicates to me that even in those days it was recognized that the scarcity and value of silver were equal to that of gold, and sometimes even greater. This might seem extraordinary. But, on reflection, it is obvious that it could not have been otherwise. For, of all the metals mixed in with the rivers' sands, none is more plentiful than gold. Silver, for examples, is never found there. It is surprising, therefore, that the greater part of the yield is found in sand, of all places, even among the most cultivated peoples; or that this is the easiest of all means of mining; and that it should yield less silver than gold? Since this is still true today, among barbarians, for example, it must follow that in ancient times gold was known before silver. The sword which King Alcinous forced Eurylaus to present to the injured Ulysses,[113] whom he had assailed, was of great value because of its silver studded hilt....

From such exchange, it must soon have become evident that since the value of the metal was always the same, it should be regulated by weight alone: that is, by quantity. Since the amount mined was also always the same, the demand general, and the quality never different; since the arts of alloying were not yet known, and since, in the crudeness of the times, no attention was given to small natural differences in fineness — it followed that these people, who gathered and traded the metals, had to establish for their greater convenience, certain weights and measures, according to which to set the value of the metal.

This is the natural and true introduction of coins and money. It is also the reason why Herodotus attributed the invention of coins to the Lydians who collected a great deal of gold from their rivers, some of which they made available to the Thyrrhenians and Phoenicians who, in turn, carried it to other regions. Coins, thus, came to acquire the universal acceptability which makes them money. Narration of these events, which comprises all of the mythology and sacred fables of Greece, can truly be said to be a confused history of the first navigation and commerce undertaken in the Mediterranean, as well as of the wars and plunder which took place in order to improve future trade. I find no other distinction between the centuries of antiquity and our own but that which runs from the great to the small. [Ferdinando Galiani, *Money (Della Moneta)*, trans. Peter R. Toscano. Ann Arbor, MI: University Microfilms, 1977, pp. 6-10.]

46. CARLO ANTONIO BROGGIA (?–1767)

Along with Galiani, Filangieri, and Genovesi, Broggia is considered to be one of the major Italian economists of the eighteenth century. Born in Naples, he traveled to Venice when he was seventeen to live with his uncle who was in business. He returned to Naples a few years later and published his *Trattato de' Tributi, delle Monete...* in 1743. Divided into two separate parts, the first dealing with tribute is the more original. The first eight of the thirteen chapters describe the various forms of tribute as well as discuss an original and complete system. Broggia emphasizes that tribute is not a necessary evil or simply a means to procure money for the state. It is, instead, an instrument for the internal and external growth and conservation of the country. The second portion, on currency, resembles an historical account and records the monetary concerns of antiquity.

CARLO ANTONIO BROGGIA, "TRIBUTE AND CURRENCY"

Chapter 1

This chapter concerns property and the necessity of taxes. In order to have security, one needs always to contribute. Those inconsiderate ones who fail to do so make a great mistake.

I shall discuss a subject that is complex and contains many truths and that I could write a good deal more about and, in doing so, be of assistance to the police, the revenue office, and both the state and commerce. But my goal here is to discuss those circumstances that are most appropriate for me and are sometimes relatively obscure. I shall use relevant examples to illustrate the points I make.

By taxes, I mean all that populations contribute in a monetary form to the government in order to conserve and enlarge both the internal and external state. First of all, people consider taxes a painful and unbearable burden not only because their rates are high but because they are handled badly. As a result little attention is paid to them as well as to principles of debt and resulting circumstances; this is true also because of the impersonal and bureaucratic manner, complete with complicated rules, in which they are legislated. The police could have an easy, short, and efficient procedure understood by all and reflecting true commercial theory. Old customs have muddied the waters and failed to achieve appropriate goals. It's possible, of course, that some of the new and useful legislature will be scorned in turn.

Then, for example, eight million taxes, if regulated well by a sound system, would no longer be considered a torment, a burden and an embarrassment; the other possibility would mean that with as few as two taxes a huge burden would result. A man can never carry a weight intended for his shoulders on his hand or finger; just as a heavy weight placed in the corner of a ship is bound to cause it to flip over, the government can never support those costs that boost primarily the prince and state. The state will inevitably decline and fall when burdened by taxes that are badly conceived and regulated.

In fact, there are some relatively small states that, despite great debt and suffering of their people, take in good revenues. There are also larger states, wealthier and more heavily populated, that have half or less the income of smaller states. This situation causes much disorder and grief. The best type of policy can combine the idea of the state with the true idea of commerce, a true conception of policy with the idea of the state.

First let us consider the sociable man who is useful to himself as well as his home and city; if any of these three categories was missing, neither the state nor the citizens themselves could survive. They would have to bear up, at any rate, because if one aspect failed there would be serious disorder, vice, and harm. There is also the obligation of taxes. These are one of many obligations for prince and country. This is to enable both to survive. If this source stopped, evil could never be eliminated, necessary goods could not be encouraged in peace or war. This is the reason why the Divine Legislator[114] specified that one has to have the debt of justice towards the government: "Render unto Caesar what is Caesar's and unto God what is God's."[115] Don't forget, as St. Paul said to the Romans, to account for given revenues, because the princes who impose them are ministers of God, and we serve Him when we obey them (even if they have been rascals) and are patient. So, return to them what is theirs. Whether duty or imposition, pay them; whether out of fear or honor, honor them. A good leader is necessary and needs to be obeyed whether out of fear or respect.

Some people rationalize and find an excuse, which amounts to fraud, even though the debt has been forced upon them.

In accordance with St. Paul's teaching, be patient with resignation for this is better even if, at times, things might seem unfair. The present government might take a turn for the worse. Then it will be up to the King of Kings and the great Father of all people to find a remedy....

We need to examine all that is just or unjust, efficient or inefficient, well distributed, or badly distributed....

Lastly, there are those who, in the hope of finding a remedy, restrict the sovereign's authority to tax without approval of the communes. Yet experience has often shown that most bad taxes are not derived in this way. I would like to discuss the reasons: taxes are designed from duty to be appointed by the communes and not by the prince; also, it should be observed that the census, which gained for Rome much wealth, would never have been used if Servius Tullius,[116] who was the despotic institutor, had to consult all the communes and put himself at the mercy of their will. In fact, we know from Livy[117] that such a just and beneficial tax was distasteful to the fathers who headed the communes. I maintain that, dealing with the principalities, the participating communes were very oligarchic. And Louis XIV, aware of their autonomy, and despite many ruthless wars, was able to bring about the most efficient remedies and with them an unexpected strength and prosperity.... Laws do not necessarily have to establish precisely what belongs to you and me. It is not the role of the government to make a doctor a perfect citizen but rather to let him prescribe necessary medicine to the sick.... [Carlo Antonio Broggia, *Trattato de tributi, delle monete, e del governo politico della sanità opera di stato*.... Naples: Pietro Palombo, 1743, pp. 1-20. (Trans. I. I.-D.)]

47. FERDINANDO IV (1751–1825)

Ferdinando IV of Naples (rule 1759–1806, 1815–25, FIG. 47) who, after the Congress of Vienna in 1814–15, called himself Ferdinando I, was known commonly as *"Il Nasone"* ("big nose"). He spoke the local dialect, sold fish he had caught himself, and otherwise cultivated a popular image; but his reign ended amid reaction and repression. Just before the French Revolution in 1789 he founded Ferdinandopolis, a planned industrial community at San Leucio near the great palace at Caserta [see 27 and FIGS. 32, 33]. It was here that he planned a vast "company" town based upon a utopian scheme. A few rows of houses were built, but there was question as to the true function of the new silk factory. The workers were referred to as the *"figli del Re"* ("the King's boys") and, despite the uplifting nature of the workers' manual cited below, local rumor implied that it was really a "front" for a harem. The title of this volume from which our passage has been obtained can be translated as *The Rise of the People of San Leucio and Their Progress toward the Glorious Present Day with the Laws Correspondent to Its Good Government*. Published in Naples in 1789, the year of the French Revolution, by the Stamperia Reale (Royal Press) this is a manual of Christian deportment, a sort of courtesy manual for workers. Even its chapters on good government include instructions for morning and evening prayer, hints on how to guard one's reputation, how to discover positive ideas, and how to avoid luxury. The intention was to encourage laborers to develop a proper frame of mind in which to serve God and king. Although Ferdinando ruled with a benevolent paternalism, his grand utopian scheme was never fully realized.

FERDINANDO IV, "THE PEOPLE OF SAN LEUCIO"

Concerning Poor Artists and the Regulation of Charity

Because of that love, which is the soul of society, and fraternal spirit, which must make each of you consider this population as a single family, if among you there is an artist without wife or children (or who is unable to earn), and a poor father fallen into misery either because of old age, sickness or other fatal misfortune (but never due to sloth), it is just that everyone helps so that these people are not reduced to begging, which is the most infamous and detestable state on earth. Hence, there will be a fund among you that will be called "Charity" from which these unfortunate people can be helped either for the rest of their lives or until they can make a living. This safe will have as its reserve a release of a monthly stipend that every manufacturer who can make more than two carlins per day will give as a donation, and fifteen grana per month by those who make less than two carlins per day.[118] This fund will be administered by the parish priest, the nobles, and art directors who will donate whatever their compassion dictates. Everyone will vote on the particular case at hand of the unfortunate person in question. The collection will be made the following way:

All the artists from every [economic] condition will be described in a statement that will be posted at the entrance of the church on the first Sunday of the month in the morning after a specific toll of the bell, (which will get the name of "Charity"). There will be the parish priest, provided that he is available (or whomever he assigns among the other priests), to receive the prescribed amount, and he will make each one write in a book that will be kept. With the charity received and in the nobles' and directors' presence, a numbered list of artists will be made with the statement in hand and with money paid so as to see if everyone has fulfilled his duty. Whoever has not carried out his obligation will be recorded on a sheet of paper, which will be posted on a board indicating the guilty; and this will be hung up next to the statement of the artists so everyone will know who is culpable. Whoever does this three times and does not pay the past debt will be canceled from the above statement and will not have any personal privilege in case of misfortune, funeral, or other troubles, as it will be said later, at the expense of the above-mentioned fund, which the nobles will supervise. This safe will be locked with three keys, one of which will be kept by the parish priest, another by the nobles, and the third by the directors. No one will be allowed to use a *grano* [one hundreth of a ducat] of it for other use except as indicated above. Each year after the election of the new nobles, the existing money will be counted and given to the newly elected along with the keys. The parish priest and the directors will always keep the keys with them, and only the ones that will prove to be unfaithful will be considered undeserving of the responsibility. As soon as the newly elected take power, they will count the incoming revenue and finally those people mentioned above will give it to me to be examined and discussed. [*Origione della popolazione di S. Leucio e suoi progressi fine al gloria d'eggi colle leggi....* Naples: Stamperia Reale, 1789, chap. XVII, pp. L-LIII. (Trans. L.N.)]

48. GIUSEPPE PALMIERI (1721?–1793/4)

Along with Broggia [46] and Genovesi [55 and 60], Palmieri is one of the three great Neapolitan economists of the period. Born in Martignano (Lecce), he died in Naples. Palmieri's early career was in the military. He joined the Royal Bourbon regiment and fought at Velletri in 1744. After years of army experience he published his famous *Critical Reflections on the Art of War* in 1761, a work translated into other languages and highly praised by Frederick the Great of Prussia (1712–1786), who made it the basis of all of his military reforms. A disciple of Genovesi, in 1783 Palmieri became administer of finance in the province of Lecce where he had returned for health reasons. In 1787 he was called to Naples by the king and, in that city, became director of the Council on Finance from 1791 until his death. Palmieri's *Reflections on Public Happiness Relative to the Kingdom of Naples* appeared in 1787; his *Economic Thoughts*, from which the following passage has been extracted, was published in 1788 and directs special attention to the economic problems of the neighboring province of Puglia. Individual chapters concentrate upon such topics as the market for silk, oil, and grain. Above all else, Palmieri expressed the spirit of reform of the Neapolitan administration prior to the Revolution of 1799.

GIUSEPPE PALMIERI, "ECONOMICS PERTINENT TO NAPLES"

Both agriculture and the arts[119] are generally viewed as being means to prosperity and subsistence. Although some economic philosophers maintain a new and different opinion that does not give credit to the arts, one still cannot deny the facts. Hence, if economic theory has declared itself as being in favor of agriculture, then practice has somewhat favored the arts. This has created competition in nations to either improve the arts or enlarge them. Ironically, the nation in which the arts flourish most is that very place despised by authors.

However, granted that the arts are important, we need to consider the conditions and circumstances necessary for competition leading to success. In doing so, we will determine the degree to which they need to exist in every society and their possible use.

We need only glance at the kingdom to see that agriculture needs to be at the forefront. An agricultural nation can not be an enemy of the arts whose only aim is its ministry; in a way, arts favor and contribute to the prosperity of agriculture.

If, having observed the kingdom, we look at the circumstances and actual state of trade with other nations, we must conclude that we could not have hoped for better revenue, livelihood, and prosperity.

Until now, the resources of the land have made, and will continue to make, profit for all nations. This has to be the main object of the government: but this does not mean that we have to disregard the arts. We will, in fact, do everything for the perfection and dissemination of the arts and, if not bringing in very much revenue, the result of which would be disastrous, that, in itself, will affect the nation's prosperity.

So, if income is based upon products of the land, it is clear that it will be in proportion to the quantity of these products and that they, in turn, will be in proportion to the quality and quantity of cultivation. Hence, to increase income, we have to improve agriculture.

Genius, art, and money are the very conditions that agriculture needs in order to be able to improve. Many are totally lacking in some or all of these attributes. If agriculture encounters only restraints, there is no hope for its improvement. The first restraint is the fiscal system. It arose out of public need in previous times, was maintained by private interests, and supported stubbornly for the good of the state. The latter was guilty of high-handed behavior in its transference of the rights of the sovereign to private individuals. The fiscal system, which operated in an absurd manner, would by now have caused widespread poverty, if it were not for people's boldness and strength.

But nature has not been able to save the nation from the painful battle wounds. The results are fields abandoned by peasants, either vexed or lazy. Furthermore, there has been an increase in the worst and most harmful class, poor enough to run contraband and rot or die in prison, and this turns out to be yet another expensive venture.

The economy, and even more morality and justice, have suffered. Fraud, dishonesty, accusations, etc. are all crimes created by such a system. Everyday we see the poison of contraband, evaded or dealt with by the rich, collected from the poor, when such contraband is sometimes the only means of survival. Public poverty...results from the justice system's blows. [Giuseppe Palmieri, *Pensieri economici relative al regno di Napoli*. Naples: Vincenzo Flauto, 1789, pp. 1-5. (Trans. I.I.-D.)]

CHAPTER 7
Jurisprudence

49. FRANCESCO D'ANDREA (1625–1698)

Figure 49

Benedetto Croce[120] refers to D'Andrea as the first lawyer in the Kingdom of Naples. Also known by the nickname for Francesco, as "Ciccio" D'Andrea, he wrote his *Avvertimenti ai nipoti*, a lawyer's memoirs in which he hails Naples as the most favorable location in which to practice law. This climate compatible with jurisprudence was, D'Andrea claims, the result of a dense population, great princes and nobles, and a capital in which European sovereigns showed interest. At that time, Naples was the center of lawsuits stemming from all the provinces of the Sacro Regio Consiglio (the Neapolitan Royal Council), which had a jurisdiction broader than that of the Parisian Parliament. D'Andrea recommends the profession of law especially to those Neapolitans who are not affiliated with a particular stratum of society or those from a lowly background because the profession provided great opportunity for a rise in status, money, and power. D'Andrea maintains that many lawyers became magistrates (especially powerful in Naples) and judges or held political offices of various sorts as a result of their profession. He cites particular cases and biographies of successful lawyers in the city. With a plethora of lawyers, the city hardly needed D'Andrea's recommendation of the vocation, although his accounts offer interesting insights into the legal and social system of that time. The following is a brief biography of the fortunate Carlo di Tappia, marquis of Belmonte, who, as D'Andrea recalls, was able to achieve great success without the usual preliminaries. Tappia and the duke of Alba helped to budget the income and expenses of the communes, which were heavily in debt, by setting up the Magistrate. A code and law of taxation was established in accordance with the 1669 census.

FRANCESCO D'ANDREA, "A LAWYER'S MEMOIRS"

The Family of Sir Regent Carlo di Tappia, Marquis of Belmonte

The regent Carlo di Tappia had been, perhaps, the only minister of the era to gain a high position without first becoming a lawyer. That was because even though he was born in Lanciano,[121] he was the son of a noble lady of that town and for this reason he was elected counselor and subsequently regent for Italy. In truth, he was the son of Spanish parents. His father was the president of the Chamber, Egidio Tappia, the owner of properties in Toledo,[122] where today the Tappia bridge is still well known. He married Isabella in Lanciano, and she too was from Tappia and not Riccia as had once erroneously been claimed by Topio[123] in the second section of his work and later by Doctor Nicolas Antonio in his *Hispanic Index*. Isabella was the daughter of the Spanish captain Francesco Tappia who had been married in Lanciano to Violante Riccia who was from a rather noble family. She had two daughters: the first married the president Tappia of the same name, although from a different family; the second married the marquis of Paglieta Pignatelli from a place near Lanciano. According to President de Franchis' resolution 261, Isabella, the mother of the regent, was called Tappia and not Riccia as a result of the genealogical tree presented to the Council at the dispute over succession to the majorat established by the regent between the duke of Diano, Don Carlo Cala, his distant nephew, and the Theatine fathers of the Loreto family.

The president Egidio [Tappia] died leaving his young son to be educated by the Spanish regent, Ribera,[124] who became judge after displaying, while still young, his famous rediscovery of essential principles. Ribera gave him a Spanish education. He became the judge of the Province two times, then judge of the Vicaria,[125] then in 1597 counselor, and finally in 1612, regent. We know this from regent Rovito's[126] resolution 69. Thus, he lived as a regent for thirty years until his death early in 1643. At that time he was dean of the Collaterale.[127]

Before being a counselor he married a very noble lady whose name was Leyva. She was the niece of the prince of d'Ascoli. He therefore acquired the title of Marquis of Castelnuovo in Abruzzo, marquis of a castle that he inherited from Violante Riccia, who was his ancestor. He then changed his title to Marquis of Belmonte, bought the land of Villamaina[128] and acquired many other properties that he described in detail....

He was known for his long life and austerity in everything he did and was therefore praised by viceroys and by the kingdom. But he obtained the name of a hard, rather than a great, minister because of his extraordinary persistence in exhausting negotiators. He would never take even an hour of rest and, with remarkable self-control, was a great observer even of the trivial. This is what was said about him: "Oh great man, engaged in doing nothing," and some very amusing stories were told. However, with his death memory of him faded. [Francesco D'Andrea, *Avvertimenti ai nipoti*, ed. Imma Ascione. Naples: Jovene Editore, 1990, pp. 167-68. (Trans. I.I.-D.)]

50. GAETANO FILANGIERI (1752–1788)

This provincial immigrant to Naples studied law instead of following the military career his father had planned for him. He was admired for his knowledge and eloquence, and appreciated by Goethe whom he met during the German philosopher's visit to southern Italy. Filangieri is representative of intellectuals who supported the regime during the latter half of the eighteenth century. He managed to gain favor from Charles (later Carlos II of Spain)[129] for his defense of a royal decree that reformed abuses in the justice system. Above all, he shared his fellow Neapolitans' concern for practical reform: economic, legal, and religious. He wrote as well on education and morals. For many years Filangieri served as secretary to the Neapolitan legation in Paris. As with Genovesi (55), Filangieri was a protégé of Tanucci. His major work, *La scienza della legislazione*, which was published in 1780, discussed the rules by which legislation ought to proceed as well as general economic concerns. His third book dealt entirely with principles of criminal justice.

Figure 50

Filangieri's *Scienza* was condemned by the Congregation of the Index[130] in 1784 because it had advocated church reform. Only an outline remains of the first part of the fifth book of the *Scienza*, which he was working on at the time of his death in Cava.[131] He had hoped to complete six volumes in all. Both flamboyant and philosophical, this passage from the first chapter of the *Scienza* discusses legislation deduced from the origin of civil societies.

GAETANO FILANGIERI, "THE SCIENCE OF LEGISLATION"

The Sole and Universal Object of Legislation Deduced from the Origin of Civil Societies

Whatever may have been the state of mankind on the foundation of civil society, the precise period of its union, the form under which it first coalesced, and the place in which it was molded into its original shape, there cannot be a doubt of the cause which produced it. A single principle gave it birth. [This was] a wish for general safety and general tranquillity. The idea, indeed, of a ferocious life previous to civil society, where, as some misanthropists have supposed, man wandered like the savage in his native forests, wild and comfortless, is perhaps a mere imaginary one. It would betray an ignorance of human nature, and the character which distinguishes us from the rest of the animal creation, to believe that we were born for such a dreary and precarious existence, or that the state of natural society were a state of natural violence. Far from being seduced by such erroneous suppositions, we may more safely admit that Providence would have formed the most perfect and august of its productions in vain, if man had not been formed for social intercourse and mutual connections.

It has given him reason, which develops and expands by communication, and in the concourse of society. In addition to imperious feeling, from which the cry of other animals in wholly derived, he has the exclusive blessing of speech. He has the inestimable advantage of attaching his ideas to certain distinct sounds agreed upon in common, and appropriated to transmit those ideas to the rest of his species. Without that instinct, which regulates the brute and directs its motions, man alone deliberates upon his actions, and to guide him in his deliberations he has the benefit of instructions from society, which he could not by any other means have drawn from any other source. He passes a longer infancy than other animals, and during its weak and helpless state he owes both his nurture and protection to society. He has different degrees of force, industry and talents, which intimate that he was designed to fill different situations. He has various inclinations, occupations and pursuits; different wants, desires and pleasures; and is susceptible of a multitude of passions useless to a solitary being. For what purpose is he warmed with the ambition of pleasing, of acquiring the esteem of others, or establishing an empire over their affections and opinions?

Chapter 7. Jurisprudence

Why are the germs of friendship, compassion and benevolence, planted in his breast, or the seeds of those amiable sentiments sown within his bosom, which ripen in every well-disposed mind? Why has he the singular desire of sharing with another a part of his existence; or why, in a word, are not his natural appetites confined within the narrow limits allotted to those of every other inhabitant of the globe, the satisfaction of his physical wants? They frequently return to him, though but for a moment, and in the void they leave him after their enjoyment, they prove their insufficiency to procure his happiness, and proclaim to him that he has intellectual, as well as corporeal wants, which are only to be gratified in society and its relations. It is reasonable therefore to conclude that society was coeval with man; and that the savage in his woods exhibits rather the picture of fallen degenerate man in an unnatural state, or in other words, the ruined degraded species, than his living image in the infancy of the world.

This primitive society coeval with man, is not, however, to be confounded with civil society, for they differ widely from each other. It would be absurd to imagine that men, though destined to live together, had in their early intercourse with each other renounced their independence, before they had learnt from experience the necessity and advantage of the sacrifice. Primitive society was not, therefore, civil society. It was strictly a natural union, where the distinctions of the noble, the plebeian, the master, and the slave, and the names of the magistrate, the laws, civil offices, impositions and punishments, were equally unknown. It was a union, where no other inequality than the inequality from force or strength existed; no laws but those of nature; no restrictions, those excepted which sprung from friendship, necessity, parental affection, and filial attachment. Its several members had not yet resigned their original independence; deposited their power in the hands of other persons; confided to their custody their rights; or entrusted the protection of their lives, their families, and honor, to any code of jurisprudence. Each individual was in fact a sovereign, because independent, a magistrate, because the guardian and protector of the law written in his breast; and a judge, from being the supreme arbiter of the disputes arising between his family and his neighbors, and the executioner of justice for the injuries he had received.

Unhappily for mankind this state could not long subsist. The beaver appears to be in the sole possession of the difficult but happy art of combining the advantages of public union with private independence.

Notwithstanding the inequality from force and strength was the only inequality that could not be extirpated in primitive society, yet in progress of time, as the human passions discovered themselves, they necessarily produced numerous disorders. Moral equality, unable to show its face in opposition to physical inequality, sunk, overpowered by its influence. The weakest individual was at the mercy of the strongest, exposed to his caprices; and even his subsistence, the pleasing but painful fruit of his meritorious toil and labor, became the object of the rapine and plunder of his more powerful neighbor. Life and honor soon ceased to be any other than precarious blessings, of which the possessor was liable at every instant to be deprived, as often as a restless and malignant spirit was united to a body more gigantic and athletic than his own. Suspicion, distrust, and fear must naturally disturb this primitive society, and a remedy was to be searched for, that would correct the evil. One only was to be found. It was discovered that physical inequality could not be destroyed without renouncing moral equality — that for the preservation of tranquillity independence was not absolutely requisite — that a public force must be established superior to private force, and that this public force could only flow from the aggregate of the whole collected mass of private force — that a moral person was wanting to represent the public will, and to be the guardian of its power — that the public force ought to be united to public reason — that the interpretation of laws, the establishment of the rights, and the regulation of the duties of each member of the community ought to be under its control — that it ought to prescribe certain determined rules of government, calculated to maintain the equilibrium between the wants of each citizen and his means of gratifying them — and lastly, that by the liberty of acquiring every requisite for personal preservation and personal tranquillity, each individual might be amply recompensed for the surrender of his original independence.

Such appears to have been the first intention of civil society and laws, and consequently the only object of universal legislation. It will be here necessary to examine what is meant under this general principle, the consequences that may be deduced from it, and to see how far every part of legislation would correspond with its common end. [Gaetano Filangieri, *The Science of Legislation*, ed. and trans. Thomas Ostell. Bristol: Emery and Adams, 1806, 1:1-9.]

CHAPTER 8
Philosophy

51. GIULIO CESARE VANINI (1585–1619)

Julius Cesar Vanini
Taurisano Neapolitanus

Figure 51

Known as "Lucilio," this restless and versatile Aristotelian philosopher and scientist was born in Taurisano de Lecce in Puglia. In spite of his birthplace, he is always thought of as Neapolitan. Vanini received a degree in law in Naples in 1606 after having already entered into the Carmelite Order as Fra Gabriele. He traveled to Padua where he studied and, in the company of his brother, moved on to countries sympathetic to the Reformation. This caused him to be under close observation by the Anglican Church. It was in London that he finally relinquished his Catholicism. After traveling also to Venice and France, in 1615 he received authority from the Church to print his *L'Amphitheatrum aeternae providentiae*. His *Dialogues* were published in Paris. Both the *Amphitheatrum* and *De admirandis naturae arcanis* were confiscated and forbidden for their threatening atheism. Vanini's approach is not a progressive one. He limits himself to old Aristotelian modes while borrowing generously from the writings of Pomponazzi, Cardano, and Scaligero[132] as well as others. Vanini died at Tolosa[133] where he had lived for several years under the assumed name of Pompeo Usciglio. The following passage from Vanini's *Amphitheatrum* considers "Ciceronian problems."

GIULIO CESARE VANINI, "CICERONIAN PROBLEMS"

The Resolutions of Boethius and Aquinas, and My Refutation of the Responses

First Problem:
It has been established that Divine Providence is infallible and unchanging. However, the concept of free will claims for itself conditions contrary to these two. For this reason, they cannot be understood. Boethius

135

in Book 5, Prose 6, of his *Consolation of Philosophy*,[134] offers three responses. the first is this: Since knowing something does not necessarily resemble the process of knowing something, it is not contradictory that knowledge be certain in itself, even though the thing about which there is knowledge by its very nature may be uncertain.

Boethius here is quite wrong because if, in fact, God can know what is uncertain to happen with the assurance that it is certain, he would also know what either will not happen, or is impossible. However, because this implies that the impossible exists and is known, this cannot be true; and, therefore, Boethius is mistaken. Also, our predecessors have proven that God does not know the impossible, nor can he know it because he prevents it from existing and as a result from being known. Likewise, since, according to inner understanding and formal logic, actions in the future are uncertain, they cannot be known as if they were certain. Indeed, such an action would be known under a condition that disagrees with the very principles it implies. Besides this, if something is known by God as certain, his mind is moved so that it is certain. Thus, he knows that that action is determined to be true but any other determined to be false. Therefore, if he knows action A to be determined true, action A is determined true. And consequently, by its very nature, action A is determined to happen, contrary to the argument of Boethius.

Moreover, his argument that knowing something does not follow the nature of knowing by which that action is able to be determined while existing as an uncertain event to me seems ludicrous. I find written in the tables of philosophy the following rule: If knowledge is to be true, there must be a likeness between what is already known and what is being learned, and its principles must be represented in this likeness. For this reason, with regards to knowing things that are conditional, the principles are uncertain. Indeed, they are, by all means, uncertain when concerning the conception of future conditions. If these principles are represented to God as being certain, the idea of divine understanding can be proclaimed false. For, knowing that something is determined true as it is happening is just like knowing that something that has yet to be determined is determined. There is a contradiction here.

Boethius' second response coincides with the first. He argues that there is no disagreement that something from one perspective has a different disposition when observed from another. From here, he does not consider the absurd consequence that human actions from a divine perspective are truly necessary occurrences in themselves. This response, the learned teacher and a theologian renowned and bestowed with many titles, Gregorio Spinola,[135] commended and proved very acutely by the conclusion that an event follows an earlier necessity and a later condition, as Aristotle teaches in *Prior Analytics* I.[136] Through this conclusion, it is evident that the result in the order would be necessary from the perspective of the first because it has a necessary cause — in fact, the cause itself is considered necessary — but from the perspective of the later, it is conditional. Since a result follows the nearest cause rather than the most remote, the result is to be proclaimed absolutely conditional, even though from the other perspective it would be necessary. He adds a very elegant example about a plant that clearly is produced by a necessary cause, the sun, and a conditional one, a seed. Nevertheless, the result is conditional rather than necessary. Thus, in the same way, even though from the perspective of divine knowledge, which is necessary, human action is necessary; because it is produced by human free will, in itself it is conditional. These ideas taken together do not allow for any impossibility. [From Luigi Corvaglia, *Le Opere di Giulio Cesare Vanini e loro fonti*, VOL. I, *Amphitheatrum Aeternae, Providentiae*. Milan: Società Anonima Editrice Dante Alighieri, 1933, Exercise XXII, pp. 126-36. (Trans. J.V.)]

52. TOMMASO CAMPANELLA (1578–1639)

This famous friar of the Counter Reformation [FIG. 37] was born of a poor family in Calabria. He came to Naples in order to study law but instead became a Dominican. Campanella, long suffering and continually devout, argued in favor of Catholicism and the reasonableness of his faith. He studied scholastic philosophy and was attracted to the ideas of Bernardino Telesio (1508–1588),[137] who unfortunately had died before the two had a chance to meet. Campanella insisted upon joining philosophy, metaphysics, theology, and the new natural science and to harness them to the cause of civil welfare. Campanella was influenced by Giovanni Pico della Mirandola[138] and like his model adopted the philosophy of Aristotle as well as Catholic orthodoxy. His major works in prose include his *City of the Sun* of 1602 which, along with the writing of More, Bacon, and Rousseau was in the tradition of the famous utopias. The fanciful first passage below, which is from the *City of the Sun*, is concerned with judgment within God's universe as well as the history of nations, customs, government, laws, and rituals. The second excerpt deals with metaphysical problems. Campanella's later *Defense of Galileo* [FIG. 59], composed in 1616, was published in 1622 [see 67].

Tommaso Campanella, *The City of the Sun:* A Neapolitan Utopia

A Poetical Dialogue between Grand Master of the Knights Hospitallers and a Genoese Sea Captain, His Guest

CAPTAIN: ...Everyone is judged by the first master of his trade, and thus all the head artificers are judges. They punish with exile, with flogging, with blame, with deprivation of the common table, with exclusion from the church and from the company of women. When there is a case in which great injury has been done, it is punished with death, and they repay an eye with an eye, a nose for a nose, a tooth for a tooth, and so on, according to the law of retaliation. If the offense is willful the council decides. When there is strife and it takes place undesignedly, the sentence is mitigated; nevertheless, not by the judge but by the triumvirate, from whom even it may be referred to Hoh,[139] not on account of justice but of mercy, for Hoh is able to pardon. They have no prisons, except one tower for shutting up rebellious enemies, and these is no written statement of a case, which we commonly call a lawsuit. But the accusation and witnesses are produced in the presence of the judge and power; the accused person makes his defense, and he is immediately acquitted or condemned by the judge; and if he appeals to the triumvirate, on the following day he is acquitted or condemned. On the third day he is dismissed through the mercy and clemency of Hoh, or receives the inviolable rigor of his sentence. An accused person is reconciled to his accuser and to his witnesses, as it were, with the medicine of his complaint, that is, with embracing and kissing. No one is killed or stoned unless by the hands of the people, the accuser and the witnesses beginning first. For they have no executioners and lictors, lest the state should sink into ruin. The choice of death is given to the rest of the people, who enclose the lifeless remains in little bags and burn them by the application of fire, while exhorters are present for the purpose of advising concerning a good death. Nevertheless, the whole nation laments and beseeches God that his anger may be appeased, being in grief that it should, as it were, have to cut off a rotten member of the state. Certain officers talk to and convince the accused man by means of arguments until he himself acquiesces in the sentence of death passed upon him, or else he does not die. But if a crime has been committed against the liberty of the republic, or against God, or against the supreme magistrates, there is immediate censure without pity. These only are punished with death. He who is about to die is compelled to state in the presence of the people and with religious scrupulousness the reasons for which he does not deserve death, and also the sins of the others who ought to die instead of him, and further the mistakes of the magistrates. If, moreover, it should seem right to the person thus asserting, he must say why the accused ones are deserving of less punishment than he. And if by his arguments he gains the victory he is sent into exile, and appeases the state by means of prayers and sacrifices and good life ensuing. They do not torture those named by the accused person, but they warn them. Sins of frailty and ignorance are punished only with blaming, and with compulsory continuation as learners under the law and discipline of those sciences or arts against which they have sinned. And all these things they have mutually among themselves, since they seem to be in very truth members of the same body, and one of another.

This further I would have you know, that if a transgressor, without waiting to be accused, goes of his own accord before a magistrate, accusing himself and seeking to make amends, that one is liberated from the punishment of a secret crime, and since he has not been accused of such a crime, his punishment is changed into another. They take special care that no one should invent slander, and if this should happen they meet the offense with the punishment of retaliation. Since they always walk about and work in crowds, five witnesses are required for the conviction of a transgressor. If the case is otherwise, after having threatened him, he is released after he has sworn an oath as the warrant of good conduct. Or if he is accused a second or third time, his increased punishment rests on the testimony of three or two witnesses. They have but few laws, and these short and plain, and written upon a flat table, and hanging to the doors of the temple, that is between the columns. And on single columns can be seen the essence of things described in the very terse style of *Metaphysics* — viz., the essences of God, of the angels, of the world, of the stars, of man, of fate, of virtue, all done with great wisdom. The definitions of all the virtues are also delineated here, and here is the tribunal, where the judges of all the virtues have their seat. The definition of a certain virtue is written under that column where the judges for the aforesaid virtue sit and when a judge gives judgment he sits and speaks thus: O son, thou hast sinned against this sacred definition of beneficence, or of magnanimity, or of another virtue, as the case may be. And after discussion the judge legally condemns him to the punishment for the crime of which he is accused — viz., for injury, for despondency, for pride, for ingratitude, for sloth, etc. But the sentences are certain and true correctives, savoring more of clemency than of actual punishment.

GRAND MASTER: Now you ought to tell me about their priests, their sacrifices, their religion, and their belief.

CAPTAIN: The chief priest is Hoh, and it is the duty of all the superior magistrates to pardon sins. Therefore the whole state by secret confession, which we also use, tell their sins to the magistrates, who at once purge their souls and teach those that are inimical to the people. Then the sacred magistrates themselves confess their own sinfulness to the three supreme chiefs, and together they confess the faults of one another, though no special one is named, and they confess especially the heavier faults and those harmful to the state. At length the triumvirs confess their sinfulness to Hoh himself, who forthwith recognizes the kinds of sins that are harmful to the state, and succors with timely remedies. Then he offers sacrifices and prayers to God. And before this he confesses the sins of the whole people, in the presence of God, and publicly in the temple, above the altar, as often as it had been necessary that the fault should be corrected. Nevertheless, no transgressor is spoken of by his name. In this manner he absolves the people by advising them that they should beware of sins of the aforesaid kind. Afterward he offers sacrifice to God, that he should pardon the state and absolve it of its sins, and to teach and defend it. Once in every year the chief priests of each separate subordinate state confess their sins in the presence of Hoh. Thus he is not ignorant of the wrongdoings of the provinces, and forthwith he removes them with all human and heavenly remedies.

Sacrifice is conducted after the following manner: Hoh asks the people which one among them wishes to give himself as a sacrifice to God for the sake of his fellows. He is then placed upon the fourth table, with ceremonies and the offering up of prayers: the table is hung up in a wonderful manner by means of four ropes passing through four cords attached to firm pulley blocks in the small dome of the temple. This done they cry to the God of mercy, that he may accept the offering, not of a beast as among the heathen, but of a human being. Then Hoh orders the ropes to be drawn and the sacrifice is pulled up above to the center of the small dome, and there it dedicates itself with the most fervent supplications. Food is given to it through a window by the priests, who live around the dome, but is allowed a very little to eat, until it has atoned for the sins of the state. There with prayer and fasting he cries to the God of heaven that he might accept its willing offering. And after twenty or thirty days, the anger of God being appeased, the sacrifice becomes a priest, or sometimes, though rarely, returns below by means of the outer way for the priests. Ever after this man is treated with great benevolence and much honor, for the reason that he offered himself unto death for the sake of his country. But God does not require death. The priests above twenty-four years of age offer praises from their places in the top of the temple. This they do in the middle of the night, at noon, in the morning and in the evening, to wit, four times a day they sing their chants in the presence of God. It is also their work to observe the stars and to note with the astrolabe their motions and influences upon human things, and to find out their powers. Thus they know in what part of the earth any change has been or will be, and at what time it has taken place, and they send to find whether the matter be as they have it. They make a note of predictions, true and false, so that they may be able from experience to predict most correctly. The priests, moreover, determine the hours for breeding and the days for sowing, reaping, and gathering the vintage, and are as it were the ambassadors and intercessors and connection between God and man. And it is from among them mostly that Hoh is elected. They write very learned treatises and search into the sciences. Below they never descend, unless for their dinner and supper, so that the essence of their heads do not descend to the stomachs and liver. Only very seldom, and that as a cure for the ills of solitude, do they have converse with women. On certain days Hoh goes up to them and deliberates with them concerning the matters which he has lately investigated for the benefit of the state and all the nations of the world.

They (the magistrates) hold great festivities when the sun enters the four cardinal points of the heavens, that is, when he enters Cancer, Libra, Capricorn, and Aries. On these occasions they have very learned, splendid, and as it were comic performances. They celebrate also every full and every new moon with a festival, as also they do the anniversaries of the founding of the city, and of the days when they have won victories or done any other great achievement....

They divide the seasons according to the revolution of the sun, and not of the stars, and they observe yearly by how much time the one precedes the other. They hold that the sun approaches nearer and nearer, and therefore by ever-lessening circles reaches the tropics and the equator every year a little sooner. They measure months by the course of the moon, years by that of the sun. They praise Ptolemy, admire Copernicus, but place Aristarchus and Philolaus[140] before him. They take great pains in endeavoring to understand the construction of the world, and whether or not it will perish, and at what time. They believe that the true oracle of Jesus Christ is by the signs in the sun, in the moon, and in the stars, which signs do not thus appear to many of us foolish ones. Therefore they wait for the renewing of the age, and perchance of its end. They say that it is very doubtful whether the world was made from nothing, or from the ruins of other worlds, or from chaos, but they certainly think that it was made, and did not exist from eternity. Therefore they disbelieve in Aristotle, whom they consider a logician and not a philosopher. From analogies, they can draw many arguments against the eternity of the world. The sun and the stars they, so to speak, regard as the living representatives and signs of God, as the temples and holy living altars, and they honor but do not worship them. Beyond all other things they venerate the sun, but they consider no created thing worthy the adoration of worship. This they give to God alone, and thus they serve him, that they may not come into the power of a tyrant and fall into misery by undergoing punishment by creatures of revenge. They contemplate and know God under the image of the Sun and they call it the sign of God, his face and living image, by means of which light, heat, life, and the making of all things good and bad proceeds....

They assert two principles of the physics of things below, namely, that the Sun is the father, and the Earth the mother; the air is an impure part of the heavens; all fire is derived from the sun. The sea is the sweat of earth, or the fluid of earth combusted, and fused within its bowels; but is the bond of union between air and earth, as the blood is of the spirit and flesh of animals. The world is a great living animal, and we live within it as worms live within us.

Therefore we do not belong to the system of stars, sun, and earth, but to God only, for in respect to them which seek only to amplify themselves, we are born and live by chance; but in respect to God, whose instruments we are, we are formed by prescience and design, and for a high end. Therefore we are bound to no Father but God, and receive all things from him....

GRAND MASTER: Oh, if you knew what our astrologers say of the coming age, and of our age, that has in it more history within a hundred years than all the world had in four thousand years before! Of the wonderful invention of printing and guns, and the use of the magnet, and how it all comes of Mercury, Mars, the Moon, and the Scorpion!

CAPTAIN: Ah, well! God gives all in his good time. They astrologize too much.

[From *Famous Utopias, Being the Complete Text of Campanella's City of the Sun,* intro. by Charles W. Andrews. New York: Tudor Publishing, 1937, pp. 308-17.]

TOMMASO CAMPANELLA, METAPHYSICAL CAUSE AND EFFECT

The Effects Must be in the Causes; Therefore the Elements and the World Must be Sentient

That no being can give to others what it does not itself possess is proved elsewhere by us and is known to many. Experience demonstrates this very well, because no light ever caused darkness, nor heat coldness, nor thorns softness, nor heavy things lightness, and so forth. True, a hot body may become cold; but coldness is not caused by the heat, nor can heat be changed into cold. Heat enclosed in cold things may be accidentally reinforced and increase, although it is not increased by the cold but by its own expansive and prolific nature, unlike things that are sterile in themselves.

Now, if the animals are sentient, as everyone agrees, and sense does not come from nothing, the elements whereby they and everything else are brought into being must be said to be sentient, because what the result has the cause must have. Therefore the heavens are sentient,[141] and so are the earth and the world, and the animals are inside them like worms inside the human belly, which are unaware of man's sense so disproportionate to their tiny knowledge.

There is no argument against the first Proposition

But they say[142]: the sun is neither animal not plant and yet makes animals and plants: it is subtle and noble and white and yet causes hardness and congeals the soil and blackens the Ethiopians under Cancer and Capricorn where it dwells the most; and fire heats and cold snow scalds the hand and fattens the land; and hot saltpeter cools beverages; and a fear, that is not cold, cools man; and one living thing kills another living thing. Many similar things, in other words, produce dissimilar things; and things are made of what they are not. Therefore, things without sense can be born of things with sense. I respond that everything made between the sky and the earth receives what it has from these two elements. So an animal is not sun but earth in which the sun's action caused spirit to be produced amid hardness. Unable to escape, spirit then organized matter and made it apt for animals' life, as will be said later on. Plants and animals receive spirit, heat, subtlety and motion from the sun, and from the earth they receive matter shaped through the artifice of this solar sense; but they receive only those things that are in the causes, even though not necessarily in the same way in which those things are in the causes. The variety between the things made and the causes comes from the admixture and violence between contraries produced by the adversity Blessed God gave the actions of the causal agents to make them instruments for stamping various models of the first Idea in matter, demonstrating his goodness in every things. Which perhaps neither the sun nor the earth understand; but sun is fire and earth causes mass, and thus they are weakened and cause mixed things that, in the shapes of the first Idea, are its instruments and first models. But sense is not a model of existence the way a shape is, but it is a thing essential to every active power, as we will soon see. So the sun and the earth must have sense. Similarly, the sun does not harden the soil by producing hardness and dryness but by uncovering the earthly hardness already there under the softness of the water, hidden and mixed, because soil is composed of essentially hard earth and malleable water. Fire acts to convert water, similar to it and less resistant to its action, first into smoke and air and then into sky, whereas the earth remains alone with its own dryness, which nonetheless a great fire can liquefy to produce fire, as seen with salt and metals in furnaces and mines.

That the sun is hot we have demonstrated elsewhere, against Aristotle, as also that it produces fire comparable to and congruent with common fire; although where it is weak it produces less. In the same way, taking away the mobile part, that conferred motion remains immobile. And thus it blackens, not by producing blackness but by showing the material blackness that was hidden under the whiteness of the hot subtle parts. If I burn this white paper, you will see white flame come out, which is the tenuous part of the paper, and gross black matter remain. If the fire keeps acting it turns the paper into glass, and if still more, it turns the paper into tenuous white air, although we have proved in our *Philosophy*[143] that the blackness of inert matter is of an inert and not of an active sort, unlike the blackness of cold matter. But from these arguments one can see that soil and coal contain nothing that is not in the sun, the earth or in matter; and the action performed by the sun, when finished, will be observed to be always subtleness and whiteness, although clouds are usually black except for the ones about to be made that have not yet received the sun's action.[144] But in similar things it always whitens and attenuates and moves even though they are few in number; a fact that can nonetheless be observed from the absence of this action in all the other things. Snow does not heat the hand, but man's natural heat, sensing the cold, unites, increases and issues from the hand to chase away what hurts its dwelling place. Snow expands because it has a natural gentle heat apt for this. Its coldness is extraneous and not essential, because no such cold constitutes and enters into the works of nature; for the sun is much more powerful than the earth. Saltpeter cools because the extrinsic coldness of wine,[145] sensing such an adverse movement and inimical odor, concentrates and increases, though if it did this for a long time it would destroy itself and the wine would heat up. When animals are afraid, a similar flight occurs of the warm vital spirit into the inner parts to avoid damage from an enemy, leaving the outer parts less warm and almost cold and allowing more air to come in, which parts tremble because they do not have enough spirit to sustain their weight. Furthermore, that the living should kill each other is an accidental and not an essential action to the living being. And in art, a natural likeness is not sought between effect and cause. This writing is done by me who am not writing, but I have the likeness of the writing in mind and give that to the paper. Every effect resembles not the instrument but the principal agent. Therefore this doctrine resembles my mind and the characters on the page resemble the pen and ink in color and thickness and subtlety, because such are the principal instruments of those characters, even though they are not principal instruments of the thinking. Thus, when someone kills another, the death is similar to the mind of the killer, not to his being; the wound is wide and large like the sword; and random killing resembles the thought of the first mover, to whom nothing is random.[146] Nonetheless, when heat kills cold, chasing it from the firewood and destroying it entirely, which happens when we throw a snowball into a great furnace, this death must be said to come from the non-being of the cold and not from the heat, because the heat only has to heat in order to kill the cold. Therefore, the heat by itself gives to the wood more heat than it is and has; but the cold, unable to stay with the heat, by accident happens to die. The possibility of perishing, which is somewhat like impotence, as I said in the *Metaphysics*,[147] threatens the cold because it is not heat, so it cannot be with that. This possibility depends on some non-being, and, by consequence, on the common nothing from which things were born. There is no necessity to dispute such fine points here that I have mentioned elsewhere. I only wish to infer that nothing gives what it does not have.

The World is a Great Mortal Animal, and What Could Be Outside It

Aristotle believes there is no full place outside the world, no void, no time, no motion, nothing. Indeed, Alexander [the Great] and many others say that outside the world God could produce nothing and that the first sphere is not in a place, because it has nothing surrounding it, but moves around always in itself. Everyone agrees that the world is still and does not move in any direction, although Democritus and Epicurus say there are infinite worlds outside our system.

I certainly do not believe God exhausted his power on this little ball, even though Copernicus thinks it is incomparably larger than the others; but I believe other things could be outside it, and God could make infinite worlds of various sorts. True, we cannot know about them if we do not receive notice of their existence from God, whom we take to be both inside and outside, and not in some place, an infinite being through whom all things are sustained. If someone in the eighth sphere tried to throw a lance and it did not go out, this would only prove that there is a resisting body, and if it went out, that there is space and a yielding body. If the sphere — therefore it is a being, and it cannot be understood to be truly nothing, neither in the mind nor outside God, because if nothingness exists, this being would then be finite and God would be finite. Indeed, if fire were infinite in every way, earth, its enemy, could not exist. Likewise, if God is an infinite being, nothingness never was nor can be. True, God is said to have made the world from nothing, because he created it out of no preexisting matter and no form, bringing this being to it from his being by simple emanation; but I will not say too much about this doctrine, having explained it in my *Metaphysics*. I will however say that one cannot know whether or not the world moves in any direction, because someone inside a covered ship does not know that it moves. I have diligently shown this to my disciple Cortese in the four books of my *Astronomy* against Aristotle, Telesio, Ptolemy and Copernicus. There I also show no one can tell by sight whether the stellar sphere or the earth moves around, because the appearance is the same if the vision moves and if the object moves; but arguing from the qualities, I stopped the motion of the heavens, removed violent motion and the division of the spheres, proving that they are one and that the wandering stars move by themselves like fish in the sea.... [From Dooley, *Italy in the Baroque*, pp. 39-47.]

53. PAOLO MATTIA DORIA (1675–1743 or 1662?–1746)

Doria was born in Genoa, the city traditionally associated with this family name, but died in Naples. Both a mathematician and philosopher, he was known generally for his erudition. Although at first Aristotelian, he came under the influence of foreign theorists and later adapted the older Platonic tradition that was more in keeping with Christian faith. His major works include *La vita civile* of 1710 and *Philosophy*, a reevaluation of Platonism, published in Amsterdam in 1728. The former discusses whether a government should be headed by a philosopher or a practitioner and the intimate connection between philosophy and pedagogy. Many of Doria's unpublished manuscripts remain to this day in the Biblioteca Brancacciana in Naples. In the following passage Doria discusses the importance of nature in determining various aspects of our existence.

PAOLO MATTIA DORIA, "THE PURSUIT OF HAPPINESS"

Introduction

It is very true that I cannot hope for an immediate and overwhelming acceptance of this work. That is because all men who are caught neglecting the intimate knowledge of things are more inclined with their passions rather than with the true reason that actual civil life depends on. The same care very little about discipline. Instead they care only for details that to them are personally useful; they place war, philosophy of the state and arts over the sciences, politics over law and justice. However, it is also true that our negative side has the tendency not to turn away from such harmful things. It is only when the damage has been done, that all this becomes intolerable. And so, when this immoderate prevalence of war over religion and law exists as we now witness, there will be terrible consequences as a result, and people will take sides. Then, we can only hope that truth and right will emanate from those who choose to embrace a leader; and I am not talking of my policy, which I believe is full of good will but still needs some improvement. I am talking about another one that is more full of knowledge and enlightened, as opposed to virtuous, and that can inspire other ardent scholars, such as myself, to make positive proposals concerning our civil society.

Of Civil Life

Without doubt the object of human desire is happiness. Everyone aims toward this appropriate end. However, human nature has not provided the means with which we can fully or partially attain it. To everyone have been given certain natural instincts that emphasize self-preservation. Each human soul has a certain yearning for truth and this would be expressed if only human nature would not be thwarted by the continual shocks given the physical natural body. Furthermore, we are always somehow guided toward the truth whenever we fall into error and misery. This soul of human nature is a good mother to the ones who know her well. But to those who defy her laws, she is a dreadful mother. In my opinion, one of the primary benefits she gives us is the instinct for unification among all people within the context of civil life. [Paolo Mattia Doria, *La vita civile*. Augusta: D. Höpper, 1710, pp. 1-12. (Trans. I. I.-D.)]

54. GIAMBATTISTA VICO (1668–1774)

Vico was concerned with the psychological and social evolution of man. The major contribution of this very famous social philosopher, whose expertise included both law and cultural history, was his "new science of humanity." His primary thesis was that since humans have created the civil world and that of nations, the principles pertaining to it arise from the modifications of the human mind. Born in Naples—his father a poor bookseller—Vico was largely self-taught.

CHAPTER 8. PHILOSOPHY

For nine years he tutored the nephews of the bishop of Ischia. He received a law degree from the University of Naples in 1694 and was professor of rhetoric there from 1699 to 1741. In 1735 he was appointed Royal Historiographer. His most celebrated writings include a metaphysical study, *The Ancient Wisdom of the Italians* of 1710, a passage from which is presented below, a biography of Marshal Antonio Carafa,[148] and three volumes of his *Universal Law* published in 1720–1722. Although all of these were written in Latin, his later works were in Italian. In his *Scienza nuova* of 1725 Vico tries to account historically for the identity of systems of law. In order to do this he relies upon the historical evolution of laws that correspond to the evolution of societies. The third excerpt is from his *Autobiography* of 1725, the same year as the *Scienza nuova*.

Figure 52

GIAMBATTISTA VICO, "THE ORIGIN AND TRUTH OF THE SCIENCES" FROM *The Ancient Wisdom of the Italians*

Why revealed theology is the most certain of all sciences — Human science is a kind of anatomy of nature — Objects of science differ in God and man — God is a being and creatures belong to being — The truly one is that which is unmultipliable — The infinite is without relation to body and is not bound by space — What are reasonings in man's mind are works in God's — Man has choice, God ineluctable will — For the Latins "separation" is the same as "diminution" — The method of division is useless with syllogisms; merely magical with numbers; blind guesswork with fire and solvents — Abstraction results from a defect in the human mind — Abstraction is the mother of human science — Man feigns for himself a world of numbers and forms — Mathematics a productive science — God defines things according to the true; man defines names — Formal definition and nominal definition were the same for the Latins — The same fate has overtaken both human science and chemistry — The sciences that are most useful to the human race are those that are the most certain — The science in which the true is synonymous with what is made is similar to divine science — The criterion of the true

149

is to have made it — The reason sciences are less certain the more they are immersed in matter — Those physical theories are approved which have something similar to our operations in them — When human truth is convertible with human good.

On the basis of these tenets about the true maintained by the ancient sages of Italy and this distinction between what is made and what is begotten, which is adhered to in our own religion, we can take it as a principle that since truth is complete in God alone, we ought to proclaim as wholly true what God has revealed to us; and we ought not to ask what the genus and mode of that truth is, because we cannot wholly comprehend it. Starting from the same premise, we can trace the origin of the human sciences, and finally we can have the standards and a criterion for distinguishing what the true sciences are. God knows all things because in Himself He contains the elements with which He puts all things together. Man, on the other hand, strives to know these things by a process of division. Thus, human science is seen to be a kind of anatomy of nature's works.

For, by way of an enlightening example, human science has dissected man into body and mind, and mind into intellect and will. And from body it has picked out or, as men say, abstracted figure and motion, and from these, as well as from all other things, it has extracted being and unity. So metaphysics examines being; arithmetic, the unit and its multiplication; geometry, shape and its dimensions; mechanics, motion from the periphery; physics, motion from the center; medicine, the body; logic, reason; and moral philosophy, the will.

This anatomy of nature produces the same results as the everyday anatomy of the human body. The more acute physicians are in not little doubt about the location, structure, and function of the bodily parts and as to whether, for example, upon death the position and structure of the living body may not have altered, because of the solidification of the liquids, the cessation of motion, and the cutting up (in the autopsy). Consequently, the functions of these same parts can no longer be explored.

For this being, this unity, this shape, motion, body, intellect, and will are different in God, in whom they are one, from what they are in man, in whom they are divided. In God they live, in man they die. For God is all things eminently, as Christian theologians say, and the uninterrupted generation and corruption of beings do not affect Him at all, because they neither increase nor decrease Him. Limited and created beings are nothing but dispositions of the unlimited and everlasting being. Only God is truly a being, whereas all the rest belong to being. On this account, when Plato speaks of "being" absolutely, he understands the Supreme Deity.[149] But what need have we of Plato's testimony when God Himself defines Himself for us? "I am who am" or "I am who is,"[150] as if to say each and every thing *is not* in comparison with Him. And our own ascetics or Christian metaphysicians preach as follows: no matter how great we are, and whatever the reason for our greatness, before God we are nothing. And since God is uniquely one because He is infinite (for an infinite being cannot be multiplied), a created unity perishes with respect to Him. For the same reason, body perishes with respect to Him, since the immeasurable does not suffer measure; motion, which is defined by space, perishes because body perishes, inasmuch as space is filled with body. Our human reason perishes because, what are reasonings in us are works in God who has within Himself what He comprehends and to whom all things are present. Finally, our will is pliable, whereas that of God is ineluctable since He has no other goal set before Him than Himself alone, since He is perfectly good.

We can observe in Latin idioms the traces of what we have been talking about. For the same verb *minuere* means both to lessen and to separate[151]; as if what we separate may not fully be any longer what has been put together, but is diminished, changed, and corrupted. Is this perhaps the reason the so-called method of division *(via resolutiva)*[152] is found useless when it is employed by the Aristotelians upon genera and syllogism, or why it is mere magic when it proceeds in algebra by means of numbers? Or why it leads nowhere when it is used in chemistry for experimentation with fire and solvents?

For these reasons, then, when man embarks on the investigation of the nature of things, he realizes at length that he cannot arrive at that nature by any means, because he does not have within himself the elements from which composite things are constituted, and that this lack arises from the limitations of the human mind, to which everything is external.... [Giambattista Vico, *On the Most Ancient Wisdom of the Italians Unearthed from the Origins of the Latin*

Language, trans. and ed. L.M. Palmer. Ithaca and London: Cornell University Press, 1988, pp. 47-50.]

GIAMBATTISTA VICO, "AN ETERNAL NATURAL STATE"

Concerning the Recourse of Human Things Taken by the Nations As They Rise Again: Conclusion of the Work on an Eternal Natural State, Ordered by Divine Providence, Containing the Best of Each Kind (of Thing)

1097. Let us then draw this work to a conclusion with Plato, creator of a fourth kind of state, whose supreme lords would be men of worth and honesty: this would be the true natural aristocracy. Providence would thus lead the nations from their origins to a state such as Plato conceived, by ordering that, when the first thunderbolts struck after the Flood, the strongest of those men of gigantic stature, who must have roamed the heights of the mountains as do the strongest of the wild beasts, should drive themselves into the depths of the mountain caves, subject themselves to a superior force which they imagined as Jove, and, amazed, proud and fierce in equal measure, humble themselves before a divinity. Nor, in this order of things human, can one understand any other plan which divine providence (could have) adopted to bring men's bestial wandering in the great forest of the earth to a halt, in order to introduce among them the order of human civil things.

1098. For here developed a world of what may be called monastic states or solitary sovereigns, under the rule of a Greatest and Best whom they themselves both invented and worshipped as, through the flare of the thunderbolts, this true light of God shone upon them: that He rules over men; so that they then imagined that all human utilities administered to them, and all the aids provided for their human needs, were gods and, as such, they feared and venerated them. And so, (caught) between the powerful constraints of a fearful superstition and the stinging incitements of a bestial lust — which must both have been very violent in such men — and because they felt that the sky's countenance demanded reverence of them, and therefore prohibited their promiscuous ways, they must have held *in conatus* the bodily impulses of their lust. Thus they began to exercise their human liberty, for this is the liberty to restrain the impulses of desire and give them a different direction, and since it comes not from the body, from which desire originates, it must belong to the mind and therefore be proper to man. And thus, under this liberty, did they change direction: by forcible seizure of women, who are naturally withdrawn and shy, whom they then dragged into their caves where, in order to mate with them, they enclosed them in continuous company for life. In this way, through these first human, that is, chaste and religious, matings, they initiated the marriages through which they bred certain children by certain women and became their certain fathers, thus founding families in which they ruled over their children and wives with cyclopean family powers proper to natures so wild and proud, in order that later, when the cities arose, men should be disposed to fear civil sovereignty. Thus providence ordered certain family states, monarchic in form, under fathers (or princes in that state) who were pre-eminent in sex, age and virtue; and these fathers, in what should be called the state "of nature" (which was the same as the state of the families) must have formed the first natural orders. For they were the pious, chaste and strong, who had settled on their lands, and being no longer able to sustain life in flight — as they had formerly in their days of ferine roaming — they had to kill the wild animals which molested them, in order to protect themselves and their families, while, since they no longer migrated in search of food, they had to cultivate their land and sow it with grain, to support themselves and their families. And all this for the salvation of nascent mankind....

IIII. But, in the light of the order of civil things reasoned out in these books, providence also reveals itself clearly to us in these three emotions: first, the wonder (of the scholars); second, the veneration which they have all hitherto entertained for the incomparable wisdom of the ancients; and third, the ardent desire by which they were inspired to seek and attain it. For these are in truth three lights of its divinity by which providence awakened in them the three most beautiful and just emotions mentioned above, which were later corrupted by the vanity of scholars and the vanity of nations, which we placed among our first axioms and have corrected throughout these books. These three beautiful and just emotions are that scholars should admire, venerate, and desire to be united with, God's infinite wisdom.

1112. In short, from the whole reasoning of this work, it must finally be concluded that this Science brings inseparably with it the study of piety, and that if one be not pious one cannot be truly wise. [From *Vico, Selected Writings*, trans. and ed. Leon Pompa. Cambridge: Cambridge University Press, 1982, pp. 259-67.]

GIAMBATTISTA VICO, "AUTOBIOGRAPHY"

...For these reasons Vico lived in his native city not only a stranger but quite unknown. His solitary tastes and habits did not prevent his venerating from afar as sages the older men who were recognized for their knowledge of letters, and envying with a genuine vexation other young men who had the good fortune to enjoy their conversation. With this attitude, which is necessary to young men who wish to make further progress and not on the say of malicious or ignorant teachers to remain all their lives satisfied with a knowledge suited to another's taste and capacity, he first came to the attention of two men of importance. One was Father Don Gaetano D'Andrea, a Theatine, who later died a most reverent bishop; he was a brother of Francesco and Gennaio [D'Andrea], both of immortal name. In a conversation which he had with Vico in a bookstore on the history of collections of canons, he asked him if he were married. And when Vico answered that he was not, he inquired if he wanted to become a Theatine. On Vico's replying that he was not of noble birth, the father answered that that need be no obstacle, for he would obtain a dispensation from Rome. Then Vico, seeing himself obliged by the great honor the father paid him, came out with it that his parents were old and poor and he was their only hope. When the father pointed out that men of letters were rather a burden than a help to their families, Vico replied that perhaps it would not be so in his case. Then the father closed the conversation by saying: "That is not your vocation."

The other was Don Giuseppe Lucina, a man of great erudition in Greek, Latin and Tuscan and in all branches of divine and human knowledge. He had made some trial of the young man's ability, and in his kind was regretting that it was not put to some good use in the city, when a good occasion offered itself to him for advancing the youth. For Don Nicola Caravita, leader of the bar in sharpness of intellect, severity of judgment and purity of Tuscan style, and a great patron of men of letters, had decided to make a collection of literary tributes to the Count of Santo Stefano,[153] Viceroy of Naples, on the occasion of his departure. This was the first collection of its kind that appeared in Naples within our memory, and it had to be printed in the narrow limits of a few days. Lucina, whose opinion was respected by all, suggested that Vico should write the oration to serve as preface to all the other compositions. And having secured this commission for the young man, he brought it to him, pointing out to him his opportunity to make himself favorably known to a patron of letters such as he had found to be his own greatest protector; and indeed the youth needed no prompting to be most eager for it. And so, because he had given up Tuscan studies, he worked out a Latin oration for that collection at the printing establishment itself of Giuseppe Roselli, in the year 1696. From then on he began to rise in fame as a man of letters; and among others Gregorio Caloprese, whom we have above mentioned with honor, was wont to call him (as Epicurus was called) the "autodidact" or "teacher of himself."... [From *The Autobiography of Giambattista Vico*, trans. Max H. Fisch and Thomas G. Bergin. Ithaca: Cornell University Press, 1944, pp. 134-36.]

55. ANTONIO GENOVESI (1712–1769)

Economist, philosopher, and author of meditations [see **60**], the Abbot Genovesi displays the versatility apparent in so many of these Neapolitan writers. Born at Castiglione near Salerno, where he taught rhetoric in the seminary, he was ordained a priest in 1737 and always remained conservative in religious practice. The following year he arrived in Naples where he was to hold the first European professorship of political economics ("commerce and mechanics"). Genovesi was greatly impressed by ideas generated by the Enlightenment. He taught both philosophy and metaphysics in 1741 as well as ethics in 1745. His last teaching assignment was in 1753. Most of his philosophical works were composed in Latin. His last years were devoted to economics, and his theories had a great effect upon political, social, and moral development not only of Naples but of Italy as a whole. His *Discorso sopra alcuni trattati d'agricoltura...in cui si tratta del vero fine delle lettere* was dedicated to the powerful Bartolomeo Intieri,[154] who had given him his professorship. Genovesi's economic theories attempted to reconcile protectionism with free competition. The following passage, from his *Academic Letters*, written with an obvious flair for the dramatic, is an onslaught of topics including happiness, virtue, education, and evil.

ANTONIO GENOVESI, "KNOWLEDGE AND IGNORANCE," FROM THE *Lettere Accademiche*

You want to extract the crab with someone else's hand. How wise you are! You are asking me if unlearned and ignorant men living down here are happier than the learned and the scientists. You are asking that (mind the cunning!) in the name of those splendid people. Therefore one might say: "Who can judge? He who can be content can enjoy life," and it is not modesty but instead most would think of it as rebellion and cynicism. So I would surely be a hero if I could shed one ray of light on the problem: but could that happen? To be reasonable, one must begin with another thought. You, as a great geometrician, know that every problem supposes another problem as well as presents the question of "is it soluble or not?" Furthermore, do you know to whom you are speaking? I'll humor you. You see: Don't frown and judge me before you have heard all I have to say. Then will you have an opinion of me? If your think I'm ignorant, which I think I might be, you men of learning would have lost out. If I were educated, which I could have been, would you want me to be something I'm not? Then I would need the constant strength of a judge, because of all those who live here. Canon, I will give you a piece of advice. You fashionable philosophers believe that there are infinite worlds out there that revolve around us. Let's turn to the wise aliens, since we are less interested in such a topic than in the human heart. This is a fact when one gets beyond pretension. You say "no" and "declare yourself." In civil wars, neutrality is not taken for granted. Therefore, I shall declare myself. "He who can be content, can enjoy life." "Oh, our Apollo!" you might say, "We don't want oracles: stop talking slowly; relinquish all politics; philosophy...." Yes, yes? I know how knights-errant think: they fight with superiority in the presence of their lady. Do we agree then? Therefore, do not agree with me necessarily if you don't want me to rebuke you.

Come on: I will declare myself. But before I do, let's make a pact. Those men of learning, those idiots, how will we deal with them? Because, my dear canon, all this happiness down here is more good temper than art; it's lower than culture, and if it's lower, too much art might spoil it.

Around these scientists, these ignorant people, are there some who are ruined and some who are virtuous? Can there be some rascals and wicked men of learning like the (simpleton) Mameluke of Scio as well as some just, honest, and human idiots who are prudent and wise in their professions? If these are the facts then the problem is already solved. Idiot or ignorant, the ruined one is always unhappy. The virtuous one lives forever for himself and is part of the joyful world. It is the law of the universe: who could ever overturn that?

Therefore, in order to be able to know the strength of the humanities and sciences we must give to them the same consistency and place them both on the same measure of virtue and vice, and weigh all equally. When this is done, I think that you can arbitrate honorably and freely.... Don't you remember in order to be less wary? Paris once said:

"Did the high and ancient empire spread its land?"[155]

What is happiness down here: I do not want "Monsignor King," or some Origene[156] follower who thinks that we are in hell to make fun of us. The happy among us is he who is less unhappy. But who is less unhappy? I believe it is he who suffers the least; he who has a less troubled, turbid, tempestuous and afflicted soul, in short the one who has less or minor pain....

A fool cannot foresee, cannot soften or avoid pain. And if sometimes a fool lives better than a wise man, it is by chance, a circumstance we should not credit, or see as reflective of knowledge, and is derived from a certain stupidity and insensitivity the result of long and continuous misery. [From *Autobiografia, lettere e altri scritti*, ed. Gennaro Savarese. Milan: Giangiacomo Feltrinelli, 1962, pp. 368-70. (Trans. J.I.-D.)]

56. MARIO PAGANO (1748-1799)

Pagano is always considered to be a Neapolitan, even though he was born in Brienza in Lucania. A jurist and teacher of Vincenzo Cuoco [see 12], Pagano's famous *Saggi politici de' principii, progressi, e decadenza della società,* was published in 1783-1785. Pagano, who came to Naples and studied under Genovesi [see 55], Pelliccia, and Gliuni among others, received his law degree and in 1770 was nominated to be the university's honored reader in Dialectics. His fields of study included erudition, literature, and philosophy; and he became renowned as a famous orator. Pagano's numerous other writings include his *Considerazioni sul processo criminale* of 1787, *Il Morte di G. Filangieri* [see 50] of 1788, and *Lettera ai censori ecclesiastici avverso le imputazioni fatte ai Saggi politici* in 1785. In addition he published several dramas that attracted the attention of P. Napoli-Signorelli,[157] the great bestower of literary fame in Naples at that time. After living in Rome and then Milan, Pagano took part in the revolution that toppled the Bourbons and helped form the provisionary government and the Comitato

Legislativo,[158] of which he became president. Pagano had the major role in creating the constitutional design of the new Parthenopean Republic. Along with over 100 prominent republican leaders he was executed by Admiral Nelson later in 1799 when the British fleet retook the city and restored the Bourbons to power. This passage from his *Saggi politici* discusses what he considers to be the two basic needs: the physical and the moral.

MARIO PAGANO, "POLITICS AND SOCIETY"

Two Sorts of Our Needs, Physical and Moral

With reference to man, we can observe two things: motion and sense; so we distinguish in him what moves and what feels, body and spirit, as these needs are not only physical but moral or a mixture of both. For they are the needs of the body, spirit, or both.

Society is not needed to merely satisfy physical needs. Instead, society is ordered by nature to achieve a moral communion of our souls. In the human spirit, there are unimaginable voids that cannot fill only our ideas, routines and inner forces. The human spirit sometimes feels its weakness unprotected and abandoned by sweet sentiment. As the body recovers its loss of strength by nourishment, so do our spirits by sharing ideas and affections with similar beings and, in this way, people are revived and their spirits regain strength. In this way, our spirits are rewarded and flourish. Therefore, moral society is as necessary to man as is food and other things that he thinks he can't live without.

Furthermore, when life is easy, man is driven toward moral society and worthy desires, to communicate to others his own ideas and feelings that he improves further by sharing them with others. One can observe this when somebody becomes depressed, which brings about a feeling of moral and physical weakness. In that case, company is the only comfort. What joy would a loner, who for many years lived like a hermit, have upon encountering another person?[159]

The mere look of another human being fills us with joy and nourishes our imagination, and this is especially true if the other person is beautiful. Among moral needs, beauty is the most sensitive of all. For our internal senses we need order and harmony so we can distinguish what is compatible and what is dissonant. So let's stimulate every sense beyond nature's expectation that we should exercise all our faculties fully. Where does this noble desire for beauty, harmony and composure of the soul come from? When the soft light of beauty and harmony enhance a Raphael painting or a sculpture of Michelangelo or music of Pergolesi, when there are those blue rays that penetrate the soul, one experiences clarity of ideas and feelings generating everywhere, all leading to a heart-felt sweet, divine, and comforting pleasure. Therefore, moral society of men and especially the beautiful sex, and I'm not discussing just physical needs, is necessary and ordered by nature itself. [Mario Pagano, *Saggi politici, de' principii, progressi, e decadenza della società*, ed. Francesco Collotti. Bologna: L. Cappelli, 1936, pp. 158-59. (Trans. I. I.-D.)]

Aspronum dum ritè Sacris Petrus expiat undis,
Alma Fides Phœbi Numina sternit humi,

Hinc Sicula cum Gente canit pia Carmina Siren,
Hinc nouus exoritur, Sole cadente dies.

Iacobus del Pe. In.

Andreas Magliar Sul Neap.

Figure 53

PART IV:
THE
SPIRITUAL
WORLD

Figure 54

CHAPTER 9
Church, Saints, and Ritual

57. FYNES MORYSON (1566–1617/30).

Although of Irish extraction, Moryson presents himself as a "Protestant English-man." His fear of, and prejudice against, Catholic tradition loom in this excerpt from his celebrated *Itinerary* of 1617. Considered to be the most authoritative account among those of the Elizabethan travelers, he recalls in the length of four volumes and with dramatic flair his early seventeenth-century voyage to Italy and other western European countries. Despite Moryson's provincialism, his description of rituals and events that transpire in the Neapolitan church do offer some insight into devotions and the intensity of veneration.

FYNES MORYSON, "A PROTESTANT VIEW OF CATHOLIC RITUAL"

> From the said Pallace the way leades right to the Kingly Gate, called Porta Reale, at which onely the King enters in solemne pompe, and from this Gate right to the West, lies a most faire and large streete called Strada Toletana, the way whereof on both sides is raised with a faire and large pavement for men to walk upon, and it hath a faire Market-place. When you come to the end of this streete, there is the Church of Saint Clara, called vulgarly San' chiara,[160] which was built by Agnes [Sancia] of Spaine, wife to King Robert [1309–1343], where are artificiall sepulchers of the said Robert (comming of the French Kings) and of his wife Agnes, and of other Kings and Princes of the French family Durazzana.[161] And there in a Chappell the Monkes day and night sing with a lamentable voice, or rather groane for the rest of their deceased soules. In the Church of Saint Dominick is an Altar, which they say, cost some twenty five thousant Crownes: and in the Vesterie lie the bodies of nine Kings in coffins of wood, covered with peuter, & having black velvet laied over them. Among these Kings are Alphonso the first, King of Aragon,[162] and Ferdinand his sonne, and Ferdinand the

163

second. And in this place also, the Monkes in like sort sing, or rather houle rest to their soules. They shew a Crucifis, which they say, did speake to Thomas Aquinas in this manner; Thomas, thou hast written well of me, what reward doest thou aske? And that Thomas should answere; No reward Lord but thy selfe onely.[163] I have heard, that Saint Bernard[164] knowing the fraudes and imposture of the Monkes, and not dissembling them, when the Image of the blessed Virgin did in like sort praise him, did with much more pietie and wisdome answere out of S. Paul, I. Cor. 14. Let women be silent in the Church, for it is not permitted them to speake.

Not farre thence are the publike schooles of the University, which the Emperour Fredericke the second founded there. In the most faire Church of the Monkes of Saint Olivet,[165] the Images of Ferdinand the first, and Alphonso the second, are so lively engraven, and doe so artificially represent them, as well in the bed dying, as upon their knees praying, with the mourning of the by-standers, (the horror of Religion being increased with lampes continually burning,) as my selfe by chance passing by this Chappel, thought I had fallen among living Princes, not dead Images; and perhaps I have seene a more sumptuous monument, but a more beautifull did I never see. [F. Moryson, Gent., *An Itinerary Containing His Ten Yeeres Travell through…Italy.* Glasgow: James MacLehose & Sons, 1907, 1:234-35.]

58. PIETRO GISOLFO (17TH C.)

W ritten by "the pious worker" Gisolfo, this is an account of Nicola de Fusco, one of many Counter-Reformation Neapolitan saints. It was published in 1682. Although relatively little is known about this author, Gisolfo had written as well a biography of Antonio de Colellis[166] in 1663. The Fusco book contains engravings by François de Louvemont after drawings by the famous painter Francesco Solimena.[167] Jean-Michel Sallmann [see General Bibliography] considers these to be among the Seicento's most beautiful book illustrations of religious subjects.

PIETRO GISOLFO, "THE LIFE OF SAN NICOLA DI FUSCO"

The Birth, Education, and Good Nature of Nicola Until Age Three

God wished this fortunate child to be born on Sunday, the day dedicated to the cult of His Divine Majesty, a little after midnight and before dawn on the 8th of February 1677. He was to give himself to God from the beginning of his life when the light of reason would arise in the midst of youthful ignorance. The child was a puzzle to many and was an example of God's approval of a ray of light that sometimes appears in the middle of darkness.

God wanted him to have as parents Bartolomeo di Fusco and Michela Ponaro, both of noble descent but even greater Christian virtue.

At the Sacred Font, he was given the name of Nicholas because his father so admired the Glorious Saint Nicholas, Bishop of Myra.[168] His father showed great reverence for this saint through homage,

Figure 55

prayer, and alms and, more specifically, by having Nicholas dress in bright blue. When nursemaids are fearful of God they often train children in external devotions, the bowing of a head before a sacred image or the striking of the chest at the sound of a church bell. They ask children to do all these things. Nicholas, however, performed all these little devotions with the greatest attention and these were things he did on his own initiative without any instruction. When his nursemaid carried him through rooms where there were images of Jesus, the Virgin, Saint Ann, or Saint Nicholas, the little child would bend his head or strike his chest before such sacred images as a sign of honor. When uncertain, he would turn to the image immediately without instruction. He would do the same at the toll of the bell and make the sign of the cross, turn to the virgin saint, and strike his little chest out of reverence and greeting.

He did all this when only six months old. When only a year old, an age when most children babble, Nicholas was exhorting his mother about the freedom of the poor. Saint Philip Benizzi[169] had done a similar thing when at the same age, seeing a few poor religious men begging for food, he said to his mother: "Do some good to the slaves of the Virgin Mary." Nicholas was much the same at the beginning of his long life. Certainly, during his first three years he showed extraordinary signs of sanctity. He relished the Lord's comparison of him to a great painter and drew a sketch on a small canvas with the intention of perfecting it. His nursemaid gave his left-over belongings to the poor. One day, when she was holding the baby Nicholas in her arms, she heard in the courtyard a poor person who begged for food. She wanted the baby to give him food with his own little hands. For that time on, every time the child heard someone begging he would turn and say: "Mama, Poor," and wouldn't stop until the alms were given.... He always kept this custom even until his last days.... [Pietro Gisolfo, *Prodigio di mature virtù nella vita di Nicola di Fusco*. Naples: Francesco Mollo, 1682, pp. 27-30. (Trans. I.I.-D.)]

59. SIGISMONDO SICOLA (17TH C.)

Sicola's verbose life of Saint Aspreno was published in Naples in 1696. The author digresses frequently as he writes of the saint's virtue and noble lineage. The engravings [FIG. 53] are by André Maillar after the drawings of Giacomo del Po.[70] This saint is one of seven (later nine) patron saints of Naples [see 61]. The major illustration is of Saint Aspreno being baptized by St. Peter, evidence, according to Sallmann, of the Roman curia's insistence that the Neapolitan church be submissive to that of Rome. The small church of Sant' Aspreno dei Crociferi in Naples is located near the Gesù delle Monache and Santa Maria dei Miracoli.

SIGISMONDO SICOLA, "SANT' ASPRENO, A PATRON SAINT OF NAPLES"

Nobility Becomes Much More Glorious When it is Joined with the Christian Religion

Whispering of the prestige of noble birth darkens the brain with mortal confusion so that the mind staggers, losing all sense.

Everyone would like to be of noble descent. It is longed for universally, and he who has never experienced nobility and thinks it is irrelevant to him really values it.

The thought of being of noble blood is so grand and gives one such dignity that it often becomes like a type of sanctity. No other condition increases the fever of ambition like this one and swells people up so they must live with that sickness, which can by treated only with its own poison. And even though all this nobility is really nothing but smoke, it is still admired....

It is true, that the great nobility that shines gloriously is derived from renowned and noble people; we should therefore praise the famous exploits of Darius, applaud in the Roman Capitol Caesar's triumphs, be astonished by the huge dominions of Alexander. Aristotle's wits, Cicero's eloquence, Tacitus' doctrine are surely not far from the world's greatest speakers. That these are valuable things cannot be denied, but we cannot consider them to be perfectly sublime for it is at that point that all their splendor plunges into the earth and it is the end of all the pomposity. Their attempts have failed. Today they are regarded as dull, lacking those very things that were once so highly valued. Their glory consists only in their name, which becomes less and less with time....

Therefore, let our Aspreno be renowned. For he lived primarily with faith in his beloved country as well as the enlightenment of charity even in the darkest moments. Let his blood indeed be noble if it is to be joined to the color red, representative of charity, and white, a symbol of the purity of baptism, for he knew how to reflect the noblest and most celestial of sacraments. Let him be associated as well with the bright sun, which is separate from the darkness of infidelity and which shows to the horizon his resplendent birth....

[Sigismondo Sicola, *La nobiltà gloriosa nella vita di S. Aspreno, primo christiano e primo vescovo della città di Napoli*. Naples: Carlo Porsile, 1696, pp. 1-5. (Trans. I.I.-D.)]

60. ANTONIO GENOVESI (1712–1769)

Usually considered to be a philosopher [see **55**], Genovesi was known also for his meditations. Although he believed that ecclesiastical authority should be limited to spiritual matters, he maintained that the state should not take land from clergy, an idea reflected later in the "enlightened" administration in Naples championed by the minister Bernardo Tanucci. His *Disciplinarum metaphysicarum elementa* (1743–1752) aroused some suspicion of heresy, and in 1748 he decided not to publish its theological companion. In the following passage from his *Philosophical Meditations* he defends religion as both wise and reasonable.

ANTONIO GENOVESI, "RELIGION AND MORAL PHILOSOPHY"

The Idea of the Work

The work that I gave to the press and is now about to be released may seem to some unnecessary or even foolhardy, and I can't say whether it was a worthwhile endeavor. Certainly, those who are aware of the enormous number of books by so many learned and venerable authors, all defenders of morality and the Christian religion, will not allow that new works be written because they will conclude that they will be of no profit except perhaps to the booksellers. It is, nevertheless, my intention to defend virtue, compassion, and human rights, which the Creator intended for all of us. As I said above, no one knows whether this is right or reasonable. But I maintain that the one thing that is right and reasonable is religion, attacked continually by those who are rebellious and impudent to both God and nature. But we, who have a great devotion to our nurturing Church, realize that it is committed to Divine Trust; consequently, we owe religion to God, the very essence of it is in us as we enter into the building, as an old and venerable priest once said. It is a unique truth and not just a trivial matter to me, although many will find this topic exhausting and foolish.

It seems we are in trouble no matter what our point of view. As far as this work being subversive, is it right or wrong? Nothing that promotes both reason and pleasure can be said to be subversive, and we can do only what is wise and reasonable. A dutiful person is not subversive no matter what the circumstances. After all, our great and excellent God doesn't need or want anything for his well-being and therefore we don't have to worry. So he who might be considered subversive has at least done his duty. Furthermore, as lofty as these critics might be, those who argue with great doctrine and learning as well as discretion and wisdom, they gain impiety in their triumph. Nevertheless (shame on this corrupt century!) there are many more sinful people around today than ever before as books illustrate while simultaneously promoting them. Crazy and brutal (appropriate words) they deny all this. They are ignorant and inconsiderate bigots driven by foolishness and wickedness. Apart from a few modern ideas that they have distorted anyway, they are all (and famous for it) armed against religion. They express themselves with a mockery and babble away. This way is not suited to men of letters and gentlemen. I believe it is necessary for all these avant-garde philosophers and experts on European literature who look askance at us to defend our common cause. Everything weak, foolish and brutal should be eliminated. They say they want reason, but fail to realize that that is a divine and noble gift. Instead, they are full of vices that make them greedy, wanting everything for their own pleasure and use. And those who support their wrong thinking, without being aware of their own limitations and mortality, want to declare war on their world, which was created and kept beautiful; they wish also to break apart the link of civil society returning to a wild and uncivilized existence. Because they are foolish, brutal and enemies of themselves and the human race, they deserve universal hatred. Instead, we should praise those who have the will to study, who deserve the love of everyone, and who are not without both a mind and human heart.... [Antonio Genovesi, *Meditazioni filosofiche sulla religione e sulla morale*. Bassano: Remondi di Venezia, 1783, pp. 368-70. (Trans. I.I.-D.)]

61. MICHAEL KELLY (1764–1826)

Michael Kelly, who wrote his *Reminiscences* in 1779 / 80, was an Irish singer, actor, composer, and theatrical manager. Other Irish travelers who kept such diaries included Fynes Moryson [see 57] and Marguerite Power, countess of Blessington (1789–1849), a novelist and mistress of the dandy Count d'Orsay, whose *Idler in Italy* was one of the last great accounts of the Grand Tour. Kelly's observation of the ceremony at San Gennaro, the gothic cathedral of Naples [FIGS. 56-57], offers an account of what is to this day one of the most famous miracles associated with a saint, the liquefaction of the blood of San Gennaro (Latin *Januarius*), still celebrated three times a year. Traditionally, San Gennaro has been considered the primary patron saint of Naples [FIG. 54], although there are six others of lesser importance as well. These minor patron saints include Agrippino, Aspreno [see 59], Aniello, Atanasio, Eusebio and Severo. During the seventeenth century Saints Gregorio Armeno and Patrizia were added. Clearly from his account Kelly displays no sympathy for, let alone belief in, the local miracle.

MICHAEL KELLY, "THE LIQUEFACTION OF THE BLOOD OF SAN GENNARO"

> I went...to visit the miracle of St. Gennaro or Januario, in the Cathedral; the King and Queen [Ferdinand IV and Maria Carolina],[171] in state, attended his saintship. There were two immense orchestras erected in the church, and all good professors, vocal and instrumental, were engaged to perform upon these occasions. The Archbishop prays, or appears to pray, while the *Te Deum* is sung. He then displays a phial, which contains the congealed blood of St. Gennaro; towards this he holds up a large wax taper, that the people may perceive it is congealed. The miracle consists, as everybody knows, in this blood dissolving before the congregation, and is

(1) Strada principale di Somma Piazza, oggi di D. Regina. (2) Antica Cattedrale di S. Restituta. (3) Chiesa, ed Ospedale di S. Andrea Apost. (4) Vicolo, che dime-
zzava tra questa Cattedrale, e l'altra del SS. Salvatore. (5) Antica Cattedrale del
SS. Salvatore, chiamata Stefania. (6) Un gran campanile della medesima. (7) Cappella di S. Pietro Apost. sotto quest'altro campanile. (8) Ospedale nell'atrio di d' Cattedrale. (9) Granajo. (10) Antico Palaggio Vescovilo. (11) Vicolo de' Munnocci, oggi di Capuana. (12) Antico Seggio di Capuana. (13) Cavallo di bronzo. (14) Strada principale di Sole, e Luna, oggi di Capuana.

Nic. d'Oratio Scul. Neap.

Figure 56

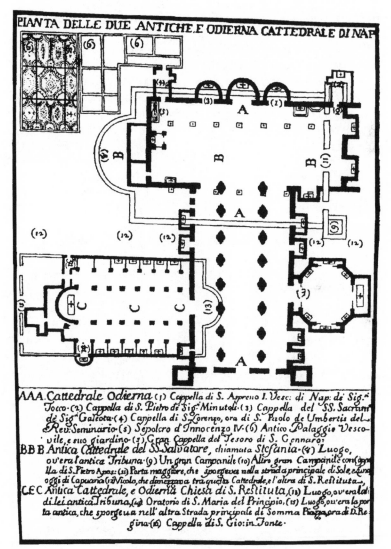

PIANTA DELLE DUE ANTICHE E ODIERNA CATTEDRALE DI NAP

AAA. Cattedrale Odierna (1) Cappella di S. Aspreno I. Vesc: di Nap: de Sig.ʳⁱ
Tocco. (2) Cappella di S. Pietro de Sig.ʳ Minutoli. (3) Cappella del SS. Sacrum
de Sig.ʳ Galeota. (4) Cappella di S. Lorenzo, ora di S. Paolo de Umbertis del
Rev: Seminario. (5) Sepolcro d'Innocenzo IV. (6) Antico Palaggio Vesco-
vile, e suo giardino. (7) Gran Cappella del Tesoro di S. Gennaro:
BBB Antica Cattedrale del SS. Salvatore, chiamata Stefania. (8) Luogo,
ov'era l'antica Tribuna. (9) Un gran Campanile (10) Altro gran Campanile con l'Appe-
lla di S. Pietro Apos: (11) Porta maggiore, che sporgeva nella strada principale di Sole, e è una
oggi di Capuana (12) Vicolo, che dinceva trà questa Cattedrale, e l'altra di S. Restituta.
CEC Antica Cattedrale, e Odierna Chiesa di S. Restituta, (13) Luogo, ov'era la
di lei antica Tribuna, (14) Oratorio di S. Maria del Principio, (15) Luogo, ov'era la por
ta antica, che sporgeva nell'altra Strada principale di Somma Piazza, ora di D. Regina (16) Cappella di S. Gio: in Fonte.

Figure 57

supposed to be performed by the saint himself. As soon as it is liquefied, the Archbishop roars lustily, "the miracle is accomplished!" The *Te Deum* is again sung, and the whole congregation prostrate themselves before the altar of the saint with gratitude and devotion, and every face beams with delight.

On one of these miraculous days, I witnessed a ludicrous scene. It happened by some accident, that the Archbishop could not make the miracle work. The Lazzaroni and old women loudly called on the Virgin for assistance. "Dear Virgin Mary! Blessed Madonna! Pray use your influence with St. Gennaro! Pray induce him to work the miracle! Do we not love him? Do we not worship him?" But when they found the Saint inexorable, they changed their note, and seemed resolved to abuse him into compliance. They all at once cried out, *"Porco di St. Gennaro!"* — "You pig of a Saint!" — *"Barone maladetto!"* — "You cursed rascal!" — *"Cane faccia gialutta!"* — "You yellow-faced dog!" In the midst of this, the blood (thanks to the heat of the Archbishop's hand) dissolved. They again threw themselves on their knees, and tearing their hair, (the old ladies particularly), with streaming eyes, cried, "Oh! most holy Saint, forgive us this once, and never more will we doubt your goodness!" [From Seward, *Naples: A Traveller's Companion*, pp. 132-33.]

62. A.M. B. W. (17TH C.)

This English author, whose last name begins with the letter B, wrote a brief history of the rituals of the papacy with a short biography of Pope Innocent XII, a Neapolitan of the aristocratic Pignatelli family. It is presented from the point of view of the foreigner and, specifically, a writer from a Protestant country who observes foreign customs in detail and with some enthusiasm. Interesting facts about this "perfect" pontiff's life are included as well. This English account was published in London in 1691, the first year of Innocent's papacy.

A.M. B. W., "INNOCENT XII, THE PIGNATELLI POPE"

Then, with the sound of Drums and Trumpets and all other sorts of Musick, he seats himself in his Chair, and being accompanied with the Cardinals and Princes, he is carried to the Lateran Palace, where, in the Portico of Benediction, he repeats again the Versicles last set down, and after crossing, he gives his Benediction, together with plenary Indulgence to the Company, which is proclaimed in Latin and Italian, as formerly; and here Money is again thrown among the People pretty liberally, and all the great Guns in the City are discharged: And after all this Ceremony is performed, the Pope betakes himself to his Litter, and with the Cardinals, Princes and Legates, with his guards and other Company he returns back to the Vatican Palace whence he came, where, being tired with all this Day's Procession and Formality, it is now time to leave him: And having spoken a word or two, in reference to the present Pope, Innocent XII, we will put an end to our Discourse.

This prelate, is by birth a Neapolitan, descended of one of the most illustrious families, in that kingdom, being the son of the prince of Minervino,[172] of the family of Pignatelli. His own brother, the duke of Terranova, is one of the grandees of Spain, and he himself possess'd great dignities in the kingdom of Naples. He came to Rome, during the pontificate of Urban VIII, who made him vice-legate of Urban. His successor, pope Innocent X, sent him inquisitor to Malta, and afterwards nuncio to Florence. Alexander VII confirm'd him in that employment for some years and afterwards sent him nuncio to Poland. Clement IX sent him with the same character to Vienna, and at his return from thence, made him bishop of Lecchi,[173] and secretary to the congregation of bishops regulars, and finally, master of his chamber. Innocent XI confirm'd him in these honours; and at the end of five years, created him a cardinal, constituted him legate of Bologna, and made him archbishop of Naples, whence his exemplary piety, discreet administration, and good works, procur'd him the esteem and veneration of all men. And these, added to his known experience in the affairs of the church, his zeal for the general interest of Christendom, and his admirable conduct in those several stations already mentioned, have advanc'd him to the chair of St. Peter.

The cardinals Cantelmi and Giudici,[174] were the principal instruments of his promotion; which they compass'd by an artifice. For, when those of the French interest, propos'd the choice of Pignatelli, these two cardinals seemed very cold, as if they did not approve their motion, or at least, look'd on it as a thing not likely to suceed, on account of the disgust that Pignatelli had given the Spanish nation, during his residence at Naples. This made the French cardinals, with the whole party of Altieri and Ottoboni,[175] more zealous for him. And when the French had given their voices for him, the Spaniards fell in and concurred with theirs; so did the zealots, and the faction of Chigi,[176] so that of 61 voices, 53 were for Cardinal Pignatelli: who was accordingly chosen and crowned, and has received the customary compliments and submissions. He has appointed Cardinal Spada, to be secretary of state, Cardinal Panciatici to be datary, and Cardinal Albani, to secretary of the chiphres. He has declar'd, that he will maintain the decrees of his predecessors, for the abolishing of nepotism; and especially those of Innocent XI for suppressing the franchises of the quarters of ambassadors; to which end, suitable orders are given out to the officers of justice. He has distributed 10,000 crowns among the poor of Rome, and 6,000 among those of Naples: has published an order, for the better supplying this city with corn; and designs to lessen the number of his guards. He has removed the nephews of the late Pope Alexander VIII from the offices they possess'd, of general of the church, governor of the Castle of St. Angelo, and legate of Avignon. He has made the bishop of Fieschi, vice-legate of Avignon; and ordered the revenues of that place, to be brought into the publick treasury. Cardinal Cantelmi, is made arch-bishop of Naples. This pope, has the character of a very good man, a lover of vertue, and a cherisher of learning, charitable in a high degree, and a hater of oppression and injustice. 'Tis on good grounds expected, that he will reform the court of Rome, and cause the primitive canons to be put in practice.

From all that has been said, it will be easie to conclude, that in common probability, the election of this pope, will change the face of affairs in Christendom; and, that the confederate princes, having the supreme bishop on their side, will be more strengthened in their league, and will be in a condition, to carry on the war with greater vigor and success, against the king of France. [A.M. B.W., *A New History of the Roman Conclave...Rites and Ceremonies...of the Pope, A Brief Account of the Life of This Present Pope Innocent XII.* London: Samuel Smith at the Prince's Arms in St. Paul's Cathedral, 1691, pp. 30-32.]

63. DOMENICO AULISIO (1639–1717)

A legal consultant and man of letters, this native-born Neapolitan was highly educated in the exact sciences, philology, and history. In 1664 he initiated the teaching of civil law at the University of Naples. Aulisio completed treatises on architecture and medicine, which were published in Naples in 1693. In addition to *Delle scuole sacre libri* of 1723, he published in that same year historical accounts on Assyrian,

Greek, and Hebrew antiquity. Like many others, Aulisio is mentioned in Pietro Giannone's *Istoria civile del regno di Napoli*, also of 1723 [see 7]. The following is a complex and multi-lingual history of the ancient theological schools and their inter-influences.

DOMENICO AULISIO, "SACRED BOOKS," BOOK I

Chapter XV

Talking about our main subject, we say that in the School of Investigation of our Lord Christ, even though the idea was held by the Rabbanimi and destined only to the doctrine of tradition, the Karraimi[177] entered into the debate without any restraint or notice.

And by believing in this, we only need the example of Christ our savior who continued to favor the Karraimi and entered without controversy into the School of Investigation and quarreled with the doctors over there. But let's observe in a more detailed manner.

Christ, our Master, despised the traditions of the Rabbanimi and approved instead the Karraimi. We get this from Saint Matthew 15 and from Saint Mark 7 where Christ refuses them as men's precepts and not of God.

Somewhere else in the traditions, where we read, for example, "that God disdained from intervening in the synagogue if there were less than ten men," it was said: "Where two or three have gathered in my name, there I shall be among them." Saint Matthew 18:20.

Chapter XXII

Thus Rabbi Abram and Rabbi Scerirà, but they do not refer to the reason for this most disgraceful act. We seek to reveal that [reason] here briefly.... Sura existed during the Greek empire, when, in the thirteenth year of Justinian, Chosroes the Elder,[178] king of Persia, collected a great army, and, entering into Sura by deceit, captured it from the Greeks, sacked and burnt it. Procopius in Book 2 of the *War of Persia*, Evagrius Book 4,[179] section 25, who write "Souros."[180]

Thus were closed the Schools (at Sura). All of this happened in the year of Our Christ 540, which corresponds to the Jewish year 4300. And it is seen, as David Ganz intended it should be understood by telling us that the Schools ceased because of the hatred of the Persian king.

Then (the Schools) re-emerged in the year of Our Christ 589, which (year) was the eighth of the Emperor Maurice,[181] when all the places on this side of the Euphrates were recovered. "When all of the East[182] held a profound peace"...as George Cedrenus writes....[183]

...In the Year of our Salvation 1039, Ezechia son of David, nephew of Saccai, was nominated Prince of Captivity two years before contending with the king. He was killed in his home and only his two sons survived. They escaped to Spain, to the city of Porzilo where they founded the academy named by the Jews the "Academy of Tolitola." This misfortune caused the ruin of the "School of Sura" and all the others of the Jews of Babylon, which disappeared completely.

In the Judaic year 4797, David Ganz in the *Offspring of David* tells us the following: At that time Sura returned under the domain of Babylon. The king was Feruz Albutaher. But then, Gelad Addaula occupied the city with arms in the year of the Egira 422. This was the year of our Redemption, 1030. He was dressed with the royal mantle by Kaimo Biamirilla Chialifa. He ruled for 13 years and 11 months. Refer to the *History* of Giogio Elmacino[184] Book 3, Chapter 7. So this is the king, who Ganz tells us about, and who closed with others the school of Sura, which survived, with some luck, for 782 years. [Domenico (Conte) Aulisio, *Delle scuole sacre libri due postumi del conte Domenico Aulisio*.... Naples: F. Riccardo, 1723, pp. 118-19. (Trans. I.I.-D.)]

64. FR. JUAN DE SAN FELIX (17TH C.)

During the Seicento, the period of the later Counter Reformation, many saints, including St. Theresa of Avila, St. John of the Cross, and St. Ignatius Loyola, were celebrated, beatified, canonized, and venerated. This Mexican account of the life of the Blessed Andrea Avellino is an indication of the widespread cultural influence of Naples disseminated through its Spanish imperial connections. This Neapolitan who was beatified 1616-1618 and canonized a century later, possibly the most popular saint of the Counter Reformation and, according to Sallmann, the first to be represented in keeping with the rules of baroque aesthetic, had been written about also in Italy by Giovanni Antonio Cangiano in his *Successi meravigliosi della veneratione del B. Andrea Avellino,* which was published in Naples in 1627.

This saint was a doctor of law before he was ordained a priest in Naples. Very popular in Rome as well as his native city, Sant' Andrea (1521–1608) is traditionally invoked against sudden death and apoplexy, of which he himself died while in prayer. He joined the Theatines in 1556 and founded houses in Piacenza and Milan where he befriended St. Charles Borromeo.[185] Because of his devotion to his particular duties as a Theatine, Sant' Andrea refused a bishopric offered him by Pope Gregory XIV. His major writings were on asceticism and edification. The following is a biographical account of this contemporary Sant' Andrea (Andres).

FR. JUAN DE SAN FELIX, "SAN ANDREA AVELLINO VENERATED IN MEXICO"

Andres Avelino, priest and confessor in the kingdom of Naples, was born in 1520. With no particular direction, life can illustrate the right path. He was treated well in a family that focused totally on the salvation of souls and the apostolic life. His parents, Juan Avelino and Margarita Apela, were genteel and kind although not wealthy. They set a good example by their integrity and good behavior. Their blessing was in the form of their virtuous son. At his baptism, Andres' parents gave him the name of Lancelot, the name of neither a saint nor an ascetic. He later changed his name to Andres. He carried the cross for Christ in the religious battle and was willing to sacrifice himself for the love of the sacred cross. As a baby, while still in his crib, he indicated the name he was to have. He constantly made the sign of the cross. His nursemaid told him: "Armed with this sacred signal you shall declare war against all enemies of Christ." He didn't care much for toys or children's games but instead devoted himself to prayer, his only consolation. He visited churches often and used to mimic the priests. His devotion for the Holy Mother of the Rosary was paramount. He also meditated on the mysteries of Christian doctrine. Everything Andres learned he taught others. He was very obedient towards his parents and showed them great respect. He was everyone's friend.

He was sent to a city near Castronovo to study spiritual exercises, cultivate his soul, and keep him away from bad company. He learned to keep his distance from the wicked and solicited the company of only those who were virtuous and studious. When Avelino was sixteen he started to blossom and possessed a beautiful face and elegant body. His soul had an innocence and from his eyes emanated thankfulness. This sometimes led to problems especially concerning one woman who tried to gain his attention romantically. He was very suspicious of her and chose to imitate a snake hiding in the weeds. He totally ignored her words. The woman, realizing she was getting nowhere, gave up. Avelino told her he was going to do God's will and he would rather blind himself than commit acts that would offend his Divine Majesty.... [Fr. Juan de San Felix, *Compendio de la vida de S. Andres Avelino Confessor, Traducida del Latin....* Trinitario, Calle de la Palma, Mexico: R.P. Fr. Juan de S. Felix, 1767, pp. 4-14. (Trans. V.M.)]

65. GIUSEPPE CAPELCELATRO (1744–1836)

Capelcelatro's famous *Riflessioni sul discorso istorico-politico*, a critique of Pietro Giannone's *History of Naples* [see 7], was published probably in 1788. Presented in the format of an elaborate dialogue between an Italian, Signor Censorini [critic(s)], and a Frenchman, Signor Ramour [love], it broaches topics such as decadence and the power of the clergy under the temporal domains, while including as well a synopsis of the history of the Two Sicilies. This tongue-in-cheek passage focuses upon the question of the clergy and celibacy from a monetary point of view.

GIUSEPPE CAPELCELATRO, "A CRITIQUE OF GIANNONE'S *History of Naples*"

CENSORINI: Here I am to pay my respects. I profit often from your goodness because you have courteously given it to me.

RAMOUR: I was waiting to talk to you about that work you left me [along] with your request for my opinion.

CENSORINI: True. I'm very curious to hear from a man of such merit.

RAMOUR: But it will be better and maybe less boring if you let me know where such an angry dispute originated and what propositions were under attack.

CENSORINI: As you like. The author, although anonymous, was believed....

Chapter 9. Church, Saints, and Ritual

RAMOUR: Slowly. I don't like to talk about authors. I'm persuaded that saints do not reveal themselves on altars until after death. Living authors always make little money. I speak of those who write about human events, legislation, history, and customs because astronomers and naturalists who deal with the sky and earth can not be bothered with man's prejudices. Therefore, they demand respect and applause, if indeed some religious idea has not been offended by the new system, as once happened to Galileo. But current times are more favorable to the study of nature.

CENSORINI: But you asked me about the origin of this dispute.

RAMOUR: That's true. But there's no need to worry yourself because you might possibly be laughed at. Everyone knows that envy, jealousy, ambition and...that's enough, I'm convinced.

CENSORINI: First of all I disliked that persistent rumor regarding the celibacy of priests. This was neither the time nor the place for the author to undertake an alien topic. One might as well pose the question of what a carriage horse has to do with celibacy? Furthermore, it is clear that criticism will undoubtedly arise over whether celibacy is opposed to the morality of Jesus Christ. And finally it is stated (although falsely so) that celibacy has ruined the clergy. In fact this practice has contributed to its revival. The advantage....

RAMOUR: That's enough for now.... Let's see things one by one and not get bogged down by all the material. It seems to me that this first debate can be seen from two aspects: it is clear that the mention of celibacy has been damaging and the manner in which it has been mentioned, false.

CENSORINI: You have gotten to the heart of the matter quickly. I admire that.

RAMOUR: I agreed with the first idea that occurred to me as I was reading. I often reread things that interest me, and when I have to pass judgment on it I usually reread with greater attention. It occurred to me that the author discussed celibacy with a goal very much in line with the intention of the book. He indicates that the principal goal of the celibacy law was the idea of profit, in other words to usurp the legacy of clergyman who died. Certainly, wives and children are not relevant to the matter. Please tell me where one can find literary references to sources of clerical power. Is this research uselessly presented under the subject of profit?

Furthermore, he refers to the apostolic canons that prohibit any usurpation regarding the election of the bishop and inheritance by his family including wives, sons, in-laws, etc. If this law had been observed in the Kingdom of Naples, the apostolic chamber would surely not have confiscated so much treasure through the so-called "collectors of the election." The author did not lose sight of this abuse: rather, he acknowledges it while reflecting that the pope, regarded as the sovereign of all clergymen, was in the habit of accepting the inheritance of the deceased and even the assets that bishops, abbeys and beneficiaries had enjoyed. [Giuseppe Capelcelatro, *Riflessioni sul discorso istorico-politico (Dialogo)*. Filadelfia: s.n., 1788?, pp. 8-12. (Trans. L.N.)]

PART V:
THE
PHYSICAL
WORLD

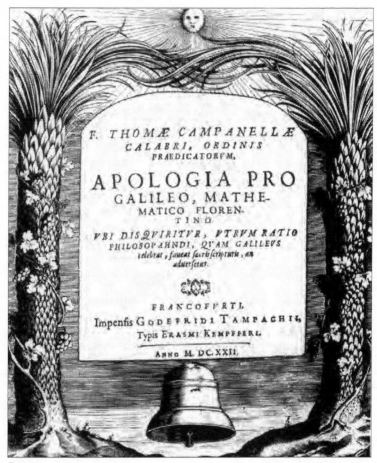

F. THOMÆ CAMPANELLÆ
CALABRI, ORDINIS
PRAEDICATORVM,

APOLOGIA PRO
GALILEO, MATHE-
MATICO FLOREN-
TINO.

VBI DISQVIRITVR, VTRVM RATIO
PHILOSOPAHNDI, QVAM GALILEVS
celebrat, faueat sacris scripturis, an
aduersetur.

FRANCOFVRTI.
Impensis GODEFRIDI TAMPACHII,
Typis ERASMI KEMPFFERI.

ANNO M. DC. XXII.

Figure 59

CHAPTER 10
Scientific Discourse and Discovery

66. GIULIO CESARE "LUCILIO" VANINI (1585–1619)

A passage from the philosophical writings of Vanini has already been presented [see **51**, FIG. **51**]. In his *De admirandis naturae arcanis* he discusses the natural sciences; and this particular excerpt refers to such botanical concerns as the shape of the thorns on roses and the manner in which pears and cucumbers grow. His naive conclusions are derived primarily from personal observation and reasoning. As in the excerpt from Capelcelatro [see **65**], the discussion is presented in the form of a dialogue between an Alexander and Iulio Cesare.

GIULIO CESARE "LUCILIO" VANINI, "ON PLANTS"

Dialogue 27

ALEXANDER: Why does a rose have a thorny stem?

IULIO CESARE: Is this not because there is a certain thinness in the stem through which rises a moist substance that is then hardened by the sun? Because a rose is a fragrant plant, is it not also a dry earthly plant because the fragrance comes out of the earthly thinness? And it produces this dry earthly substance, which is diffused through the entire plant, so that the plant may swiftly dry out and the odor must, therefore, be emitted. It does not seem harmonious with nature that the odor is drawn out into the leaves since they have fallen off quickly. Therefore, it is drawn out through the skin through which the future humor bursts out in the shape of thorns because the odor cannot cut through it without a sharp point.

ALEXANDER: But, good doctor, why are the thorns in the shape of pyramids?

IULIO CESARE: Does not each thorn diminish from base to point because, as the surrounding air compresses it, gradually it increases its parts? This is what happens even in plants themselves as they are thinner at the top. Or can we attribute an even more subtle reason for the pyramid shape? The base is nearer to the nutrients and is also wider; at the same time, the thorn is narrower at the point because it is further from the food. Thus both the form of stems and almost all plants are this way.

ALEXANDER: But in pear trees and cucumbers, it is different. For they grow bigger at their ends.

IULIO CESARE: This happens because of the thinness and slipperiness of the humor. For it cannot hold itself together but flows to where it can more easily go.

ALEXANDER: This garden is decorated with many little flowers. Look at it, I ask you, and ponder how, because the sharpness of garlics and the taste innate in them excites and inflames the emotions. For emotions, which grow weak in the cold, are aroused by heat.

We...can see that roses, which suffer for a long time the heat of the day, lose their reddish color. This is the reason: The native heat, helped by heaven, draws out the color naturally to a certain shade which, without this help, it would not be able to achieve. When this process is completed, the different color, as it absorbs moisture, destroys those thin parts of the plant in which the initial color had its origin....We can also see that wax exposed to the sun loses its color.... Because honey is extracted from wax, even those parts breathe out from whose thinness the color is produced.... [From Luigi Corvaglia. *Le opere di Giulio Cesare Vanini e le loro fonti.* VOL. 2. *De admirandis naturae arcanis.* Milan: Società Anonima Editrice Dante Alighieri, 1933, pp. 151-67. (Trans. J.V.)]

67. TOMMASO CAMPANELLA (1578–1639)

Campanella is perhaps the most versatile of all these Neapolitan writers and was known for his poetry [see 31] as well as his philosophy [see 52]. The following is taken from the latter, his famous *Defense of Galileo,* composed early in 1616 and published in 1622, just ten years before the Italian physicist and astronomer presented his own dialogue on the two chief systems of the world [FIG. 59]. Called before the Roman Inquisition, Galileo was forced to abjure belief in the earth's movement around the sun. Here, using questions from the Bible and early church writers, Campanella attempts to topple the critics' own "certainties."

TOMMASO CAMPANELLA, "A DEFENSE OF GALILEO"

I reply to the second argument by denying that the teachings of Galileo are opposed to all the Scholastics and to the Fathers. For even though his teachings do not agree literally with some of them, still they agree in intention. For the Fathers wished to have the truth presented to them; however they did not speak in philosophical matters as direct witnesses but as men who quoted the opinions of others. Therefore in such matters preference should be given to direct witnesses rather than to the Fathers, just as today Christopher Columbus is preferred over Lactantius, Procopius, Ephrem,[186] and other holy doctors, and as Magellan is preferred over St. Thomas, Anthony, and others.

Moreover in support of this I will prove first, that some theologians have embraced philosophical teachings which are more opposed to Scripture and to the holy doctors than are the teachings of Galileo; second, that many of the Fathers and scholastics agree with Galileo; and third, that Scripture agrees more with Galileo than with his adversaries.

Proof of the first point.

That the heavens, and especially the stars, are not composed of a fifth type[187] of matter, but of the four elements or perhaps only of fire, was once taught by all philosophers and by Saints Augustine, Ambrose, Basil, Justin, Cyril, Chrysostom, Theodoret,[188] Bernard in his sermon *"Mulier amicta sole,"*[189] and by the Master of the Sentences.[190] In Book IV of his *Hexameron*[191] Ambrose proves this from Scripture, where it is said, "The heavens will perish and all will wear out like a garment" [Ps. 101:26-27; Heb. 1:10-11]. Philoponus[192] says the same thing when he explains the books of Aristotle's *De caelo* against Aristotle and in favor of the Christians.

Nevertheless, without being condemned, as they say, by the Scriptures, many scholastics say that the heavens are composed of a fifth type of matter. But Ambrose has attacked this in innumerable places as an imaginary and diabolical invention, as have Justin and Basil also. And when St. Thomas discusses Aristotle in Part I[193] where he explains the text of Moses concerning the work of the six days of creation, he first outlines both views, i.e., the opinion of the philosophers and the Fathers and the opinion of Aristotle. But then in Questions 65, 66, 67, 70, and 71, he consistently teaches that the former agrees better with the text of Scripture, while Aristotle's view is in disagreement, which only a fool would not notice.

Moreover the Scripture of God testifies that the sun in itself is most hot and most luminous. For Genesis I [1:16] speaks of "the greater light"; and the sun's heat is mentioned in Psalm 18 [18:7], in Wisdom 2 [2:3], in Ecclesiasticus 43 [43:2-4], and many other places; and Wisdom 17 [17:5] speaks of the illumination of fire and of "the brilliant flame of the stars." That is the way things are, and that to think otherwise is heresy, is taught by Ambrose in Book IV of his *Hexameron*, and Basil agrees, as also do Augustine, Chrysostom, Justin, Bernard, Origen, Philoponus, and all the Fathers I have ever read. In the Church's Ambrosian hymn we sing, *"Iam sol rededit igneus."*[194]

Nevertheless, other Scholastics think that the sun in itself is not hot, without being marked as heretics, and the Church does not prohibit this opinion. Even Aristotle himself, the author of this theory, says that there is no light in the sun, as is clear in *De caelo*,[195] II,7, where he teaches that light and heat are produced by the friction of the air, which both Simplicius and Alexander agree is Aristotle's view. In his *De substantiae orbium coelestium* Averroes states that Aristotle denied that there is any light or heat in the sun. More recent authors, who do not accept Aristotle's teaching, have restored light to the sun. But indeed if light should be attributed to the sun so that Scripture would not be contradicted, then so also should heat be attributed to the sun. However Aristotle denied that there is light in the sun, for otherwise it would be composed of fire.

Nevertheless many modern writers disagree with Aristotle and the literal meaning of Scripture, and they are not condemned. Should Galileo then, who proves his teachings from sense evidence, be prohibited from observing the book of God? I will omit discussion of other views that long ago were held to be part of the faith but which are now known by common experience to be false; for example, that the antipodes do not exist; that the land near the equator is uninhabitable; and that heaven or hell is located in the other hemisphere or in the islands of the blest. I will pass over the fact that Procopius, Eusebius,[196] and others maintained from Scripture that the earth floats on water, while others who held the contrary were not condemned, and now experience has shown that the former were wrong. These facts are in Galileo's favor.

Proof of the second point

To begin with, the question of whether or not the earth is in the center of the world is in no way a dogma of the faith, as St. Thomas was quoted in our fourth assertion, and as was stated by the Fathers and later by the Scholastics. For in the first place Lactantius in book III, chapter 23, Procopius, Diodorus bishop of Tarsus,[197] Eusebius bishop of Emissa, Justin his *Questiones ad orthodoxos*, and others have taught that the earth is not in the center of the world and that the heavens are not spherical. Chrysostom held the same view in his homilies 6 and 9 on Genesis; and in his homily 31 on the Letter to the Romans he says that humans do not know where hell is, which Augustine also taught in *De civitate dei*, XXII, 16, and Peter Lombard[198] in *Sententiae*, IV, 44, and St. Thomas in *Opusculum* 11, Article 25.[199]

The fact that hell is located in the center or in some other part of the earth can be deduced from the word *"inferno"* [hell] and from what the Apostle says in Ephesians 4 [4:9], "Christ descended to the lower regions of the earth." Hence hell is there, unless we assume that there are other earths. And David, speaking of Christ descending to the lower regions, says, "You will not abandon my soul in hell" [Ps. 15:10], as the Apostle Peter explains in Acts 2 [2:27]. Therefore we do not know whether the earth is in the center of the world.

If someone were to hold that the infernal darkness, which Christ called "exterior,"[200] is located outside this world, as Origen[201] conjectured in his commentary on Matthew and as Chrysostom thought in his commentary on the Letter to the Romans, then there are other worlds outside of our world. The censors condemned this idea in Galileo because they had not carefully examined the Scriptures and the books of the holy Fathers. But what is beyond controversy is that in his homily 7 on the First Letter to the Thessalonians, Chrysostom[202] says that we can know that the earth is cold, dry, and dark, but nothing more, and especially its location and situation in the world, etc. Therefore Scripture does not teach us what is at the center rather than at the circumference.

Furthermore Chrysostom teaches that we do not know whether the earth is in motion or at rest, for he limits what we can know about it to the three conditions mentioned above, i.e., coldness, dryness, and darkness. Agreeing with Chrysostom are Theophylactus,[203] Lactantius, Augustine, Procopius, Diodorus, Eusebius, and others;

and Justin maintains that the earth is not in the center. Therefore I do not understand why our theologians today, without any prior mathematical proofs or experience or revelation, think that they know for certain that the earth lies motionless in the center of the world, and that to think otherwise contradicts the Fathers and the Scholastics, whom they have not read.... [Tommaso Campanella, *Defense of Galileo the Mathematician from Florence*, trans. and intro. by Richard J. Blackwell. Notre Dame and London: University of Notre Dame Press, 1994, pp. 86-89.]

68. TOMMASO CORNELIO (1614–1684)

Cornelio was a mathematician, physicist, and physiologist. After traveling through Italy and staying in Florence and Rome he returned to Naples in 1649, bringing with him works of both Italian and foreign naturalists, including those of France and England. Cornelio was impressed by the philosophy of Descartes, Gassendi, and Hobbes. In 1651 he and others were, upon the advice of Francesco D'Andrea [49], awarded a chair in mathematics at the university. These other chairs included Di Capua's in medicine [69], Aulisio's [63] in law, and Messere's in Greek. Cornelio is representative of the scientific and philosophic revolution that occurred during the second half of the Seicento. All this rendered possible the scientific foundation of Aristotle and Galileo. Here he comments on the digestive system of the dove.

TOMMASO CORNELIO, "DIGESTION"

Meanwhile, at this point, we should admire the ability doves have to nourish their young during their first few days of "milk." Certainly, if the gullet of a dove-chick, newly born into the world, should be extended, at once a mass of many shiny-white little bodies pasted together rushes out, a mass which — having curdled in the bellies of the young — displays not only a dazzling white color, but also an odor and a taste very much like milk. This substance is placed into the gullet of the chick who, by it, becomes larger in time and gets bigger doses, just as if it had a child in its womb. Indeed, there is not doubt that doves have this in common with all birds who feed their young by storing food in their gullets.

At birth, the stronger ones are sustained with food and drink. The food is broken down by the teeth and saliva out of their own ducts, especially out of the tonsils and tongue, small glands that emit moisture into the beak regularly; and, thus the food is made damp and, then, is worked over by the frequent agitation of the tongue itself, which often rolls it down into a softer mass. At last, when it has been prepared like this, the food is forced out of the gullet into the stomach.

Now the stomach is the storage bin for food and drink. Its great strength, in fact, is in collecting and changing everything it receives, whether these foods are dry or moist so that, after they are collected and digested, they are dispensed into the entire body. All digestion is accomplished by the force of heat; food is digested by body heat, and it is softened by a moist fluid and is boiled down to liquid form, according to Hippocrates and Aristotle, whom the Medici followed confusedly....

When chemists observe that rocks, metals, and other hard substances that have been immersed in certain liquids dissolve and diminish, they determined that food is digested in the stomach by the very same process.... [Thomae Cornelii Consentini, *Progymnasmata Physica*, ed. Lionardo Di Capua. Venice: Bartholomaei, 1683, pp. 76-80. (Trans. J.V.)]

69. LIONARDO DI CAPUA (1617–1695)

Di Capua was a physician who, along with Tommaso Cornelio [68], helped to found the Academy of Investigators in Naples. It survived into the middle of the eighteenth century and exercised considerable influence upon Vico [54], many ideas of whom would not have evolved without this academy. This "translation" of Di Capua was published in London in 1684 and was "made English" by F.L. Gent. Here Di Capua analyzes the art of doctoring in his day and concludes that it has "greatly advanced." The passage is, above all, a defense of the profession.

LIONARDO DI CAPUA, "THE PRACTICE OF MEDICINE"

But let not any one therefore believe, that the Physicians gained such a liberty by transgressing their Rules; for it proceeded rather from the utmost necessity of the publick, and is, as it were an effect of the Art of good Government: for I am verily perswaded, that even the memory of the Mystery of the Medicine would have been utterly extinguished, if Physicians had been proceeded against according to the rigor of Justice. And what man indeed, unless he were exceeding dull and stupid, or extreamly rash, would ever have vainly spent his Time and Endeavours in the pursuit of an Art (if Medicine, which has not any certain and fixed Rule in its operations, may possibly be so called) in it self displeasing, and hard to be obtained, and in its Events very dubious: say displeasing, for what can be more offensive and disgustful, than continually to converse with sick persons and daily to see and hear the Miseries of others, and that many times without being any ways able to remedy them. It is also difficult to undertake, and always uncertain in its success; because in the curing of the Sick, not only the skill of the Physician, but also Fortune and Chance claim their share: from whence arose this common Proverb: "A Physician had need be born under a fortunate Constellation."

And O how exceeding often does it happen, that contrary to all human expectation, as Celsus[204] writes: Expectation is likewise frustrated, and that man dies, of whom the Physician was secure before. And Hippocrates himself, although esteemed a most profound and skilful Physician, yet confesses, That he gained more Reproach than commendations by his Profession. And therefore it is exceeding difficult, or rather impossible always to judge, whether the unhappy success of distempers proceeds from…the Physicians, or from the Nature of the disease, or from some other internal Cause, into which no humane Wisdom or Knowledge can penetrate…. Besides that in the Bodies of Animals are wont to be ingendred poisons, and that oftentimes presently, by sudden precipitation and Coagulation; and the man, whom not only others, but even Apollo and Aesculapius themselves would have judged most sound and healthful, may have within him Imposthumes,[205] and other secret distempers, which, when he least thinks of it, may be able to cause his death, and that at the very Instant when the Medicins are prepared: wrongfully therefore are the Remedies blamed, and not the evil quality of the distemper. And besides this, some good Medicines which are esteemed good and conducint to the Health of man, may oftentimes occasion such disturbance within the Patients body, as may bring on his death, before we with our shallow understandings can prevent it, as Celsus testifies. It will not therefore be the Physicians fault, if sometimes his Patient grows worse by his Remedies; nor can Laws ever determine any thing herein. But come, let us grant, that a method of Curing may by Law be prescribed to Physicians, how can they be punished for transgressing it? or how can the Crime be so clearly manifested, that they may be proceeded against in form of Law?

CHAPTER 10. SCIENTIFIC DISCOURSE AND DISCOVERY

The Art of Medicine is at this day so greatly increased and advanced, that it seems to strive for Superiority with the most illustrious and most noble Studies, its Jurisdiction to penetrate even into the most remote and extreme Confines of Nature;... It appears, that Hercules, from whom the Herculean Panacea took its Name, cured only with Plants; as also did Isis...and Apollo...and Bacchus, by whose means, as Plutarch tells us, that most powerful and pleasant Medicine, Wine, was first found out, and brought into esteem; and the great vertue of Ivy of marvellous efficacy in repairing the Evils caused by the too excessive use of Wine, was made known to the World; Bacchus, saith he, was accounted an Excellent Physician, not only because he found out the use of Wine, a most pleasing sort of Physick, but for that he also taught the use of Ivy, and caus'd his Followers, in the midst of their Cups, to crown their Temples with it, as being that which by its coolness repels the Vapors from the head. Herbs alone were likewise made use of by Aesculapius, the Inventor of the Asclepian Panacea.... [Lionardo Di Capua, *The Uncertainty of the Art of Physick, Written in It. by the Famous Lionardo di Capoa, and made English by F.L. Gent.* London: Fr. Clark, for Thomas Malthus, 1684, pp. 1-15.]

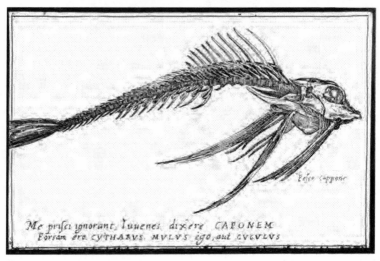

Figure 60

NOTES

CHAPTER 1

1. Pliny the Younger's letters. In a few he gives a vivid and dramatic account of this major eruption of 79 C.E., in which his father was killed. See note 34.

2. Roman miles.

3. Strabo of Amasya in Pontus (b. 63 B.C.E.). A Greek geographer and historian, he saw little of Italy. His major literary contribution was *Geography*. Dione refers to Dionysius of Halicarnassus (fl. c.20 B.C.E.), who was a Greek historian and teacher of rhetoric. He came to Rome to study Latin and wrote the twenty-volume *Roman Antiquities*.

4. Torre del Greco, Annuziata, Resina, and Portici, all extant, are towns to the southeast on the coast near Herculaneum.

5. "The Gennaro" probably refers to the region around the "duomo," the cathedral of Naples, dedicated to San Gennaro, in the central part of the city. San Gennaro is associated as well with the dangerous eastern extremity of Naples toward Vesuvius near Portici. At the Bridge of the Magdalene (Ponte Maddalena) the head of the saint was sometimes brought in order to miraculously subdue the fury of Vesuvius. See Sir William Hamilton, *Campi phlegraei* (Naples: P. Fabris, 1776).

6. Roman Emperor, Titus, ruled during the first century C.E.. Theodoric was king of the Ostrogoths, c.454–526 C.E.

7. The ancient name for the city, founded in the seventh century B.C.E., was a derivation of *Parthenope*, the siren who loved Odysseus and drowned herself at his rejection. Some time around 474 B.C.E. a new city, *Neapolis* in Greek, was founded next to the site of Parthenope.

8. Toppi [reading 17] also refers to a person being clothed in purple, which is traditionally a royal or imperial color. Toppi's reference, however, is to a "holy purple," which indicates a cardinal of the Church.

9. Charles of Anjou (1266–1285), first Angevin king, who made Naples his capital.

He built the Castel Nuovo. In 1282, with the Sicilian Vespers, he lost Sicily to the Aragonese.

10. Henry of Lorraine, fifth duke of Guise and archbishop of Reims, died in 1664. As a result of his unsuccessful attempts to conquer Naples, he was imprisoned in Spain from 1648 to 1652.

11. The viceroy at that time was Rodrigo Ponce de Leon, duke of los Arcos, who ruled from 1646 to 1648.

12. Posillipo, in the western part of Naples, offers an impressive view of the bay and is, to this day, a fashionable section of the city.

13. *Doppie, zecchini* and *scudi* are currencies. A *doppia* is approximately equivalent to a ducat, and one equals two *scudi*.

14. San Gennaro is the major patron saint of Naples. See note 5.

15. Cardinal Ascanio Filomarino (1583–1666) was archbishop of Naples. An excellent man, much esteemed by the people, he brought about reconciliation between anti-Spanish and anti-noble rebels and the viceroy of the kingdom. In addition, he was a patron of the arts, in particular the baroque painter, Massimo Stanzione. There is a portrait of him in the Corsini Collection, Florence; and his family chapel is in the church of SS. Apostoli, Naples.

16. Alexander VII (b. 1599 and pope from 1655 to 1667) was bishop at Nardo (Puglia) and inquisitor at Malta. Perhaps best known for his contribution toward the Peace of Westphalia in 1648, the conversion of Queen Christina of Sweden, and the beatification of St. Francis de Sales.

17. The viceroy, Fernando Joaquin Fajardo, marquise of los Velez (1675–1683).

18. Valtellina, Chiavenna, Tirano, and Coiro are representative of his military victories in northern Italy.

19. *Cocogna* (or *cuccagna*) is derived from Cockaigne (or Cockayne), the land of pleasure and plenty, an imaginary medieval utopia in which rivers were of wine, houses of cake, etc. The first references are from the thirteenth century in the French *Fabliau Cocaigne* and the English poem, "The Land of Cockaygne."

20. Vicaria (Sede dei Tribunali or Seat of the Tribunals). The Castel Capuano was commonly known as "La Vicaria" because in 1540 Don Pedro de Toledo transferred all the different courts of justice to this palace, where they are still located. Originally, a prison existed beneath it.

21. The eighteenth-century Giuseppe Maria Galanti is famous for his *Descrizione delle due Sicilie*. Using statistics, he insists upon the importance of the provinces in the kingdom of Naples, which he believes were neglected at the expense of the city.

NOTES

CHAPTER 2

22. Translated here as "legendary king," *re baie* probably refers to the town of Baiae (Latin) or Baia (Italian) on the coast of Campania at the Campi Flegrei (burning fields). The location is known for its warm baths, many named after classical gods.

23. "Larue" may refer to *lar, laris* m. (Latin s.) or *lares* (Latin pl.), tutelar household gods.

24. *Bene de me scripsisti, Thoma.* "Thomas, you have written well of me." The full exchange continues with Christ: "What reward do you ask? Thomas: "No reward, Lord, but yourself only." See note 163 and Fynes Moryson [57].

25. "Padri Olivetani" refers to those of Monte Oliveto in Naples. See note 165.

26. "The learned Alexand. ab. Alexandro" refers to Alessandro d'Alessandro (c.1461–1523) who wrote *Dies geniales* in 1522.

27. *Onacratulus* is the pelican.

28. *Manucodiata* is the bird of paradise.

29. Federico Pesche, late seventeenth-century engraver who worked in Italy.

30. *Seggio di Nido*, literally "nest seat," refers to one of several conventions of nobles in the city of Naples. The other *seggi* included the Capuana, Montagna, Porto, and Portanova, all of whom sent representatives to the city council. (Although no *seggio* was representative of the poor, there was one that was associated with the wealthy upper-middle class.) The centrally located *Seggio di Nido* was to the east of the central Via Toledo and not far from Naples' gothic cathedral dedicated to San Gennaro. The *seggi* were disbanded in 1800. Pietro Giannone gives an account of the *seggi* in his *History of Naples*. For member families, see Enrico Bacco, *Naples: An Early Guide*, ed. and trans. Eileen Gardiner. (New York: Italica Press, 1991), pp. 132-36.

31. Holy purple. See Mazzella [4] and note 8.

32. King Conradin, Conrad the Younger, (1252–1268), duke of Swabia, born in Bavaria and beheaded during the Angevin conquest, is representative of the romantic hero, "lamented by maidens and poets." His execution represents the end of the Hohenstaufen dynasty. Still remembered in the nineteenth century, he was immortalized by Thorwaldsen who executed a marble statue of him, which stands to this day in the church of the Carmine.

33. The French writer and publisher Antonio Bulifon (late seventeenth century), who settled in Naples in 1670, was known primarily for his *Lettere*. His shop was sacked in 1707 after the arrival of the troops of Charles VI.

34. This quotation is actually from Pliny's *Natural History*, II.95 rather than III.99 as quoted by Sarnelli: "— the places called breathing holes, or by other people jaws of hell —ditches that exhale a deadly breath...." Pliny I and II wrote about the volcanic region around Naples. Pliny the Elder (23/4–79 C.E.) was killed by the most famous eruption of Vesuvius. Book III of the 37 volumes of his *Natural History* deals with geography and ethnography and includes the region around Naples. Pliny the Younger (61/2–c.113 C.E.) is famous for his *Letters*. A few of these, including a famous one to Tacitus, describes his father's demise from the eruption of Vesuvius in 79 C.E. See Braccini [2].

35. Small-caliber long guns operated by a matchlock and in use from around 1400 C.E.

CHAPTER 3

36. Giovanni Battista Caracciolo ("Battistello," 1570–1637). Jusepe de Ribera (1591–1652) was born in Jativa, Spain, but settled in Naples probably some time between 1610 and 1615. Massimo Stanzione (1585–1656) probably died in the plague.

37. Marie de' Medici (1573–1642), queen consort and regent of France, married to Henri IV of France, mother of Louis XIII.

38. Michelangelo Merisi da Caravaggio (1573–1610) from Lombardy, active primarily in Rome, also Naples, Malta, and Sicily; Annibale Carracci (1560–1609) part of the famous Bolognese family, including brother Agostino and cousin Ludovico.

39. See Gerald Ackerman, "Gian Battista Marino's Contribution to Seicento Art Theory," *The Art Bulletin* 42 (1961): 326–36.

40. The Holy Shroud of the house of Savoy in Turin and still located in that city. Although Marino considered it to be a painting, the shroud is, at present, being tested for its authenticity as the burial shroud of Christ. Few today believe it could be any sort of painting.

41. Mathematical perspective came into use during the early fifteenth century and is usually attributed to the Florentine theoretician-architect, Filippo Brunelleschi. When perspective is applied to a single object, it is referred to as foreshortening.

42. Caravaggio's *Medusa* of c.1597 is still extant in the Uffizi Gallery, Florence. The gorgon's head traditionally was displayed on the shield of Perseus and, in this case, is symbolic of the invincible power of the Medici duke.

43. The painter "Domenichino" is Domenico Zampieri of Bologna (1581–1641).

44. The sculptor Alessandro da Bologna Algardi (1595–1654).

45. The painter-architect Pietro Berrettini, known as Pietro da Cortona (1596–1669).

196

46. The Roman church of San Giovanni Decollato (the beheaded St. John the Baptist) is located near Santa Maria della Consolazione and Santa Maria in Cosmedin and not far from the ancient Theater of Marcellus. Salvator Rosa was in Rome from c.1635 through the late 1630s.

47. Most of these references are to sixteenth-century Venetian and seventeenth-century Bolognese painters. Passeri was sympathetic to the classical traditions of Bolognese painting and implies that association with these artists is with the best.

48. Zoilus (4th century B.C.E.) was a Cynic philosopher known for his bitter literary criticism of Plato, Homer, and others.

49. Gian Lorenzo Bernini (1598–1680) was the greatest sculptor and architect of the seventeenth century. Most of his work, including the baldacchino and colonnade of St. Peter's, churches, and fountains, is located in Rome.

50. Rosa's letter to Ricciardi is published by Limentani in *Poesie e lettere inedite di Salvator Rosa* (Florence: L.S. Olschki, 1950), pp. 110-12.

51. Giorgio Vasari (1511–1574) Florentine biographer, painter, and architect, his major contribution is his *Lives of the Artists*.

52. Filippo Baldinucci (1625–1696) historian, connoisseur, art counsellor, and philosopher. His biography was written by his son, Francesco Saverio. Baldinucci's major literary contribution was *La Veglia* (Lucca: Iacinto Paci, 1684, republished in Florence in 1765, and subsequently).

53. Nicola Vanni was an engraver who worked in Rome from c.1750 to 1770.

54. See also note 4.

55. Carlo Nolli, Nicola d'Orazi, and Roccus Pozzi were all eighteenth-century engravers. Only d'Orazi is fairly well known for having collaborated during the middle of the century with his brother Carlo on these prints illustrating the antiquities of Herculaneum.

56. Tifata is the Mons Tifata, once the site of a temple of Jupiter.

57. Capua is a town east and north of Naples on the Volturno River. The ancient city, which figured prominently in Hannibal's struggle against Rome, was destroyed in 456 C.E. The new city was founded in 856.

58. Consul Spurius Postumius (Albinus), 2nd century B.C.E., built the Via Postumia in northern Italy, linking Genoa, Cremona, and Mantua.

59. The Caudine Valley, or Caudine Forks described by Livy, is between Sant'Agata and Moiano and between Naples and Foggia.

60. "Samnites" is a Roman name for warlike tribes in the mountainous center of southern Italy. Tradition holds that they are an offshoot of the Sabines. Their language was Oscan. The first Samnite War (between the Romans and Samnites over the rule of the southern Italian region of Campania) was declared in 343 B.C.E. and ended in 341. The second was from 342 to 327 B.C.E. The third and final Samnite War ended in 290 B.C.E.

61. Charles de Bourbon (1734–59) was generally known as Charles III after his title as king of Spain. His queen was Maria Amalia. See FIG. 33.

CHAPTER 4

62. There is word-play here on the word for "radish" and the similar words for "open this!"

63. Alcides is Herakles.

64. Alpheus, the major river of the Peloponnesus, Greece, is in Greek mythology associated with a river god who was the lover of Arethusa.

65. In Greek mythology Arethusa was a nymph who loved Alpheus. Her name was given to a spring in Elis and to another on the island of Ortygia near Syracuse.

66. Greek mythology's Proteus was the old man of the sea, the shepherd of the sea's flocks, who had the ability to prophesy but was reluctant to do so.

67. The Pindus Mountains are between Thessaly and Epirus. Hippocrene, referred to as "the fountain of the horse," is associated with a spring on Mt. Helicon (Boetia) sacred to Apollo and the nine muses.

68. Ennius (Quintus) (239–169 B.C.E.), the "father of Roman poetry," was the greatest of the early Latin poets. In addition, he wrote tragedies. His greatest literary contribution was a narrative poem concerning the story of Rome, the *Annales*.

69. Gaius Valerius Catullus (84?–54 B.C.E.) usually considered to have been the greatest lyric poet of Rome.

70. *Sampogna* is a collection of Marino's poems also from 1620.

71. The town of Melito is to the south of Naples toward Reggio and near Cantanzaro.

72. Chiaia(no) is near the sulphurous Campi Flegrei (burning fields) to the west of the city.

73. Today a park, Astroni refers to a volcanic crater west of Naples near the Lago d'Agnano and the Cave of the Dog.

74. Along with the Academy of the Ardenti (fervent), the Oziosi (idlers) Academy was one of the two "academies of the wits." Its emblem bears the inscription NON PIGRA VIES. See F. De' Pietri, *I problemi accademici*. (Naples: F. Savio for G.D. Montanaro, 1642).

75. Rosa's "The Witch" was published by Limentani. See note 50.

76. This quotation is taken from a well-known Neapolitan nursery rhyme.

77. The word *ceccarella* still refers to the vagina.

78. The academy known as Arcadi(a) was a naturalist society. Another of its members was the late baroque painter Francesco Solimena (1657–1747).

CHAPTER 5

79. For the academies see notes 74 and 78.

80. Julius Pollux, Greek grammarian, second century C.E.. Wrote *Onamasticon*.

81. Purple color. See notes 8 and 31.

82. Tiresias, Philostetes, and Telephus were characters in the plays of Aeschylus, Euripides, and Sophocles.

83. *Hypotyposis* or *prosopopoeia* is "word painting," i.e., "personification."

84. Cesare Ripa, *Iconologia*, or *Vero descrittione dell'imagini universali cavate dell'antichità et da altri luoghi* (Rome: Heredi di Giovanni Gigliotti, 1593); Giovan Pietro Valeriani, *Hieroglyphica, sive, De sacris Aegyptorum litteris commentarii* (Basel: Michael Isengrin, 1556).

85. Deuteronomy 22:5.

86. Salomon Gesner, *Orattio de personis sive larvis* (Hamburg: Gundermann, 1636).

87. *El arte nuevo de hacer comedias* (Madrid: Alfonso Martin, 1613), pp. 281-82.

88. *De jure naturae et gentium* (Frankfurt: Knock, 1694), 6.1:30.

89. The most famous Seneca is Lucius Annaeus (4 B.C.E.–65 C.E.), who was born in Cordova, Spain, and studied in Rome. He was known as a rhetorician and a philosopher. Valerius Maximus, fl. c.20 C.E., Latin author of historical anecdotes. St. Cyprian, d. 258 C.E., bishop of Carthage and martyr, orator and teacher of rhetoric.

90. Magnes the Athenian, fifth century B.C.E., writer of comedy.

91. Suidas was a tenth-century Greek lexicographer.

92. Giovambattista Giraldi Cintio, *Discorsi intorno al comporre de i romanzi delle comedie, e delle tragedie* (Venice: Giolito De Ferrari, 1554).

93. *De Humana physiognomonia* (Naples: Longo, 1599), 1:14, 15.

94. Joseph Nicolas Delisle (1688–1768), French astronomer who proposed the diffraction theory of the sun's corona.

95. Giovanni Antonio Medrano da Sciacca (Agrigento) (1703–?). During the latter part of the century he worked on minor additions to the Palazzo Reale in Naples.

96. Angelo Carasale da Napoli (fl. 1740). Famous almost exclusively for the building of the Teatro San Carlo.

97. Most of these eighteenth-century composers studied music in Naples. Their achievement is first and foremost in opera and occasionally, and secondarily, in instrumental performance. Niccolo Piccinni (1728–1800), born in Bari, studied in Naples, became associated with the *opere buffe* and, in all, composed about fifty operas. Antonio Sacchini (1730–1786), born in Florence, died in Paris, studied and taught music in Naples. Francesco di Maio (Gian Francesco di Maio 1732–1770), organist at the Neapolitan court. Tommaso Traetta (1727–1779), studied in Naples with Popora and Durante, was Catherine the Great's opera director. Pietro Alexandro Guglielmi (1728–1804), conductor and composer of about 100 operas. Pasquale Caffaro (or Cafaro 1716?–1787), employed at the Royal Chapel, was a specialist in singing and harpsichord. Giovanni Battista Ferradini (1710–1791), composer of operas and oboist at the Munich court. Nicolo Jomelli (1714–1774), composed operas for the major Italian houses.

98. Apostolo Zeno (1668–1750). Born in Venice, he was an Italian librettist and literary scholar, historian, editor, and critic. Composer of *Lucio Vero, Griselda, Aminta,* etc. Replaced by Metastasio at the Viennese court.

99. "La Gabrielli" (Caterina Gabrielli, 1730–1796), the most famous soprano in eighteenth-century Naples, was much in demand and had an international reputation.

CHAPTER 6

100. Sir Walter Raleigh (1552–1618), explorer and soldier, wrote his collected works, including his *History of the World*, later published in eight volumes. Thomas Mun (1571–1641) in his *Discourses* presented the first clear statement on the balance of trade. Sir Josiah Child (1630–1699), English merchant and economist, wrote *Brief Observations Concerning Trade and the Interest of Money* in 1668, *A New Discourse of Trade* in 1668–90. Sir William Temple (1628–1699) was a statesman, diplomat, and writer.

101. The Levant refers to the Mediterranean coastlands of Asia Minor and Syria and sometimes includes the coastline from Greece to Egypt.

102. The government's financial difficulties forced it to sell the right to collect revenue at prices so low that the tax farmers' return on investments was very

high. See Brendan Dooley, *Italy in the Baroque: Selected Readings* (New York and London: Garland Publishers, 1995), p. 172; and Domenico Sella, *Italy in the Seventeenth Century* (New York and London: Longman, 1997), pp. 94-95.

103. The Signoria was the ruling body in Venice and was comprised of the doge, six ducal councillors, and three heads of the Council of Forty. See Frederic C. Lane, *Venice: A Maritime Republic* (Baltimore and London: Johns Hopkins University Press, 1977), pp. 399-405 et passim.

104. The merchant Marcantonio De Santis wrote the then much-acclaimed *Discorso intorno alli effetti che fa il cambio in Regno* (Naples: Constantino Vitale, 1605).

105. Complex poison antidotes.

106. Chemicals.

107. Although Rome and Venice published more than Naples during this period, this statement is a great exaggeration. Not only was the Regia Stamperia affiliated with Naples, but so was the French publisher Bulifon, Constantino Vitale, Antonio di Fusco, Pietro Palombo, F. Riccardo, Lodovico Canallo, and others.

108. For arquebuses, see note 35. Morions are open helmets of the sixteenth and early seventeenth centuries. Typically, they have a flat or turned-down brim and a crest from front to back. Corselets refer to suits of light armor (often three-quarter length) from the sixteenth century and later.

109. Royal Council.

110. For *scudo*, see note 13.

111. King Carlo I of Spain (1500–1558), king of Spain from 1516. As Charles V Hapsburg, he was Holy Roman Emperor from 1519 to 1556 and the last to be crowned by the pope.

112. Pentateuch refers to the first five books of the Old Testament (i.e., the Torah). "Homeric Poems" is a term commonly used to indicate the whole cycle of early Greek epics, including the *Odyssey* and the *Iliad*.

113. Homer mentions King Alcinous, grandson of Poseidon and king of the Phaeacians on the island of Scheria. He is associated with Odysseus (Ulysses) as well as argonautic legend.

114. Christ.

115. Matthew 17:24-27.

116. Servius Tullius (578–534 B.C.E.), sixth legendary king of Rome.

117. Titus Livius (59 B.C.E.–17 C.E.), the most celebrated Roman historian.

118. Currency. The carlin was an ancient Neapolitan coin, rated at one-tenth of a ducat, worth about 4d.

119. Arts here implies crafts, the work of artisans formerly associated with the guild system.

CHAPTER 7

120. Benedetto Croce, *History of the Kingdom of Naples,* ed. H. Stuart Hughes, trans. Frances Frenaye (Chicago and London: University of Chicago Press, 1970), p. 137.

121. Lanciano is near Termoli, between Ancona and Foggia. See Karl Baedeker, *Handbook for Travellers: Southern Italy and Sicily* (Leipzig: Baedeker, 1900), 3:194.

122. Toledo, in central Spain, was the capital until 1560 when Philip II moved it to Madrid.

123. Probably a reference to Toppi, who composed an index of prominent citizens and professions of Naples [**17**]. There were several such indexes, including that of Campanile [**16**].

124. Although three Spanish viceroys of Naples bore the name Ribera, because of the chronology it is likely that this one was the last, Juan Alfonso Enriquez de Ribera, Almirante de Castilla (1644–1646).

125. For the Vicaria, see note 20.

126. Croce, *History*, p. 137, mentions an S. Rovito who collaborated with Carlo Tappia on a general code and body of laws on taxation.

127. "Collaterale" refers to the Council in the *principio composti* of several ministers. See Pietro Giannone, *Dell'Istoria civile del Regno di Napoli* (Naples: Niccolo Naso, 1723), 3:546-59.

128. Villamaina is an estate, not a town.

129. Charles II of Spain (1665–1700), last of the Neapolitan Hapsburg monarchs.

130. The *Index Librorum Prohibitorum (Index of Prohibited Books)* of the Roman Catholic Church.

131. Cava dei Tirreni is near Passiano north of Salerno.

CHAPTER 8

132. Pietro Pomponazzi (1462–1525), Italian philosopher who represented Renaissance Aristotelianism. Wrote on the immortality of the soul, predestination, and free will. Geronimo (or Girolamo) Cardano (1501–1576), Italian physician, mathematician,

and astrologer from Pavia, wrote books on scientific and philosophical subjects. Joseph Justus Scaligero (Scaliger) (1540–1609), renowned scholar of the classics and science, was the son of J.C. Scaliger of scientific and literary fame.

133. Tolosa is near Bilbao in northeastern Spain.

134. Anicius Manlius Severinus Boethius (480–524 C.E.), Roman scholar, philosopher, theologian, and statesman.

135. The Spinola family, known for its ancient origins, wealth, and power, were rivals of the Doria family in Genoa. Its most famous member was Ambrose Spinola, a general for the Spanish army who died in 1630.

136. Aristotle's treatises on logic include his *Prior* and *Posterior Analytics*.

137. Bernardino Telesio (1508–1588), philosopher and man of letters.

138. Giovanni Pico della Mirandola (1463–1494), famous Italian philosopher and scholar who, second only to Marsilio Ficino, represented Renaissance Platonism.

139. Hoh is the elected chief priest of Campanella's utopia. Others priests include Pon, Sin, and Mor.

140. Aristarchus of Samos (fl. 270 B.C.E.), Greek astronomer, first to claim that the earth revolves around the sun. Philolaus (2nd half of the 5th century B.C.E.), Greek philosopher of the Pythagorean school. Interested also in astronomy.

141. Reference to *cielo* (the sky and space) could imply heavenly spheres of the Aristotelian universe as well as the Christian paradise.

142. Those who disagree with Campanella.

143. *Philosophia Realis* (Frankfurt: Tampach, 1623).

144. The action of the sun causes darkness.

145. Saltpeter was used in artificial refrigeration.

146. Random killings are as hard to understand as are God's ways.

147. *Metaphysics* (Paris: Denis Langlois, 1638).

148. See reading 10 by Filamondo. Marshal Antonio Carafa is included under "Capitani" in Raffaelle Maria Filamondo, *Il genio bellicoso di Napoli*, p. 54. Also included are Francesco Maria, Emmanuele, and Geronimo Carafa.

149. A probable reference to Plato's *Paramenides* as filtered through Neoplatonic thought.

150. Exodus 3:13-14.

151. Vico's two senses: "to lessen" and "to chop into smaller bits." See p. 49 n. 7 of the cited source edition of this text.

152. A classificatory scheme, based upon genus and species, first used by Plato. See source text, p. 150 n. 8.

153. Count of Santo Stefano (Conde de San Esteban), Fernando de Benavides (1687–1695).

154. Bartolomeo Intieri (1676–1757), born in Florence, died in Naples. Mathematician concerned with practical means of agriculture. Intieri established the first chair of economic science and commerce in Naples. This was awarded first to Genovesi.

155. This is part of a verse from Casa's sonnet, "La bella greca onde il pastore ideo."

156. For Origen, see William King, author of *De origine mali* (Dublin: Andrew Crook, 1702). An Origenist is a follower of the Greek-Christian philosopher Origen, who considered the physical world to be a place of atonement for souls. See source text, p. 370 n. 5.

157. Pietro Napoli-Signorelli (1731–1815), man of letters, critic, and dramatic poet who wanted to bring a reform to Neapolitan comedy. Napoli-Signorelli lived in Spain from 1765 to 1783 and taught dramatic poetry in Milan, Pavia, and Bologna. In 1799 he adhered to the Republic and became part of its legal commission. His comedies include *La Faustina*.

158. Legislative Committee.

159. Cicero's *De officiis*, 1.1.

CHAPTER 9

160. Santa Chiara, a large, early fourteenth-century church in Naples, is located near the Gesù Nuovo. Its eighteenth-century ceramic cloister (Chiostro delle Clarisse) is famous.

161. King Robert "the Wise" (1309–1343) of Anjou was not married to Agnes but first to Violante d'Aragona and secondly to Sancia of Majorca. Their monument in the church is by Giovanni and Pacio Bertini. The Durazzana family were associated originally with the Albanian seaport of Durazzo, long an Angevin possession.

162. Alphonso I, king of Naples (1442–1458) (and V, king of Aragon), was known as "the Magnificent." "Ferrante" (1458–1494) was Ferdinand, his son. Ferdinand II (1495–1496) was known as "Ferrantino."

163. See Evelyn's account of this same crucifix [15]. Also n. 24.

164. There was more than one saint named Bernard. This is probably St. Bernard of Clairvaux (1090–1153), a church doctor, canonized in 1174, who left ten spiritual treatises, over one hundred sermons, and five hundred letters.

165. St. Olivet (Monte Oliveto) is the same as the church of Sant'Anna dei Lombardi in Naples. See note 25.

166. Gisolfo's biography of Antonio de Colellis, who was affiliated with the new Spanish Carmelite mysticism in Naples, was published in 1663. See Jean-Michel Sallmann, *Naples et ses saints à l'age baroque, 1540–1750* (Paris: Presses Universitaires de France, 1994), pp. 34, 64, 145, 158, 271, 275, 299, 307.

167. Francesco Solimena da Canale di Serino (1657–1747), famous late baroque Neapolitan painter. François de Louvemont (or Lauvemont) was an obscure engraver documented in 1648 at Nevers and later in Paris.

168. St. Nicholas, archbishop of Myra, d. 324 C.E. He is associated with numerous miracles, and St. Bonaventure recounted stories of him.

169. St. Philip Benizzi (or Benizi) (1233–1285), doctor who was born in Florence and studied in Paris and Padua before joining the Servite Order, of which he later became general. In 1269 he went into hiding in order to avoid becoming pope.

170. Giacomo del Po (1652–1726), painter and architect from Rome who worked in Naples.

171. Ferdinand IV (1759–1825) of Naples, III of Sicily, and I of the Two Sicilies; and Maria Carolina of the house of Bourbon. [FIG. 47 and reading 47]

172. There is a Murgie di Minervino in southern Italy near Barletta.

173. Lecchi might refer to Lecce in southern Italy or to Lecco.

174. Jacopo Cardinal Cantelmi, a Neapolitan descended from the dukes of Popoli, who lived in the late seventeenth century. Francesco Cardinal Giudici, governor of Rome, was descended from the feudal nobility, one of whom was the count of Castres. Both became cardinals in 1690 during the time of Pope Alexander VIII (1689–1691). See Ludwig Pastor, *History of the Popes*, 23 vols. (London: Kegan Paul, 1923-40), 23:543, 570.

175. These are prominent, papal families. Clement X (1670–1676) was of the Altieri; Alexander VIII (1689–1691) was an Ottoboni.

176. The Chigi were another papal family, that of Alexander VII (1655–1667).

177. *"Rabbanimi"* (rabbis) refers to Jewish scholars and teachers; *"Karraimi"* indicates members of a Jewish movement originating in Persia during the eighth

century. *"Karism"* rejected oral tradition and challenged the authority of the rabbinites, the teachers of the Talmud.

178. Chosroes (or Khosrau) the Elder, "the Famous," king of Persia, (reigned 531–579 C.E.), Sassanian monarch of Persia.

179. Procopius, (end 5th–6th century C.E.), Byzantine historian and private secretary to Belisarius, he went to Constantinople after the capture of Ravenna. His writings consist of historical accounts, unpublished memoirs, and documentation of the buildings of Justinian. Evagrius Scholasticus (c.536–early 7th century) Byzantine historian who wrote his *Ecclestiastical History* in six volumes. He explicitly summarized Procopius.

180. The city can be spelled Souron or Soura.

181. The Emperor Maurice is Mauricius Flavius Tiberius (c.539–602), Eastern Roman emperor who fought in the Persian War.

182. The East is the Roman-Byzantine administrative district of "Oriens."

183. George Cedrenus (11th century), wrote *Synopsis historiarum,* a world history from creation to 1057. See Migne, *Patrologia Graeca,* 1865, 86.2:2743.

184. George Elmacin (Jirjis al-Makin, 1205–1273), Christian Arab historian, author of a world chronicle, *Majmu'-al-Mubarak.*

185. San Carlo Borromeo (d. 1584), cardinal and later archbishop of Milan, remembered for his charity, as well as for the foundation of schools, seminaries, and hospitals.

CHAPTER 10

186. Lactantius Firmianus (c.260–c.340 C.E.), known as "the Christian Cicero," wrote *Divinarum institutionum libri septem.* For Procopius, see note 179. Ephrem (Ephraim the Syrian or Saint Syrus, 306–373 C.E.), a doctor of the church, was the most celebrated writer among the Syrian fathers and famous for his hymns, homilies, and commentary on the Old Testament.

187. Aristotle's first four elements (earth, water, air, and fire) compose all objects in the world, that is, within the orbit of the moon. All else is of the immutable "fifth essence" or "quintessence," which experiences local, circular, and eternal motions.

188. Theodoretus of Cyrus (c.393–458 C.E.), *Questiones in Genesim* I. There are also his commentaries on Psalm 18 and on the Epistle to the Hebrews 19.

189. Revelations 12:1.

190. "Master of the Sentences" is a reference to Peter Lombard (see note 199). Sometimes referred to as simply the Master, he wrote the *Libri IV Sententiarum* (c.1150), taken from the church fathers, especially Augustine.

191. Ambrose, *Hexameron*, IV, 3, 10; 8, 31.

192. John Philoponous (or Philoponus) (5th–6th century C.E.) was a writer of the philosophical school of Alexandria. Known as the Grammarian, he wrote voluminous commentaries on Aristotle.

193. Thomas Aquinas, *Summa theologica*, 1.65-74.

194. "Now the fiery sun sets," from Ambrose's Hymn II, first verse. See Migne, *Patrologia Latina* (PL) 16:1476.

195. Aristotle, *De caelo* II, 7 (289 a 20).

196. Eusebius of Caesarea (c.260–c.340 C.E.), bishop and scholar who wrote an *Ecclesiastical History* up to 324 C.E.

197. Diodorus of Tarsus (d. 392 C.E.), teacher of John Chrysostom, biblical commentator. Only fragments of his writings survive. He preferred a literal rather than allegorical reading of Scripture.

198. Peter Lombard (1100–1160), bishop of Paris, wrote *Quaestiones in librum secundum sententiarum*. See note 191.

199. Thomas Aquinas, *Responsio ad lectorem Venetum de articulis XXXVI (Opusculum II)*, Article 25.

200. Matthew 8:12, 22:13, 25:30.

201. Origen, *In Matthaeum commentariorum series*, 69. See Migne, PL 13:1710-11. See note 156.

202. John Chrysostom, *In Epistolam ad Thessalonios homilia VII*, 4. See Migne, PL 62:438.

203. Theophylactus of Archrida (c.1038–1108), bishop of Bulgaria.

204. Aulus Cornelius Celsus (1st century C.E.), Roman author of a wide-ranging encyclopedia, of which only eight books, *De medicina*, survive.

205. Imposthumes are abscesses.

CHRONOLOGY

1504	Expulsion of the French by Gonzalo de Cordoba, the first viceroy, known as "el Gran Capitan."
1510	Opposition to introduction of the Spanish Inquisition.
1536	Charles V, Holy Roman Emperor (Charles IV of The Two Sicilies) visited Naples. Construction of the Via Toledo initiated.
1538	Eruption of Vesuvius.
1547	Successful protest against the Spanish Inquisition. Viceroy Pedro de Toledo's stern repression marks the end of the "golden" years of Spanish rule.
1582	Giordano Bruno's *The Candle Bearer.*
1586	Church of Gesù Nuovo begun.
1587	Fire in Pozzuoli to the west of Naples.
1588	Defeat of the Spanish Armada.
1600	Giordano Bruno burned at the stake in Rome. Construction of the Palazzo Reale begun.
1601	Pio Monte della Misericordia founded.
1602	Campanella's *City of the Sun.*
1606–7	The painter Caravaggio's first visit to Naples.
1609–10	Caravaggio's final visit to Naples and death in 1610.
1610	George Sandys, English traveller, begins his journey.
1610–16	Viceregency of the Conde de Lemos brings significant social reforms.
1611–12	First visit of Bolognese painter Guido Reni.
1616 (c.)	Jusepe de Ribera, Spanish painter, settles in Naples.
1616	First edition of Enrico Bacco's *Description of the City of Naples.*
1617	Fynes Moryson's 4-volume account of his travels, which included Naples.
1618–48	Thirty Years War.
1623	Giovanni Battista Marino, *Adonis.*
1623–44	Papacy of Urban VIII (Barberini).
1623–56	Cosimo Fanzago became master of works at the Certosa di San Martino.
1625	Death of poet Giovanni Battista Marino.

1626–30	Arrival of the painter Artemisia Gentileschi.
1629–30	First visit of Diego Velazquez, the Spanish painter.
1630	The painter Domenichino arrives from Bologna via Rome.
1631	Eruption of Vesuvius.
1634	Giovanni Lanfranco, painter from Parma, arrives. Capaccio's *Guido de' forestieri*.
1634–36	Giovanni Battista Basile, *The Pentameron*.
1638–47	Economic hardship after Spanish involvement in the Thirty Years War.
1639 (c.)	Painter Salvator Rosa leaves Naples.
1642	Last "parliament" of the barons.
1643	John Evelyn in Italy and Naples.
1647	Revolt led by the fisherman Masaniello.
1650	French defeated at Portolongone.
1649–50	Diego Velazquez's second visit.
1652	Death of Jusepe de Ribera and Artemisia Gentileschi.
1654	Duc de Guise leads French offensive at Castellammare.
1656	Plague in Naples with loss of at least half of the population. Painter Mattia Preti arrives.
1671	Spread of Cartesianism alarms the Inquisition.
1672	Eruption of Vesuvius.
1674–78	French occupy Messina.
1685	First performance of Domenico Scarlatti's first opera, *Pompeo*.
1686	Inquisition prosecutes "atheists" (1686–1693).
1688	Major earthquake.
1690	Foundation of the Arcadia.
1691–1700	Pope Innocent XII of the Pignatelli family.
1692	First of Carlo Celano's five editions of his city guide.
1693	Plague and earthquake. Inquisition condemns friends of Vico.
1694	Salvator Rosa's *Satires*.
1697	Laying out of the Riviera di Chiaia.
1700	Felipe V (Spanish Bourbon) becomes king of Naples by inheritance.
1702	Visit of Felipe V (April–June).
1703	University reform.
1706	Reinhard Keiser's opera, *Massagnello*.
1706–10	Handel in Italy.
1707	Austria occupies Spanish Naples.
1708	Gian Vincenzo Gravina, *On the Nature of Poetry*.
1710–36	Giovanni Battista Pergolesi.

Baroque Naples, 1600–1800

1713	Emperor Charles VI (Austrian Hapsburg) recognized as king of the Two Sicilies.
1715	Eruption of Vesuvius.
1723	Pietro Giannone, *The Civil History of the Kingdom of Naples.*
1723–50	L.A. Muratori, *Historians of Italy.*
1724	Metastasio, *Dido Forsaken.*
1725	Vico's *Scienza Nuova* published.
1728–29	Vico's *Autobiography.*
1730	Handel's opera *Parthenope.*
1732	Metastasio's *Attilius Regulus.*
1733	Production of Pergolesi's *La Serva Padrona*, the first *opera buffa.*
1734	Kingdom of Naples conquered by Charles de Bourbon (later Carlos III of Spain). Charles becomes the first Bourbon king of the Two Sicilies. Monarchy returns to Naples. Festival of the *"Cuccagna"* initiated.
1737	Construction and opening of the Teatro di San Carlo.
1738	Formal excavations begun at Herculaneum. Construction begun on the royal palaces of Portici and Capodimonte.
1739-40	Lady Mary Wortley Montague in Naples.
1743	Capodimonte porcelain factory established.
1744	Battle of Velletri; Austria defeated.
1745	Death of the late baroque painter Francesco Solimena.
1748	Formal excavations at Pompeii and Paestum begin.
1751	King Charles commissions Ferdinando Fuga to build the Albergo dei Poveri.
1752	Construction of the Palace of Caserta begun.
1759	King Charles abdicates to become Carlos III of Spain.
1759–1825	Ferdinando IV king.
1759–67	Bernardo Tanucci, minister for Foreign Affairs, Justice, and Household.
1764	Sir William Hamilton becomes British Minister to Naples.
1768	Marriage of Ferdinando IV and Archduchess Maria Carolina of Austria.
1770	Ferdinando Galiani, *Dialogues on the Wheat Trade.*
1777	Museo Borbonico (Archeologico) founded.
1787	Goethe visits Naples.
1780-83	Gaetano Filangieri, *The Science of Legislation.*
1789	The French Revolution begins.
1799	Naples invaded by the French. Parthenopean Republic founded. Republic overthrown by Cardinal Ruffo and his Calabrian peasants with the aid of English fleet under Horatio Nelson. King Ferdinando IV returns to Naples.
1806	French invade. Joseph Bonaparte installed as "King Joseph Bonaparte."

RULERS OF NAPLES

VICEROYS

1504–1507	Consalvo de Córdova
1507	Juan de Aragon, count of Riparcorsa
1508	Antonio Guevara
1509–22	Raimundo de Cardona
1522–24	Carlos de Lannoy
1524–26	Andrea Carafa
1527–28	Hugo de Moncada
1529–30	Filiberto de Châlons-Orange
1530–32	Cardinal Pompeo Colonna
1532–53	Pedro de Toledo, marquis of Villafranca
1553–55	Cardinal Pedro Pacheco de Villena
1555	Bernardino de Mendoza
1555–58	Fernando Alvarez de Toledo, duke of Alba
1558	Juan Manriquez de Lara
1559–71	Perafan de Ribera, duke of Alcala
1571–75	Antonio Perronot, cardinal of Granvelle
1575–79	Inigo Lopez Hurtado de Mendoza
1579–82	Juan de Zuniga, prince of Pietraperzia
1582–86	Pedro Giron, duke of Ossuna
1586–95	Juan de Zuniga, count of Miranda
1595–99	Enrique de Guzman, count of Olivares
1599–1601	Fernando Ruiz de Castro, count of Lemos
1601–1603	Francisco de Castro (Regent)
1603–10	Juan Alonso Pimentel, count of Benavente
1610–16	Pedro Fernandez de Castro e Andrada, count of Lemos
1616–20	Pedro Giron, duke of Ossuna
1620	Cardinal Borgia
1620–22	Cardinal Antonio Zapata (delegate)

1622–29   Antonio Alvarez de Toledo, duke of Alba

1629–31   Fernando Afan de Ribera, duke of Alcala

1631–37   Manuel de Guzman, count of Monterey

1637–44   Ramiro de Guzman, duke of Medina de las Torres

1644–46   Juan Alfonso Enriquez de Ribera, admiral of Castile

1646–48   Rodrigo Ponce de Leon, duke of los Arcos

1648   Don Juan Jose of Austria

1648–53   Inigo Velez de Guevara y Tassis, count of Onate

1653–58   Garcia de Avellaneda y Haro, count of Castrillo

1658–64   Gaspar de Bracamonte, count of Penaranda

1664–66   Pascual, Cardinal of Aragon

1666–72   Pedro Antonio de Aragon

1672–75   Antonio Alvarez, marquis of Astorga

1675–83   Fernando Joaquin Fajardo, marquis of los Velez

1683–87   Gaspar de Haro, marquis of Carpio

1687–95   Francesco de Benavides, count of San Esteban

1695–1702 Luis de la Cerda, duke of Medinaceli

1702–1707 Juan Manuel Fernandez Pacheco de Acuna

1707   Giorgio Adamo, count of Martinitz

1707–1708 Wirico Filippo Lorenzo, count of Duan

1708–1710 Cardinal Vincenzo Grimani

1710–13   Carlo Borromeo, count of Arona

1713–19   Count of Daun

1719   Juan Venceslao, count of Gallas

1719–21   Wolfgang Hannibal de Schrattenbach

1721–22   Marcantonio Borghese

1722–28   Cardinal Michele Federico de Althan

1728   Cardinal Joaquin Portocarrero

1728–33   Luigi Tomaso Raimondo, count of Harrach

1733–34   Giulio Visconti, count of Pieve

SOVEREIGNS

SPANISH HOUSES OF HAPSBURG AND BOURBON

1598–1621 Felipe III

1621–65   Felipe IV

1665–1700 Carlos II, "the Bewitched"

1700-1707 Felipe V (Bourbon king of Spain, 1700-1746)

HOUSE OF AUSTRIA

1707–34   Charles of Austria (II of Spain, Holy Roman Emperor Charles VI)

NEAPOLITAN HOUSE OF BOURBON

1734–59   Charles de Bourbon (son of Felipe V) (1759–88 Charles III of Spain)
1759–1825 Ferdinando IV (I of the Two Sicilies). Deposed by French 1799, 1806-15
1825–30   Francesco I
1830–59   Ferdinando II
1859–60   Francesco II

ALPHABETICAL LIST OF
READINGS

Anonymous. *Relatione della Cavalcata Reale: Seguita in questa fedelissima Città di Napoli il di 14 Gennaro 1680*. Naples: Lodovico Canallo, 1680, p. 11.

Aulisio, (Conte) Domenico. *Delle scuole sacre libri due postumi del conte Domenico Aulisio....* Naples: F. Riccardo, 1723, pp. 118-19.

B.W., A.M. *A New History of the Roman Conclave...Rites and Ceremonies...of the Pope, A Brief Account of the Life of this Present Pope Innocent XII*. London: Samuel Smith at the Prince's Arms in St. Paul's Cathedral, 1691, pp. 30-32.

Bacco, Enrico. *Naples: An Early Guide*. Ed. and trans. Eileen Gardiner. Introds. Caroline Bruzelius and Ronald G. Musto. New York: Italica Press, 1991, pp. 8-10.

Basile, Giovanni Battista, *Il Pentamerone or The Tale of Tales*. Trans. Sir Richard Burton. London: Horace Liveright, 1893, pp. 45-51.

Battista, Giuseppe. "Beautiful Eyes." In Giuseppe Guido Ferrero, *Marino e i Marinisti*. Milan and Naples: Riccardo Riccardi Editore, 1954, p. 1005

Bayardi, Octavio Antonio. *Le pitture Antiche d'Ercolano....* 4 vols. Naples: Regia Stamperia, 1765, 4:229-30.

Braccini, Giulio Cesare. *Dell'Incendio fattosi nel Vesuvio*. Naples: Gioviano di Lucca, 1632.

Broggia, Carlo Antonio. *Trattato de tributi, delle monete, e del governo politico della sanita opera di stato....* Naples: Pietro Palombo, 1743, pp. 1-20.

Calzabigi, Ranieri de. *Poesie*. Livorno: Stamperia dell'Enciclopedia, 1774, 2:273-74.

Campanella, Tommaso. *A Defense of Galileo the Mathematician*. Trans. and intro. Richard J. Blackwell. Notre Dame and London: University of Notre Dame Press, 1994, pp. 86-89.

—. *Famous Utopias, Being the Complete Text of Campanella's City of the Sun*. Intro. by Charles W. Andrews. New York: Tudor Publishing, 1937, pp. 308-17.

—. "Metaphysical Cause and Effect." In *Italy in the Baroque: Selected Readings*. Ed. and trans. Brenden Dooley. New York and London: Garland Publishers, 1995, pp. 39-47.

—. Selected writings. In George R. Kay, ed. *The Penguin Book of Italian Verse*. Baltimore: Penguin Books, 1960, pp. 203-17.

Campanile, Giuseppe. *Notizie di nobiltà. Lettere di Giuseppe Campanile*. Naples: Lui Antoni di Fusco, 1672, pp. 351-52.

Capaccio, Giulio Cesare. *La vera antichità di Pozzuolo descritta da Giulio Cesare Capaccio secretario dell' inclita città di Napoli*. Rome: Filippo de Rossi, 1652, pp. 123-24.

Capelcelatro, Giuseppe. *Riflessioni sul discorso istorico-politico (Dialogo)*. Filadelfia: s.n., 1788?, pp. 8-12.

Castelli, Pietro. *Incendio del Monte Vesuvio*. Rome: Giacomo Mascardi, 1632.

Celano, Carlo. "Landmarks: The Church of the Carmine." In Desmond Seward, *Naples: A Traveller's Companion*. New York: Atheneum, 1986, pp. 192-98.

Cerlone, Francesco, "Pulcinella's Duel." In Henry D. Spalding, *A Treasury of Italian Folklore and Humor*. Middle Village, NY: Jonathan David Publishers, 1980, pp. 171-73.

Colletta, Pietro. "The Cocagna of 1734." In Seward, *Naples: A Traveller's Companion*, pp. 139-41.

Cornelio, Tommaso. *Thomae Cornelii Consentini Progymnasmata Physica*. Ed. Lionardo Di Capua. Venice: Bartholomaei, 1683, pp. 76-80.

Cortese, Giulio Cesare. *Opere poetiche*. In appendix to *La Tiorba a Taccone de Felippo Sgruttendio de Scafato*. Ed. Enrico Malato. Rome: Edizioni dell'Ateneo, 1967, 1:62-63.

Cuoco, Vincenzo. "The Revolution of 1799." In Massa Nunzia, ed., Benedetto Croce, trans. *Napoli guida, Guide-Naples, Reiseführer Neapel*. Naples: Graphotronic Edizioni, 1994., pp. 139-40.

D'Andrea, Francesco. *Avvertimenti ai nipoti*. Ed. Imma Ascione. Naples: Jovene Editore, 1990, pp. 167-68.

De Dominici, Bernardo. "The Architect Cosimo Fanzago," and "Jusepe de Ribera, 'Spagnoletto'." From *Vite dei pittori, scultori ed architetti napoletani*. Naples, 1884, 3:118-21.

Della Porta, Giovanni Battista. *Albumazar: A Comedy (1615), by Thomas Tomkis*, Ed. Hugh G. Dick. Berkeley and Los Angeles: University of California Press, 1944, pp. 78-79.

Di Capua, Lionardo. *The Uncertainty of the Art of Physick*. Trans. F.L. Gent. London: Fr. Clark for Thomas Malthus, 1684, pp. 1-15.

Donzelli, Giuseppe (Barone di Dogliola). *Parthenope liberata*. Ed. Antonio Altamura. Naples: F. Fiorentino, 1970.

Doria, Paolo Mattia. *La vita civile*. Augusta: D. Höpper, 1710, pp. 1-12.

Evelyn, John. *The Diary of John Evelyn, Kalendarium 1620–49*. Ed. E.S. de Beer. Oxford: Clarendon Press, 1955, 2:325-32.

Ferdinand IV. *Origine della popolazione di S. Leucio e suoi progressi fine al gloria d'eggi colle leggi*.... Naples: Stamperia Reale, 1789, pp. L-LIII.

Filamondo, Raffaele Maria. *Il genio bellicoso di Napoli*. Naples: Domenico-Antonio Parrino, 1714, p. 30.

Filangieri, Gaetano. *The Science of Legislation*. Bristol: Thomas Ostell, Emery and Adams, 1806, 1:1-9.

Fontanella, Girolamo. "To Tears." In Ferrero, *Marino e i Marinisti*, p. 849.

Galiani, Ferdinando. *Money (Della Moneta)*. Trans. Peter R. Toscano. Chicago: Loyola University, 1977, pp. 6-10.

Gaudiosi, Tommaso. "Woman Possessed." In Ferrero, *Marino e i Marinisti*, p. 1084.

Genovesi, Antonio. *Autobiografia, lettere e altri scritti*. Ed. Gennaro Savarese. Milan: Feltrinelli Editore, 1962, pp. 368-70.

—. *Meditazioni filosofiche sulla religione e sulla morale*. Bassano: Remondi di Venezia, 1783, pp. 368-70.

Giannone, Pietro. "Masaniello Remembered." In Seward, *Naples: A Traveller's Companion*, pp. 89-90.

Giraffi, Lord Alexander. "Masaniello's Revolution of 1647." In Dooley, *Italy in the Baroque*, pp. 272-75.

Gisolfo, Pietro. *Prodigio di mature virtù nella vita di Nicola di Fusco*. Naples: Francesco Mollo, 1682, pp. 27-30.

Kelly, Michael. "The Liquefaction of the Blood of San Gennaro." In Seward, *Naples: A Traveller's Companion*, pp. 132-33.

LaLande, Joseph-Jerome Lefrançais De (Chevalier). "Neapolitan Theater." In Seward, *Naples: A Traveller's Companion*, pp. 168-69.

Manso, Giovanni Battista. *Poesie nomiche*. Venice: Francesco Baba, 1635, p. 147.

Marino, Giovanni Battista. "The Formal Elements of Painting." In Jonathan Brown and Robert Enggass, *Italian and Spanish Art, 1600–1750: Sources and Documents*. Evanston, IL: Northwestern University Press, 1972, 1:33, 75, 83.

—. Selected Poems: "Beautiful Slave," "Broken Vows," Daphne into Laurel," How to Steal," "Inconstant Love," "Leave Taking," "Woman Washing Her Legs," from Dooley, *Italy in the Baroque*, pp. 458-59.

— *Sospetto d'Herode*. In Claes Schaar and Jan Svartvik, eds. *Marino and Crashaw, Sospetto d'Herode*. Lund: C.W.K. Gleerup, 1971, pp. 37-39, 1:28-29.

Mazzella, Scipio. *Parthenopeia, or the History of the Most Renowned Kingdom of Naples and the Dominions, There unto annexed and the Lives of all their Kings.... (The Second Part Continued to these Present Times, 1654 by James Howell)*. London: Humphrey Moseley, 1654, 1:28-29.

Metastasio, Pietro. "Liberty," and "While Writing Olympiad." In Kay, *Penguin Book of Italian Verse*, pp. 228-33.

Moryson, Fynes. *Moryson, F. Gent. An Itinerary Containing His Ten Yeeres Travell through...Italy*. Glasgow: James MacLehose and Sons, 1907, 1:234-35.

Pagano, Mario. *Saggi politici: De' principii, progressi, e decadenza della società*. Ed. Francesco Collotti. Bologna: L. Cappelli Editore, 1936, pp. 158-59.

Palmieri, Giuseppe. *Pensieri economici relative al regno di Napoli*. Naples: Vincenzo Flauto, 1789, pp. 1-5.

Parrino, Domenico. "Observe and Enjoy Naples." In *Nuova guida de' forastieri per osservare, e godere le curiosità piu vaghe, e piu rare della fedeliss(ima) gran Napoli, città antica...* Naples: n.p., 1725, pp. 243-45.

Passeri, Giambattista. "The Painter, Salvator Rosa." In Brown and Enggass, *Italian and Spanish Art*, 1:128-30.

Perrucci, Andrea. "The Choosing of Costumes." In Dooley, *Italy in the Baroque*, pp. 500-504.

Ritijs, Fra Massimo. In James B. Clifton, "Images of the Plague and Other Contemporary Events in Seventeenth-Century Naples." Ph.D. diss. Princeton: Princeton University, 1987, pp. 197-98.

Rosa, Salvator. "Letter to Giovanni Battista Ricciardi." In Brown and Enggass, *Italian and Spanish Art*, 1:132-33.

—. "The Witch." In Brown and Enggass, *Italian and Spanish Art*, 1:134-35.

San Felix, Fr. Juan de. *Compendio de la vida de S. Andres Avelino Confessor, Traducida del Latin....* Trinitario, Calle de la Palma, Mexico: S. Felix, 1767, pp. 4-14.

Sarnelli, Pompeo. *Guida de forestieri per Pozzuoli, Baja, Cuma, e Miseno*. Naples: N. Rossi, 1789, pp. 7-9.

Serra, Antonio. "Venice versus Naples." In Dooley, *Italy in the Baroque*, pp. 305-6, 308-9, 310.

Sgruttendio, Filippo. "The Place and Manner of Falling in Love," and "Wounded by Love." From *Opere poetiche*. In appendix to *La Tiorba a Taccone de Felippo Sgruttendio de Scafato*, pp. 517-18

Sicola, Sigismondo. *La nobiltà gloriosa nella vita di S. Aspreno, primo christiano e primo vescovo della città di Napoli*. Naples: Carlo Porsile, 1696, pp. 1-5.

Sigismondo, Giuseppe. *Descrizione della città di Napoli e suoi borghi*. Naples: Fratelli Terres, 1788-89, 3:108-9.

Stigliani, Tommaso. "Gift from a Flower." In Ferrero, *Marino e i Marinisti*, p. 645.

Toppi, Nicolo. *Biblioteca napoletana, et apparato a gli huomini illustri in lettere di Napoli, e del Regno.…* Naples: Antonio Bulifon, 1678.

Torcia, Michele. *Elogio di Metastasio, poeta cesareo*. Naples: s.n., 1771, pp. 18-20.

Turbolo, Gian Donato. *Discorsi sopra le monete del Regno di Napoli*. Naples: s.n., 1629, pp. 25-29.

Vanini, Lucilio "Cesare" and Luigi Dorvaglia. *Le opere di Giulio Cesare Vanini e loro fonti: Amphitheatrum Aeternae, Providentiae*. Milan: Società Anonima Editrice Dante Alighieri, 1933, pp. 126-36.

Vanvitelli, Luigi. *Dicharazione dei disegno del Reale Palazzo di Caserta.…* Naples: Regia Stamperia, 1756, pp. II-III.

Vico, Giambattista. "An Eternal Natural State." In *Selected Writings*. Ed. and trans. Leon Pompa. Cambridge: Cambridge University Press, 1982, pp. 259-67.

—. *The Autobiography of Giambattista Vico*. Trans. Max H. Fisch and Thomas G. Bergin. Ithaca, NY: Cornell University Press, 1944, pp. 134-36.

—. *The New Science of Giambattista Vico*. Trans. Thomas G. Bergin and Max H. Fisch. Ithaca and London: Cornell University Press, 1991.

—. *On the Most Ancient Wisdom of the Italians, Unearthed from the Origins of the Latin Language*. Trans. with intro. L.M. Palmer. Ithaca and London: Cornell University Press, 1988, pp. 47-50.

Zazzera, Francesco. *Della nobiltà dell'Italia*. Naples: Giovanni Battista Gargano and Lucretio Nucci, 1615-18.

BIBLIOGRAPHY

GENERAL AND INTRODUCTORY

Barzaghi, Antonio. *Il presepe nella cultura del '700 a Napoli*. Treviso: Matteo, 1983.

Bernier, Olivier. *Pleasure and Privilege: Life in France, Naples, and America 1770–90*. Garden City: Doubleday, 1981.

Bouvier, René and Andre Lafforgue. *La vie napolitaine au xviiieme siècle*. Paris: Hachette, 1956.

Buchanan, Daniel H. "The Kingdom of Naples: 1650–1750." Ph.D. diss. New Haven: Yale University, 1953.

Capecelatro, Gaudioso Domenico. *Una capitale, un re, un popolo*. Naples: A. Gallina, 1980.

Caratelli, Giovanni Pugliese. *Il Rinascimento dell'età barocca*. Storia e Civiltà della Campania. Naples: Electa, 1994.

Carpanetto, Dino and Giuseppe Ricuperati. *Italy in the Age of Reason, 1685–1789*. Trans. Caroline Higgitt. London and New York: Longman, 1987.

Cione, Edmondo. *Il paradiso dei diavoli: Napoli dal 400 all'800*. Milan: Longanesi, 1949.

Cochrane, Eric. *Italy 1530–1630*. Ed. Julius Kirshner. London and New York: Longman, 1988.

Collison-Morley, Lacy. *Naples Through the Centuries*. London: Methuen, 1925.

Cortese, Nino. *Cultura e politica a Napoli del Cinque al Settecento*. Naples: Edizioni Scientifiche Italiane, 1965.

Croce, Benedetto. *Storie e leggende napoletane*. Milan: Adelphi, 1991.

De Franciscis, Alfonso, Daniela del Pesco Spirito, et al. *Campania*. Rudolf G. Carpanini et al., trans. Naples: Electa for the Banco Nazionale del Lavoro, 1977.

De Mura, Cesare. *Napoli fra rinascimento e illuminismo*. Naples: Electa, 1991.

De Seta, Cesare. *Napoli*. Rome and Bari: Laterza, 1981.

Di Mola, Alfonso M. *Lo specchio e l'olio: Le superstizioni degli Italiani*. Rome and Bari: Laterza, 1993.

Dooley, Brendan, ed. and trans. *Italy in the Baroque: Selected Readings*. New York and London: Garland Publishers, 1995.

Doria, Gino. *Bambocciate napoletane*. Naples: Fiorentino, 1961.

—. *Del colore locale e altre intrepretazioni napoletane*. Rome and Bari: Laterza, 1930.

—. *Settecento napoletano*. Turin: ERI, 1962.

Fuiano, Michele. *Insegnamente e cultura a Napoli nel Rinascimento*. Naples: Libreria Scientifica, 1971.

Furnari, Mario, ed. *'700 napoletano: Cultura popolare a Napoli nel diciotessimo secolo*. Naples: A. Gallina, 1980.

Gambardella, Alfonso. *Naples: Portrait of a City*. Genoa: Sagep Editrice, 1993.

Gunn, Peter. *Naples: A Palimpsest*. London: Chapman and Hall, 1961.

Haskell, Francis. *The Age of the Grand Tour (1720–1820)*. New York: Crown Publishers, 1967.

Ingamells, John. *A Dictionary of British and Irish Travellers in Italy, 1701–1800*. New Haven & London: Yale University Press, 1997.

Labrot, Gerard. *Baroni in città: Residenza e comportamenti dell'aristocrazia napoletana, 1570–1734*. Naples: Società Editrice Napoletana, 1979.

Mastellone, Salvo. *Pensiero politico e vita culturale a Napoli nella seconda metà del seicento*. Messina: G. D'Anna, 1965.

Miranda, Gaetano. *Breve storia del carnevale a Napoli*. Naples: Colonnese, 1971.

Montanelli, Indro. *Roma e Napoli nel settecento*. Milan: Rizzoli, 1976.

Negro Spina, Annamaria. *Napoli nel settecento: Le incisioni di Antoine Alexandre Cardon*. Naples: Giannini, 1989.

Petraccone, Claudia. *Napoli dal cinquecento all'ottocento: Problemi di storia demografica e sociale*. Naples: Guida, 1969.

Pezzullo, Adele. *Napoli nel settecento: Architettura, pittura, scultura*. Naples: Società Editrice Napoletana, 1980.

Sella, Domenico. *Italy in the Seventeenth Century*. New York & London: Longman, 1997.

Steegmuller, Francis. *A Woman, A Man, and Two Kingdoms*. New York: Alfred A. Knopf, 1991.

Strazzullo, F. *Napoli, i luoghi e le storie*. Naples: Guida, 1992.

I. HISTORY OF THE KINGDOM AND CITY OF NAPLES

Acton, Harold. *The Bourbons of Naples, 1734–1825*. New York: St. Martin's Press, 1956.

BIBLIOGRAPHY

Alisio, Giancarlo. *Napoli nell'ottocento, (Storia della città)*. Naples: Electa, 1992.

Calabria, Antonio, and John A. Marino, eds. *Good Government in Spanish Naples*. New York: Peter Lang, 1990.

Ceva Grimaldi, Francesco (Marchesi di Pietracatella). *Memorie storiche della città di Napoli*. Bologna: A. Forni, 1976.

Chorley, Patrick. *Oil, Silk, and Enlightenment in xvmith-Century Naples*. Naples: Istituto Storico, 1965.

Colletta, Pietro. *Storia del reame di Napoli dal 1734 fino al 1825*. Milan: E. Oliva, 1848.

Coniglio, Giuseppe. *I vicere spagnoli di Napoli*. Naples: F. Fiorentino, 1967.

—. *Il viceregno di Napoli nel secolo xvii*. Rome: Storia e Letteratura, 1955.

Croce, Benedetto. *History of the Kingdom of Naples*. H. Stuart Hughes, ed., Frances Frenaye, trans. Chicago and London: University of Chicago Press, 1970.

De Bildt, Baron, Christine de Suede et Cardinal Azzolino. *Lettres Inedités, 1666–1668*. Paris: Librairie Plon, 1899.

De Renzi, Salvatore. *Napoli nell' anno 1656*. Naples: De Pascale, 1867. Reprint ed., 1968.

De Seta, Cesare. *Storia della città di Napoli: Dalle origini al settecento*. Rome and Bari: Laterza, 1973.

D'Onofrio, Vincenzo. *Giornali di Napoli dal 1660 al 1680*. Naples: Società Napoletana di Storia Patria, 1934-43.

Doria, Gino. *Storia di una capitale*. Naples: Guida, 1935.

Giglioli, Constance. *Naples in 1799: An Account of the Revolution of 1799 and the Rise and Fall of the Parthenopean Republic*. London: J. Murray and New York: E.P. Dutton, 1903.

Gleijeses, Vittorio. *La storia di Napoli: Dalle origini ai nostri giorni*. 3 vols. Naples: Società Editrice Napoletana, 1974-81.

Knowlton, David C. "Masaniello and the Rising of 1647-8 in Naples." Ph.D. diss. Ithaca, NY: Cornell University, 1906.

Leopardi, Anselmo Cosimo. *Masaniello: Chi è, che cosa ha fatto, dove*. Naples: Laurenziana, 1972.

Maiorini, Maria Grazia. *Il viceregno di Napoli, introduzione all raccolta di documenti curata da Giuseppe Coniglio*. Naples: Giannini, 1992.

Marshall, Christopher R. "*Causa di stravaganze*: Order and Anarchy in Domenico Gargiulo's *Revolt of Masaniello*." *The Art Bulletin* 83.3 (1998): 478-97.

Musi, Aurelio. *La rivolta di Masaniello nella scena politica barocca*. Naples: Guida, 1989.

Padiglione, Carlo. *Dizionario delle famiglie nobili italiane o straniere importanti predicati di ex feudi napoletani e descrizione dei loro blasoni*. Bologna: A. Forni, 1976.

Pagden, Anthony. *Spanish Imperialism and the Political Imagination, 1513–1830*. New Haven: Yale University Press, 1990.

Rovito, Pier Luigi. "La rivoluzione costituzionale a Napoli (1647–48)." *Rivista Storica Italiana* 98 (1986).

Russo, Giuseppe. *La città di Napoli dalle origini al 1860*. Naples: Società per Risanamento di Napoli, 1960.

Sella, Domenico. *Italy in the Seventeenth Century*. London and New York: Longman, 1997.

Storia di Napoli. 10 vols. Naples: Società Editrice Storia di Napoli, 1975-81.

Villari, Rosario. *The Revolt of Naples*. James Newell and John A. Marino, trans. Cambridge, MA and Cambridge, England: Polity Press, 1993.

Visco, E. *La politica della S. Sede nella revoluzione di Masaniello*. Naples, 1923.

Vivenzio, Nicola. *Dell'istoria del Regno di Napoli e suo governo dalla decadenza dell'Imperio Romano infino al Re Ferdinando IV*. Naples: A Spese del Gabinetto Letterario, 1848.

2. GUIDES, DIARIES, AND TRAVELERS' ACCOUNTS

Baedeker, Karl. *Italy, Handbook for Travelers: Southern Italy and Sicily*. Leipzig: Karl Baedeker, 1900.

Bellani, Luigi, F.F. *I libri di viaggio e le guide della raccolta*. 3 vols. Rome: Sussidi Eruditi, 1957.

Brilli, Attilio. *Il Viaggio in Italia: Storia di una grande tradizione culturale dal XVI al XIX secolo*. Milan: Silvana Editoriale, 1987.

Delle Donne, Vincenzo, ed. *Naples, Capri & the Coast*. Boston: Houghton Mifflin Company, 1995.

De Seta, Cesare. *L'Italia del Grand Tour: Da Montaigne a Goethe*. Milan: Electa, 1992.

Doria, Gino. *Via Toledo, Cava dei Tirreni*. Naples: Di Mauro, 1967.

Gleijeses, Vittorio. *La guida storica, artistica, monumentale, turistica della città di Napoli e dei suoi dintorni*. 4th ed. Naples: Società Editrice Napoletana, 1979.

Massa, Nunzia, ed. *Napoli guida (Guide Naples, Reiseführer Neapel)*. Naples: Graphotronic Edizioni, 1994.

Morton, C.V. *A Traveller in Southern Italy*. New York: Dodd, Mead, 1969.

Porter, Jeanne Chenault. "Reflections of the Golden Age: The Visitor's Account of Naples." In *Parthenope's Splendor: Art of the Golden Age in Naples*. Jeanne Chenault Porter and Susan Munshower, eds. Papers in Art History from The Pennsylvania State University 7. University Park: Pennsylvania State University Press, 1993, 11-47.

Riedle, Beate. "Untersuchungen zur Kunst Neapols in Reiseberichten von 1550–1750." Ph.D. diss. Munich: Ludwig-Maximilians-Universität, 1977.

Schudt, Ludwig. *Italienreisen*. Vienna: Schroll, 1959.

Sells, A. Lytton. *The Paradise of Travellers: The Italian Influence on Englishmen in the Seventeenth Century*. Bloomington: Indiana University Press, 1964.

Seward, Desmond, ed. *Naples: A Traveller's Companion*. New York: Atheneum 1986.

Touring Club Italiano. *Napoli e dintorni*. Guida d'Italia. Milan: TCI, 1960.

3. ART, ARCHITECTURE, ARCHAEOLOGY

Ackerman, Gerald. "Gian B. Marino's Contribution to Seicento Art Theory." *The Art Bulletin* 18 (1961): 326-36.

Blunt, Anthony. *Neapolitan Baroque and Rococo Architecture*. London: A. Zwemmer, 1975.

Bologna, Ferdinando, ed. *Battistello Caracciolo e il primo naturalismo a Napoli*. Naples: Electa, 1991.

Bossa, Renato, Franco Mancini, Leonardo Di Mauro, Renato Ruotolo, eds. *Civiltà del Seicento a Napoli*. Naples: Electa, 1985.

Brown, Jonathan and Robert Enggass, eds. *Italian and Spanish Art, 1600–1750: Sources and Documents*. Evanston, IL: Northwestern University Press, 1972.

Cantone, Gaetana. *Napoli barocca*. Rome and Bari: Laterza, 1992.

Cassani, Silvia, Daniela Campanelli and Fiammetta Chiuazzi, eds. *Napoli: Città d'arte*. Naples: Electa, 1986.

Causa, Raffaello. *L'Arte nella Certosa di San Martino a Napoli*. Cava dei Tirreni: Di Mauro, 1973.

Cautela, Gemma, ed. *Napoli sacra: Realtà e proposte per il centro storico*. Naples: Electa, 1986.

Clifton, James D. "Images of the Plague and Other Contemporary Events in Seventeenth Century Naples." Ph.D. diss. Princeton: Princeton University, 1987.

Colton, Judith, George Hersey, Stephen Pepper, and John T. Spike, eds. *A Taste for Angels: Neapolitan Painting in North America, 1650–1750*. New Haven: Yale University Art Gallery, 1987.

De Velay, Philippe. *A l'ombre du Vesuve: Collections du Musée national d'archéologie de Naples*. Paris: Musées de la Ville de Paris, 1995.

Ferrari, Oreste and Giuseppe Scavizzi. *Luca Giordano*. 3 vols. Naples: Edizioni Scientifiche Italiane, 1966.

Galante, Gennaro and Nicola Spinosa. *Guida sacra della città di Napoli*. Naples: Società Editrice Napoletana, 1985.

Gleijeses, Vittorio. *Il colle di San Martino a Napoli: Il Museo a la Certosa, Castel Sant'Elmo*. Naples: Società Editrice Napoletana, 1979.

Guadagno, Giuseppe. *Pompeii, Herculaneum and Stabiae: The Buried Cities*. Venice: Edizioni Storti, 1973.

Lechner, George S. "Tommaso Campanella and Andrea Sacchi's Fresco of Divina Sapienza in the Palazzo Barberini." *The Art Bulletin* 58 (1976): 97-108.

Litchfield, R. Burr et al., eds. *The Golden Age of Naples: Art and Civilization under the Bourbons, 1734–1805*. Vols. 1-2. Detroit and Chicago: The Detroit Institute of Arts with the Art Institute of Chicago, 1982.

Muscettola, Stefania Adamo and Patrizia Gastaldi, eds. *Archeologia urbana e centro antico di Napoli: Atti del convegno 1983 (1984) 3*. Naples: Istituto per la storia e l'archeologia della Magna Grecia, 1983.

Museo di Capodimonte. *Civiltà del '700 a Napoli, 1734–99*. Naples: Museo e Gallerie Nazionali di Capodimonte, 1979-80.

Pane, Roberto. *Architettura dell'età barocca in Napoli*. Naples: Politecnica, 1939.

Perez-Sanchez, Alfonso E. and Nicola Spinosa. *Jusepe de Ribera (1591–1652)*. New York: Metropolitan Museum of Art and Harry N. Abrams, 1992.

Prota-Giurleo, Ulisse. *Scritti inediti e rari*. Naples: Arte Tipografica, 1988.

Ricerche sul '600 napoletano. Milan: Edizioni "L & T," 1984–.

Roworth, Wendy W. "The Evolution of History Painting: Masaniello's Revolt and Other Disasters in Seventeenth-Century Naples." *The Art Bulletin* 75.2 (1993): 219-34.

Schutze, Sebastian and Thomas Willette. *Massimo Stanzione: L'opera completa*. Naples: Electa, 1992.

Scott, Jonathan. *Salvator Rosa: His Life and Times*. New Haven and London: Yale University Press, 1995.

Whitfield, Clovis and Jane Martineau, eds. *Painting in Naples, 1606–1705: From Caravaggio to Giordano*. London: Weidenfeld and Nicolson, Royal Academy of Arts, 1982.

4. LITERATURE

Consiglio, Alberto, ed. *Antologia dei poeti napoletani*. Milan: Mondadori, 1986.

Cropper, Elizabeth. "The Petrifying Art: Marino's Poetry and Caravaggio." *Metropolitan Museum Journal* 26 (1991): 193-212.

De Mura, Ettore. *Poeti napoletani dal seicento ad oggi*. Naples: A. Marotta, 1973.

Dizionario letterario Bompiani degli autori di tutti i tempi ed di tutte le letterature. Vol. 9. Milan: Bompiani, 1971.

Ferrero, Giuseppe Guido. *Marino e i Marinisti*. Milan and Naples: Riccardo Riccardi, 1954.

Gleijeses, Vittorio. *I proverbi di Napoli*. Naples: Edizioni del Giglio, 1978.

Headley, John M. *Tommaso Campanella and the Transformation of the World*. Princeton: Princeton University Press, 1997.

Kay, George R., ed. *The Penguin Book of Italian Verse*. Baltimore: Penguin Books, 1960.

Mirollo, James. *The Poet of the Marvelous: Giambattista Marino*. New York: Columbia University Press, 1963.

Morisani, Ottavio. *Letteratura artistica a Napoli*. Naples: Gausto Fiorentino, 1958.

Pieri, Marzio, ed. *G.B. Marino: La Galleria*. Collana di Testi e Documenti. 2 vols. Padua: Liviana Editrice, 1979.

Salvo-Cozzo, Giuseppe. *Sulle notizie biografiche e bibliografiche degli scrittori napoletani fioriti nel secolo XVII*. Palermo: Virzi, 1876.

Schaar, Claes and Jan Svartvik, eds. *Marino and Crashaw, Sospetto d'Herode*. Lund Studies in English 39. Lund: C.W.K. Gleerup, 1971.

Simon, Roger and D. Gidrol. "G.B. Marino e la musica del '600." *Studi seicenteschi* 14 (1973).

Spalding, Henry D. *A Treasury of Italian Folklore and Humor*. Middle Village, NY: Jonathan David, 1980.

Stefanile, Mario. *Labirinto napoletano: Studi e saggi letterari su scrittori di ieri e di oggi*. Naples: Edizioni Scientifiche Italiane, 1958.

Tilgher, Adriano. *Ottocento napoletano ed oltre*. Naples: Montanino, 1959.

Trolano, Rosa, ed. *Poeti e prosatori del settecento*. Rome: G. e M. Benicasa, 1994.

5. THEATER AND MUSIC

Bianconi, Lorenzo and Renato Bossa, eds. *Musica e cultura a Napoli dal XV al XIX secolo*. Florence: L.S. Olschki, 1983.

Canessa, Francesco, ed. *Il melodramma a Napoli nell'ottocento*. Naples: Guida, 1982.

Clubb, Louise George. *Giovanni Battista della Porta, Dramatist*. Princeton: Princeton University Press, 1965.

Croce, Benedetto. *I teatri di Napoli dal rinascimento all fine del secolo decimottavo*. Milan: Adelphi, 1992.

D'Alessandro, Domenico Antonio and Agostino Zino, eds. *La Musica a Napoli durante il seicento: Atti del convegno internazionale di studi*. Rome: Edizioni Torre d'Orfeo, 1987.

De Matteis, Stefano. *Lo specchio della vita: Napoli, antropologia della città del teatro*. Bologna: Il Mulino, 1991.

Giacomo, Salvator. *Storia del Teatro San Carlino: Contributo alla storia della scena dialettale napoletana, 1738–1884*. Naples: Berisio, 1967.

Greco, Franco C. *La scena illustrata: Teatro, pittura e città a Napoli nell'ottocento*. Naples: T. Piranti, 1995.

Griffin, Thomas E. "The Late Baroque Serenata in Rome and Naples: A Documentary Study with Emphasis on Alessandro Scarlatti." Ph.D. diss. Los Angeles: University of California, 1983.

——. *Musical References in the* Gazzetta di Napoli *1681–1725*. Berkeley, CA: Fallen Leaf Press, 1992.

Larson, Keith A. "The Unaccompanied Madrigal in Naples from 1536 to 1654." Ph.D. diss. Cambridge, MA: Harvard University, 1985.

Lazarevich, Gordana. "The Role of the Neapolitan Intermezzo in the Evolution of Eighteenth-Century Musical Style: Literary, Symphonic and Dramatic Aspects, 1635–1735." Ph.D. diss. New York: Columbia University, 1970.

Lyonnet, Henry. *Pulcinella & C.: Le théâtre neapolitain*. Paris: Société d'Éditions litteraires et artistiques, 1901.

Parker, Roger, ed. *The Oxford Illustrated History of Opera*. Oxford and New York: Oxford University Press, 1994.

Prota-Giurleo, Ulisse. *I teatri di Napoli nel '600: La commedia e le maschere*. Naples: Fausto Fiorentino, 1962.

Rak, Michele. *Napoli gentile: La letteratura in "lingua napoletana" nella cultura barocca (1596–1632)*. Bologna: Il Mulino, 1994.

Robinson, Michael F. *L'Opera napoletana: Storia e geografia di un'idea musicale settecentesca*. Venice: Marsilio, 1984.

——. *Naples and Neapolitan Opera*. New York: Da Capo Press, 1972, 1984.

Trevisani, Giulio, ed. *Teatro napoletano*. Bologna: Fenice, 1957.

6. ECONOMICS AND SOCIAL SCIENCES

Calabria, Antonio. *The Cost of Empire: The Finances of the Kingdom of Naples in the Time of Spanish Rule.* Cambridge: Cambridge University Press, 1991.

Colapietra, Raffaele. *Problemi monetari negli scrittori napoletani del seicento.* Rome: Accademia Nazionale dei Lincei, 1973.

Contino, Elvira. *Mire di espansione commerciale del Regno di Napoli nel secolo xviii: Progetti di compagnie con le Indie Orientali.* Naples: Edizioni Scientifiche Italiane, 1990.

Galasso, Giuseppe. *Napoli spagnola dopo Masaniello: Politica, cultura, società,* Naples: Edizioni Scientifiche Italiane, 1972; Florence: Sansoni, 1982

Luca, Mario de. *Gli economisti napoletani del Settecento e la politica dello sviluppo: Saggio storico-dottrinario sulle vie allo sviluppo.* Naples: Morano, 1969.

Plunz, Richard, ed. *San Leucio: Vitalità di una tradizione. Traditions in Transition.* New York: Wittenborn, 1973.

Romano, Ruggiero. *Le commerce du royaume de Naples avec la France et les pays de l'Adriatique au xviiie siècle.* Paris: Armand Colin, 1951.

Rosa, Luigi di. *I cambi esteri del regno di Napoli dal 1591 al 1707.* Vol. 2. Naples: Banco di Napoli, 1955.

Tagliacozzo, Giorgio. *Economisti napoletani dei secoli xvii e xviii.* Fasano: L. Cappelli, 1987.

Vidal, Enrico. *Il pensiero civile di Paolo Mattia Doria negli scritti inediti, con il testo del manoscritto "Del Commercio del Regno di Napoli."* Milan: A. Giuffrè, 1953.

Vinci, Lucia. "Civiltà del 600 e 700 a Napoli." *Punto 4 (Caserta)* 15 (1984).

7. JURISPRUDENCE

Colapietra, Raffaele. *L'Amabile fierezza di Francesco d'Andrea.* Milan: Giuffrè, 1981.

Giustiniani, Lorenzo. *Memorie istoriche degli scrittori legali del Regno di Napoli: Raccolte da Lorenzo Giustiniani.* Naples: Stamperia Simoniana, 1787-78. Microfilm 1964, 1970.

Massamormile, Mario Pisani, ed. *Napoli e i suoi avvocati.* Naples: Società Editrice Napoletana, 1975.

Moschetti, Cesare Maria. *Questioni di diritto pubblico marittimo negli scritti dei giuristi napoletani dalla prima metà del Seicento.* Naples: Giannini, 1984.

Rovito, Pier Luigi. *Le garanzie giurdiche.* Naples: Jovene, 1981.

Villani, Antonio. *Gaetano Filangieri e l'illuminismo europeo: Atti del convegno....* Naples: Guida, 1991.

8. PHILOSOPHY

Addante, Pietro. *Antonio Genovesi e la polemica antibayliana nella filosofia dell '700: Contributo di Ricerche Storico-Filosofiche.* Bari: Centro Ricerche Storico-Filosofiche, 1972.

Beligioioso, Giulia. *Cultura a Napoli e cartesianesimo: Scritti su G. Gimma, P.M. Doria, C. Cominale.* Galatina: Congedo, 1992.

Consiglio, Alberto. *Dizionario filosofico napoletano: Detti, motti, e proverbi.* Rome: G. e M. Benicasa, 1971.

Fulco, Adrienne. "A Study of the Political Ideas of Giambattista Vico's *New Science*." Ph.D. diss. New York: City University of New York, 1982.

Mazzotta, Giuseppe. *The New Map of the World: The Poetic Philosophy of Giambattista Vico.* Princeton: Princeton University Press, 1999.

Oldrini, Guido. *La cultura filsofica napoletana dell'Ottocento.* Rome and Bari: Laterza, 1973.

—. *Napoli e i suoi filosofi: Protagonisti, prospettive, problemi del pensiero dell'Ottocento.* Milan: F. Angeli, 1990.

Pompa, Leon, ed. and trans. *Vico: Selected Writings.* Cambridge: Cambridge University Press, 1982.

Tessitore, Fulvio. *Da Cuoco a De Sanctis: Studi sulla filosofia napoletana nel primo ottocento.* Naples: Edizioni Scientifiche Italiane, 1988.

9. CHURCH, SAINTS, AND RITUAL

Amabile, Luigi. *Il santo officio della inquisizione in Napoli: Narrazione con molti documenti inediti.* Rubbettino: Soveria Mannelli, 1987.

Fantasia, Matteo. *I Papi Pugliesi.* Fasano: Schena Editore, 1987.

Lopez, Pasquale. *Riforma cattolica e vita religiosa e culturale a Napoli: Dalla fine del cinquecento ai primi anni del settecento.* Naples: Istituto Editoriale del Mezzogiorno, 1964.

Osbat, Luciano. *L'Inquisizione a Napoli: Il processo agli ateisti, 1688–1697.* Rome: Storia e Letteratura, 1974.

Pastor, Ludwig. *The History of the Popes from the Close of the Middle Ages, Drawn from the Secret Archives of the Vatican and Other Original Sources.* 23 vols. London: Kegan Paul, 1923-40.

Pignatelli, Diego. *Catalogo di libri stampati e manoscritti disegni, incisioni ed acquerelli riguardanti Innocenzo XII (Pignatelli).* Rome: Officina Poligrafica Romana, 1902.

Pironti, Pasquale. *Un processo dell'Inquisizione a Napoli.* Naples: Edizioni Pironti, 1976.

Robertazzi Delle Donne, Enrica. *L'Espulsione dei Gesuiti dal Regno di Napoli.* Naples: Libreria Scientifica Editrice, 1970.

Sallmann, Jean-Michel. *Naples et ses saints a l'âge baroque (1540–1750).* Paris: Presses Universitaires de France, 1994.

10. SCIENTIFIC DISCOURSE AND DISCOVERY

Crispini, Franco. *Metafisica del senso e scienza della vita. Tommaso Cornelio.* Naples: Guida, 1975.

De Sanctis, Riccardo. *La nuova scienza a Napoli tra '700 e '800.* Rome: Laterza, 1986.

Gatto, Romano. *Tra scienza e immaginazione: Le matematiche presso il Collegio gesuitico napoletano (1552–1670).* Florence: L.S. Olschki, 1994.

Lomanaco, Fabrizio e Maurizio Torrini. *Galileo e Napoli.* Naples: Guida, 1987.

Torrini, Maurizio. *Tommaso Cornelio e la ricostruzione della scienza.* Naples: Guida, 1977.

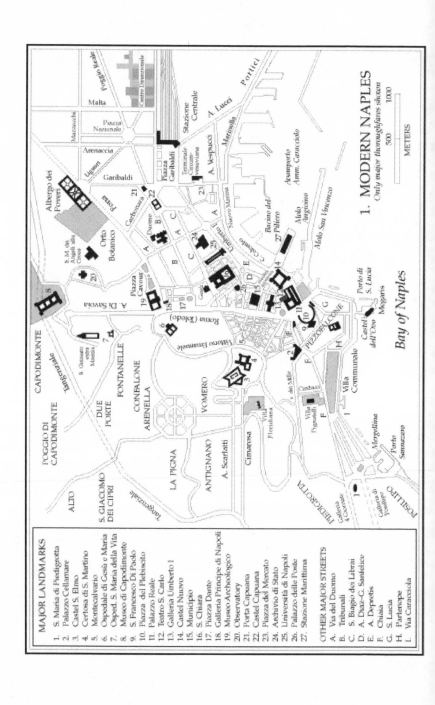

1. MODERN NAPLES

Only major thoroughfares shown

0   500   1000
METERS

MAJOR LANDMARKS

1. S. Maria di Piedigrotta
2. Palazzo Cellamare
3. Castel S. Elmo
4. Certosa di S. Martino
5. Montecalvario
6. Ospedale di Gesù e Maria
7. Osped. S. Maria della Vita
8. Museo di Capodimonte
9. S. Francesco Di Paolo
10. Piazza del Plebiscito
11. Palazzo Reale
12. Teatro S. Carlo
13. Galleria Umberto I
14. Castel Nuovo
15. Municipio
16. S. Chiara
17. Piazza Dante
18. Galleria Principe di Napoli
19. Museo Archeologico
20. Observatory
21. Porta Capuana
22. Castel Capuana
23. Piazza del Mercato
24. Archivio di Stato
25. Università di Napoli
26. Palazzo delle Poste
27. Stazione Marittima

OTHER MAJOR STREETS

A. Via del Duomo
B. Tribunali
C. S. Biagio dei Librai
D. A. Diaz–G. Sanfelice
E. A. Depretis
F. Chiaia
G. S. Lucia
H. Partenope
L. Via Caracciola

Bay of Naples

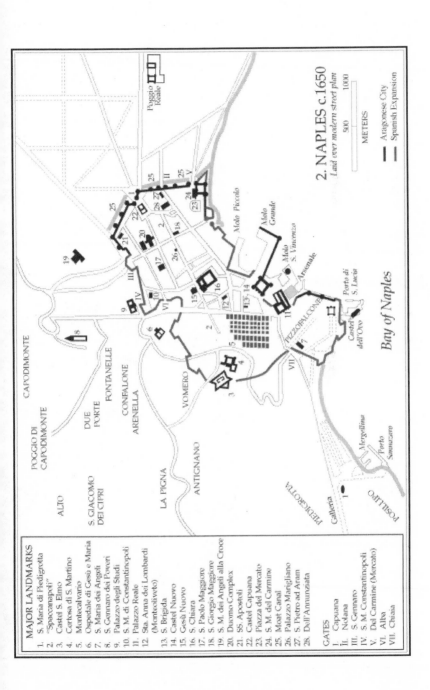

MAJOR LANDMARKS

1. S. Maria di Piedigrotta
2. "Spaccanapoli"
3. Castel S. Elmo
4. Certosa di S. Martino
5. Montecalvario
6. Ospedale di Gesù e Maria
7. S. Maria dei Angeli
8. S. Gennaro dei Poveri
9. Palazzo degli Studi
10. S. M. di Constantinopoli
11. Palazzo Reale
12. Sta. Anna dei Lombardi
    (Monteoliveto)
13. S. Brigida
14. Castel Nuovo
15. Gesù Nuovo
16. S. Chiara
17. S. Paolo Maggiore
18. S. Giorgio Maggiore
19. S. M. dei Angeli alla Croce
20. Duomo Complex
21. SS. Apostoli
22. Castel Capuana
23. Piazza del Mercato
24. S. M. del Carmine
25. Moat Canal
26. Palazzo Maregliano
27. S. Pietro ad Aram
28. Dell'Annunziata

GATES

I. Capuana
II. Nolana
III. S. Gennaro
IV. S. M. Constantinopoli
V. Del Carmine (Mercato)
VI. Alba
VII. Chiaia

2. NAPLES c.1650

Land over modern street plan

METERS

500   1000

━━━ Aragonese City
═══ Spanish Expansion

Bay of Naples

CAPODIMONTE

POGGIO DI
CAPODIMONTE

ALTO

S. GIACOMO
DEI CIPRI

DUE
PORTE

FONTANELLE

CONIFALONE
ARENELLA

VOMERO

LA PIGNA

ANTIGNANO

PIEDIGROTTA

Galleria

POSILLIPO

Mergellina

Porto
Sannazaro

Castel
dell'Ovo

Porto di
S. Lucia

Arsenale

S. Vincenzo

Molo

Molo
Grande

Molo Piccolo

PIZZOFALCONE

Poggio
Reale

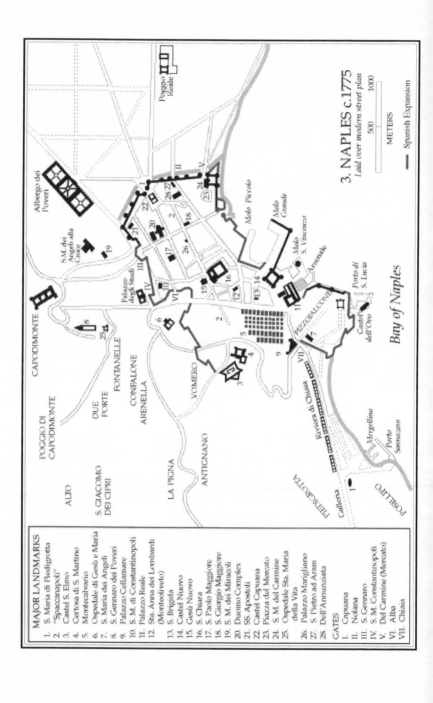

MAJOR LANDMARKS

1. S. Maria di Piedigrotta
2. "Spaccanapoli"
3. Castel S. Elmo
4. Certosa di S. Martino
5. Montecalvario
6. Ospedale di Gesù e Maria
7. S. Maria dei Angeli
8. S. Gennaro dei Poveri
9. Palazzo Cellamare
10. S. M. di Constantinopoli
11. Palazzo Reale
12. Sta. Anna dei Lombardi (Monteoliveto)
13. S. Brigida
14. Castel Nuovo
15. Gesù Nuovo
16. S. Chiara
17. S. Paolo Maggiore
18. S. Giorgio Maggiore
19. S. M. dei Miracoli
20. Duomo Complex
21. SS. Apostoli
22. Castel Capuana
23. Piazza del Mercato
24. S. M. del Carmine
25. Ospedale Sta. Maria della Vita
26. Palazzo Marigliano
27. S. Pietro ad Aram
28. Dell'Annunziata

GATES
I. Capuana
II. Nolana
III. S. Gennaro
IV. S. M. Constantinopoli
V. Del Carmine (Mercato)
VI. Alba
VII. Chiaia

3. NAPLES c.1775

Laid over modern street plan

METERS

500   1000

500   1000

— Spanish Expansion

Bay of Naples

INDEX

INDEX

INDEX

G

Gabrielli, Caterina (La) XL, 109
Galanti, Giuseppe Maria XLIX, 21
Galazia 59–60
Galeota, Giacomo Capece 33, 38
Galiani, Ferdinando XLIII, XLVI, L, 119–20;
    Della Moneta 120–22
Galilei, Galileo XLV, XLIX, 138, 184, 186, 187–88
Galizia 3
Galuppi, Baldassare XL
Ganz, David 175, 176
Gargiulo, Domenico XXX
Garibaldi, Giuseppe XXVIII
Gassendi, Pierre L, 188
Gaudiosi, Tommaso 89; "Woman Pos-
    sessed" 89
Gelad Addaula 176
Geloira, countess 4
Geneva 15
Genoa XLIII, 28, 110, 147
Genovesi, Antonio XLV, XLVI, XLVII, 21,
    122, 126, 131, 155, 167; *Lettere Acca-
    demiche* 155–57; *Meditazioni filosofiche*
    167–69
Gent, F. L. 189
gentile civile. See Naples: administrative
    system: bureaucracy
Gentileschi, Artemisia XXXV
Gesner, Salomon 103
Gessi, Francesco 54
Giannelli, Basilio XLVI
Giannone, Pietro XXX, XLVII, XLIX, 14,
    175, 178; *Istoria civile del Regno di
    Napoli* 15–16
Giordano, Luca XXXV, 33, 38, 39–41
Giotto XXXI, XXXIV
Giovanna II, queen 38
Giraffi, Alexander XXX, 7, 11; *Exact History
    of...the Revolution in Naples* 11–14
Giraldi Cintio, Giovambattista 103
Gisolfo, Pietro 164; *Prodigio di mature virtù
    nella vita di Nicola di Fusco* 164–66
Giudice
    Domenico, duke of Giovenazzo 40
    Nicola, prince of Cellamare 40
Giudici, Francesco, cardinal 173

Gliuni, N. 157
Gluck, Cristoph W. 95
Goethe, Johann Wolfgang von XXXIII, XLVI, 131
Gonzaga, Ferdinand 70
Gorgon 47
Gravina, Gian Vincenzo XXXIX, 93
Great Britain LI, 7, 27, 68, 120
    economic theory 113
Gregory XIV, pope 177
Grottaglie in Cecce 89
Guercino (G. F. Barbieri) 49
Guglielmi, Pietro Alexandro 109
Gugliemo of Agrisoglio, cardinal 40
Guzman, Manuel de XLI

H

Halley, Edmond 107
Hamilton
    Emma XXXIII, XXXVI; William XXXIII
Handel, George Frederick XXXII, XL
Hannibal 26, 59
Hapsburg Empire XXIX, XXXIV
    Austria 17; Spain XXVIII; tax policies XXXI
Hare, Augustus XXXIII
Harlequin XLI. *See also* Naples: theater:
    Pulcinella
Henry of Lorraine, duke of Guise XXX, 9
Henry VIII, of England 113
Herculaneum XXXIV, XXXV, XXXVII, 4, 39, 55,
    57–58
Hercules 191
Herod 69
Herodotus 121
Hesperides 21
Hippocrates 189, 190
Hobbes, Thomas 188
Hohenstaufen duke of Austria 34, 35, 40
Homer 121
Honorius III, pope 34
Horace XXXVII
Hospitallers 138
Howard, Thomas, earl of Arundel 27
Howell, James 7
Hutton, Edward 11

I

Imparato, Girolamo 38

237

Index

Palmieri, Giuseppe xLIII, 126–27; *Pensieri economici* 127–28
Paris xxIx, 27, 95, 107, 119
  College de France 108; Parliament 129; salons 119
Parma xxxv, 21, 88, 110
Parmigianino (G. F. M. Mazzuoli) 49
Parrino, Domenico Antonio 37, 38; *Nuova guida de' forestieri* 38–39
Passeri, Giambattista 48; *Vite dei pittori, scultori e architetti* 48–51
Pateano, Ericio 19
Pedro de Toledo xLV, 24, 37
Pedro of Aragon 35
Pedro of Portugal 3
Pelliccia, N. 157
Peray, N. 70
Pergolesi, Giovanni Battista xL, 94, 159
Perrucci, Andrea 101–2; *Dell'arte rappresentiva* 102–4
Pesche, Federico 31
Petersburg 110
Petrarch, Francesco xxxI, 67, 83
Philip III, king of Spain 3
Philip v, king of Spain 20
Philoctetes 102
Philolaus 142
Philoponus 185, 186
Phoenicians 121
Piacenza 177
Piccini, Niccolò xL, 109
Pico della Mirandola, Giovanni 137
Pietro da Cortona 48, 51
Plato 151, 152
Pliny
  the Elder 4
  the Younger xxvII, xxxIII, xxxvII, 4, 5
Plutarch xxvIII, 103, 191
Po, Giacomo del 166
Poland 173
Polignano 36
Polyphemus 82
Pompeii xxxIV, xxxv, xxxvII, 4, 39
Pomponazzi, Pietro 135
Ponaro, Michela. *See* Saints: Nicola de Fusco
Pontano, Giovanni xxxviii
Porpora, Niccolo 94

Portici 5, 39, 57
Portolongone, battle of xxIx
Porzilo 176
Poussin, Nicolas 45
Power, Marguerite 169
Pozzi, Roccus 58
Pozzuoli xxIx, xxxI, 29, 36
  antiquities 26; Monte Barbaro 26; caves 26; temple of Serapide xxxIV
Presti, Bonaventura 40
Preti, Mattia xxxvI, 38
Procida 29
Procopius 175, 185, 187
Proteus 64
Ptolemy, Claudius 142, 147
Pufendorf, Samuel 103
Puglia 127, 135
Punch. *See* Naples: theater: Pulcinella

Q

Quevedo, Francisco xxxvIII

R

Rabbanimi 175–76
Rabbi Abram 175
Rabbi Scerirà 175
Raimondo, prince xxxIII, L
Raleigh, Walter 113
Rama, Andrea 13
Ramsay, Allan xxxv
Raphael 159
Rasura, Nugno 3
Redi, Francesco L
Reggio in Emilia 87
Renaissance
  humanism xxvII; naturalism 80; religious thought 90
Reni, Guido xxxv, 49, 54
Resina 5
Ribera
  Juan Alfonso Enriquez de 130
  Jusepe de xxxII, xxxv, xxxvI, xxxvII, 41, 45, 53–57
Riccia 130
Riccia, Violante 130
Ricciardi, Giovanni Battista 51
Rieti 35

243

INDEX

This Book Was Completed on January 15, 2000
at Italica Press, New York, New York and
Was Set in Monotype Dante and Adobe
Bodoni. It Was Printed on 60-lb
Natural Paper by BookSurge,
U. S. A. / E. U.

Made in the USA
Lexington, KY
01 February 2019